The Essential Feature

THE ESSENTIAL FEATURE

**Writing for Magazines
and Newspapers**

Vicky Hay

Columbia University Press
New York

Columbia University Press
New York   Chichester, West Sussex

Copyright © 1990 Columbia University Press
All rights reserved

Library of Congress Cataloging-in-Publication Data

Hay, Millicent V., 1945–
    The essential feature : writing for magazines and newspapers /
Vicky Hay.
        p.   cm.
    Includes bibliographical references and index.
    ISBN 0-231-06886-7
    ISBN 0-231-06887-5 (pbk.)
    1. Feature writing.   2. Journalism—authorship.   I. Title.
PN4784.F37H39   1990
808'.06607—dc20   90-1985
                                      CIP

Printed in the United States of America

c 10 9 8 7 6 5 4 3 2 1
p 10 9 8 7 6

Book design by Ken Venezio

Acknowledgments and Copyrights

"Sound Effects." From "The Talk of the Town." *The New Yorker*, March 21, 1988. Copyright © 1988. Reprinted by permission of *The New Yorker* Magazine, Inc.

Page Stegner. "The Arizona Strip of Clarence Dutton." *Arizona Highways*, September 1988. Copyright © 1988 by Page Stegner. Reprinted by permission.

William Strunk and E. B. White. *The Elements of Style*. 3rd edition. New York: Macmillan Publishing Co., 1979. Copyright © 1979.

Steve Twomey. "How Super Are Our Supercarriers?" *The Philadelphia Inquirer*, October 5, 1986. Used by permission.

John Updike. "Witty Dotty." *The New Yorker*, April 25, 1988. Copyright © 1988. Reprinted by permission.

Eva Zeisel. Quoted in "The Present Moment," by Susannah Lessard. *The New Yorker*, April 13, 1987. Copyright © 1987 by Susannah Lessard. Reprinted by permission.

Special thanks to:

John L. Hay, whose support made this book possible
Merrill Windsor, a fine editor and a natural teacher
Christine Mitchell, who generously helped with the artwork
Martha Blue, for her helpful review of the chapters on ethics, libel, copyright, and contracts

Contents

Introduction

This book exists for two purposes:

1. To suggest to beginning writers what it takes to write a successful magazine or newspaper feature; and
2. To fill a gap among the books available for feature-writing courses.

When I began teaching the feature article, I found several excellent guides. None, however, covered all the ground: research, language, writing and organizational skills, and the facts of life in a tough, competitive business. Nor did many offer full-length examples of the kind of story students will eventually have to write. As a result, I was asking my students to buy three books: a text, a style guide, and a compendium of mentorly advice such as Zinsser's *On Writing Well*. *The Essential Feature* attempts to gather all those elements into one. It will serve not only as a guide for a single course but as a permanent resource for those students serious enough to continue writing nonfiction.

To return to the book's first *raison d'être*, as a magazine editor I receive submissions from very accomplished free-lance writers, from working journalists, and from amateurs who crave to be Writers with a capital W. Certain qualities mark the most successful contributors.

Ability to get the facts. Good nonfiction is based on solid, thorough research. I have tried to communicate this by devoting three chapters to the subject.

Passion for accuracy. The best writers are willing to check and double-check their work. Chapter 9, in particular, emphasizes this.

Honesty. Some writers—dare one utter it?—are innocent of the most basic principles of personal and professional ethics. It should go without saying that we do not plagiarize, we do not misrepresent ourselves or the facts, and we do not deceive our colleagues. Because, unfortunately, this appears *not* to go without saying, I have harped on the issue through several chapters.

Ability to tell a story. All too often, feature editors receive efforts by young reporters who can write excellent hard news pieces but who have not yet learned the literary technique demanded by the feature story. Chapters 6 and 7 confront this problem, and I have tried to reinforce my points throughout part 2.

Understanding of the market. In this department, amateur writers are often the strongest because they imbibe the principles of the marketplace from self-help books. Journalists and j-school graduates can be oddly naive about the need to know a publication's readers before attempting to write for it—probably because they receive much of their training in-house and so never have to match their styles to a variety of markets.

Part 2 offers eight selections as samples of nonfiction subgenres. I have chosen several prize-winning stories and selected examples from both newspapers and magazines. Even those that have not won awards showcase real skill and talent. I hope this book will help develop similar talent among its readers.

Millicent V. (Vicky) Hay
Phoenix, Arizona

The Essential Feature

I

WRITING FOR PUBLICATION

1

What Is a Feature Article?

A feature article is a type of journalistic story that entertains and informs. By "entertain" we don't necessarily mean "amuse." We mean the story engages the reader's attention. It may appear in magazines, newspapers, or newsletters, but it is always directed at a specific audience and publication. Because its language is popular, simple, and often casual, it looks easier to write than it is. In truth, a successful feature requires meticulous research, attention to accuracy, intelligent thought and organization, and considerable writing talent.

In this book, we will treat the feature article as a single genre—a literary type which, like the short story or novel, has its own conventions. Within this genre, we include both magazine and newspaper features. Although the two show distinct differences, the structure is similar. Once you understand the basic architecture, you can adapt it to the needs of most publications.

Newspaper features are usually done on a tight deadline. The reporter may conduct briefer interviews than would a magazine writer, and his research may be (but is not always) less extensive. The newspaper reporter attempts to take an "objective," third-person stance, and to that end eschews literary techniques such as telling the story from a participant's point of view, extensive dialogue, and lengthy, detailed description. He hides his opinion and tries to present all sides of the story in a disinterested manner. Newspaper features are usually (but not always) shorter than magazine articles: 40 column inches, or about 1,600 words, might be considered long. Leads are often shorter and punchier than a magazine feature's, and it is more important to get as much information as possible near the top of the story.

In contrast, the magazine editor thinks a 1,500-word story is short. Magazine articles may run upwards of 3,000 words, although an average length is 2,000 to 2,500 words. The magazine writer may take a somewhat more literary approach to her subject, freely using devices you see in fiction, such as characterization, point of view (relating the action through a character's eyes), narrative, description, and dialogue. Transitions, which help the reader move logically from one point to the next, may be more sophisticated. The writer may be less "objective," interpreting the facts and events to fit her viewpoint. Too, because magazines usually have longer deadlines than newspapers, the writer has more time for in-depth, wide-ranging research.

Another important difference between magazine and newspaper writing exists. Newspapers are still in the business of reporting the news. Many lesser magazines—the ones that form the bulk of this market—have a different agenda: they survive solely on the strength of advertising revenues. For this reason, newspapers are more likely to publish investigative journalism. Except for fearless publishers and those publications with access to a wide spectrum of advertisers, such as *Common Cause* or *The Atlantic*, few magazines will allow writers to expound on what is called the "negative" side of an issue. Magazines tend to carry "happy news," human interest stories, and service pieces upon which the advertising department can hang a pitch to media buyers—and which have small potential to offend. This is why, for example, you rarely see a magazine story that discusses how the tobacco lobby has managed to control Congress and maintain its heavily subsidized industry despite its product's proven hazards: tobacco companies are major advertisers in national and regional magazines.

Magazine and newspaper features take many forms, eight of which are described in the second half of this book.

THE NONFICTION INDUSTRY

Feature writing has taken an important place in late twentieth-century journalism, largely because of economic and technological forces beyond the control of the newspapers and magazines that use such stories. Skim the front page of any big-city newspaper and you will likely see at least one long piece that opens with a fiction writer's lead, rather than the standard who-what-when-where-why lead of the hard news story. That article is likely to take a point of view or to examine the issues and forces behind the news; it may try to cast light on the human beings involved in the news, or study the history behind an event; and it may run to an epic 3,000 words or more. This makes the front page quite different from the front pages we read a decade ago.

Now leaf through a few magazines on the supermarket or bookstore rack. They, too, have changed over the past few years. You don't find much short fiction, the staple of the great general-interest magazines that pleased our parents and supported many a free-lance writer. Indeed, you won't find many general-interest magazines at all: competing for newsstand space are such titles as *Games, Chocolatier, Motocross Action, Mustang, Walking,* as well as the familiar *Field and Stream, Seventeen,* and *Ladies' Home Journal.* These special-interest magazines publish nonfiction, because publishers believe that's what readers want. Much, if not most, of that nonfiction appears in feature articles.

The many reasons behind these changes boil down to two: television and money. Televised newscasts cover spot news far more efficiently than do daily newspapers. By the time you read a hard news story, chances are you've already seen it on the evening news, as a bulletin, or on an early-morning t.v. "magazine." To compete, newspapers publish more magazine-like articles. The *Wall Street Journal* runs three carefully written and edited feature stories on its front page and two or three shorter features on the front page of the second section. One Sunday in 1987, the *New York Times* ran 110 stories that fit the feature format, ranging in subject matter from the Beatles and the Boy Scouts to an analysis of Oliver North's character. Suburban papers, struggling against monopolistic urban newspapers as well as television, focus on hometown news rich in human interest and local importance.

Too, when newspapers responded to feminist activism during the 1960s by recasting their women's pages into "leisure" or "style" sections, they found the feature article appealed to men as well as women. With this revelation, the genre found a wider readership, and now it appears as often on the business pages as in the food or society section.

Magazines also have had to respond to the effects of television. Apparently the public now satisfies its urge for short escapist fiction in half-hour sessions before the tube. Interest in magazine fiction has fallen in a curve that traces the drop in American literacy. Already fighting this trend, general-interest magazines were hit with a 400 percent increase in second-class postage between 1970 and 1974. This blow killed many popular general-interest magazines, among them *Look* and the old *Life*. With a few exceptions, such as *Reader's Digest*, magazines that appeal to many tastes and interests died like dinosaurs, to be replaced by smaller, more agile special-interest books. By and large, the industry now consists of specialized publications: regionals, city magazines, television guides, sports, music, hobby, religious, trade, and company magazines. A whole mini-industry of "custom publishers" exists, producing controlled-circulation magazines for businesses that want to reach their own customers or employees.

THE FEATURE VS. OTHER KINDS OF NONFICTION

Let's silhouette the feature article by defining what it is not:

• The feature is not a research paper nor its real-world sibling, a journal article. It does involve research, usually more than you would perform for a college term paper. But the nature of that research—most often, interviews—is different and its documentation is looser. This does not mean you don't tell your readers where you got your facts; only that you do so in the text, in a readable way —never in footnotes or parentheses.

Nor, or course, will you purloin information or words from other writers. You must be very careful not to reproduce anyone else's work without acknowledging it. Your editor will expect you to provide a list of sources with their addresses and phone numbers, to save transcripts and tapes of interviews, and to list any published works you used.

Research papers and journal articles are characterized by footnotes and bibliographies, long paragraphs, and often by academic or technical jargon. All these are taboo in journalistic writing. As an undergraduate in English literature, I was told that a good paragraph should run about one and a half typed, double-spaced pages, a rule that served me well through a collegiate career extending all the way to the terminal degree. My first editor greeted this principle with a disgusted snort. In writing for the mass media, paragraphs are short because most readers lose heart when they see a mass of gray space. The white space between paragraphs (or "grafs") breaks up the page and pulls the reader through the copy. Paragraphs for feature articles are well-developed, with effective transition, topic sentences, and argument, but they normally are shorter than the academic or professional paper's.

• The feature article is not a hard news story. Reporters still organize news articles in the classic inverted pyramid: the key information (who what when where why) appears in the first paragraph or two, and the remaining material comes in descending order of importance. This allows an editor to cut copy to fit space simply by lopping off the final paragraphs.

The feature may present its information in exactly the opposite order: it sometimes delivers its message in the last paragraph. Depending on the market, the feature may not put the "five w's" in the first paragraph. A typical feature lead is usually quite different from the news story's; it lures the reader into the piece, using concrete imagery or striking statements.

In addition, the feature may be less objective than the hard news article. The feature writer is permitted—often expected—to take a stand, although that stance may be expressed subtly, through choice and organization of detail rather than by overt editorializing. Again, this depends on the market. A general-circulation newspaper will rarely allow a writer to express as much opinion as would an alternative paper or some of our livelier magazines.

Feature articles contain longer, better-developed paragraphs than do news stories. Hard news is presented in one- or two-sentence paragraphs, because editors find this format is easiest for unsophisticated readers to follow. Smooth transitions, logical structure, nuance, and thorough exploration of ideas are more important to the feature story than to the hard news piece.

• The feature article is not a review. It is true that some restaurant, book, and dramatic reviews follow a featurelike format. However, a good feature requires more research than a couple of trips to an eatery, and it is not a piece of literary or dramatic criticism.

• The feature article is not a column. Dear Abby and Miss Manners do not write features. Neither, most of the time, does Ellen Goodman or even Mike Royko.

• The feature article is not usually an essay. The essayist treats a single subject in a brief literary composition, usually from an intimate, personal point of view. She makes no attempt to cover the subject completely. The feature writer, while he may select a very limited focus, does try to touch on all the points within that field of view. He may use the first person or relate an experience of his own to engage the reader or to make a point, but the bulk of the article presents information the writer has gathered through interviews, observation, or reading.

• The feature article is not an editorial. While the writer may allow her point of view to show, her primary purpose is not to opine but to inform.

• The feature article is not a filler. Fillers are short blurbs that occupy space around longer pieces, such as the ones you find at the end of *Reader's Digest* or *New Yorker* pieces. Sometimes fillers occupy whole departments, like *New York's* "Best Bets" or *Boys' Life's* "Think & Grin." These are the one-liners of the journalist's world. A feature story is fully developed, with a lead, a thesis, several paragraphs of information, and a windup. Such pieces rarely run less than 800 words.

• A feature article is not an advertorial, a phony magazine article whose sole purpose is to hype paying advertisers. Feature stories are journalism, not ad copy.

NOW THAT WE KNOW WHAT A FEATURE ISN'T . . .

. . . What *is* it? It's a long, nonfiction story, 800 to 3,000 or more words, written in clear, simple language and dressed out rather casually. It resembles a newspaper story in that it is always factual and its writer is expected to adhere to high standards of accuracy and honesty. It is based on solid research, which usually takes the form of interviews, personal observation, or groundwork in libraries and public records. But unlike a news story, it begins with a lead like a fictional opening and presents facts in a more flexible manner. The writer may take an obvious point of view, and the story may use fictional techniques to *show* rather than tell the reader what is going on. In short, it's a hybrid that requires you to combine a reporter's skills with a storyteller's art.

REPORTING AS LITERATURE

The feature article as a form has been handled by the finest journalists and mishandled by the worst hacks in the business. Because it lends itself to anything from slack-jawed awe to hard-hitting investigation, it invites writers of all stripes. Most people who can write a simple sentence can learn to craft a workmanlike feature story.

A few, very gifted writers have taken the feature beyond craft, proving that the form lends itself to art. This development began with the so-called New Journalists, when several feature writers of the 1960s—notably Gay Talese, Jimmy Breslin, and Tom Wolfe—realized that they could combine the fictional technique of the novel with reporting. The result, says Wolfe, was "the discovery that it was possible in nonfiction, in journalism, to use any literary device, from the traditional dialogisms of the essay to stream-of-consciousness, and to use many different kinds simultaneously, or within a relatively short space . . . to excite the reader both intellectually and emotionally."

Norman Sims has called this group "the literary journalists," a term embracing the now-established New Journalists and their younger followers. "Reporting on the lives of people at work, in love, going about the normal rounds of life," Sims observes, "they confirm that the crucial moments of everyday life contain great drama and substance." *The Essential Feature* can't make you an artist. You'll have to do that for yourself. But it will map the basic principles of writing and selling the feature article.

Meanwhile: read. If you want to spend your life in journalism, read and follow the best. Read the New Journalists—Hunter Thompson, Tom Wolfe, Richard Rhodes, Jane Kramer, Joan Didion, John McPhee. Read their predecessors—George Orwell, Lillian Ross, A. J. Liebling, James Agee, John Hersey, Joseph Mitchell. Read their heirs—Richard West, Mark Kramer, Sara Davidson, Tracy Kidder, Mark Singer. And watch the new generation: William Least Heat Moon, Charles Bowden, Bob Greene, and many more. You'll meet these writers in national magazines like *The Atlantic*, *The New Yorker*, and *Esquire*, in some of the better regionals, such as *Philadelphia*, *Texas Monthly*, or *New York*, and in alternative publications such as *Village Voice*, *The Boston Phoenix*, and *Mother Jones*. As you go through this book, you will find lists of recommended reading. These are more than decorative. Get to know the best in the business: they will help you learn your craft.

−30−

FOR PROJECTS OR DISCUSSION

1. Bring a metropolitan newspaper's Sunday edition to class. Identify as many features as you can, and explain how they differ from the paper's other content. What is the average length of the features you noted? One inch of copy, one column wide, contains about 40 words.

2. Select a substantial feature from this newspaper or from a magazine of your choice—it should be at least 1,500 to 2,000 words long—and try to extrapolate the amount of research that went into it. How many people are quoted? How much fact appears to have come from printed sources? How much from direct observation or investigation? Is any information repeated? Can you find any sentences that do not carry at least one fact? If so, why are those sentences there?

3. Bring in a feature by one of the authors mentioned in the section titled "Reporting as Literature." Discuss how their work differs from the writing you ordinarily see in your local city maga-

zine or newspaper. What works best in this person's writing? What, if anything, seems to fall short? Why?

SUGGESTED READING

Folio: The Magazine for Magazine Management, a monthly periodical. Often runs informative articles for editors and writers.

Larry L. King. *None But a Blockhead*. New York: Viking, 1986. Sometimes hilarious, sometimes touching insider's story—tells you what it's like to make a living as a free-lance writer.

Leonard Mogel. *The Magazine*. Engelwood Cliffs, N.J.: Prentice-Hall, 1979. A useful overview of what goes into magazine production.

William Ruehlmann. *Stalking the Feature Story*. Cincinnati, Oh.: Writers Digest Books, 1977. An old favorite.

Daniel R. Williamson, *Feature Writing for Newspapers*. New York: Hastings House, 1975. Although out of date in some respects, it remains a useful guide to the newspaper feature.

2

Developing and Selling a Story Idea

• One of my students, a quarter horse enthusiast, sold a story on establishing a county riding trail to *Western Horseman*.

• A history buff won a statewide contest for a piece about the founding of a local city; the award included publication in the state historical society's respected journal.

• A cat-lover sold a story on a European country's feline protection plan to *Cats*.

• And a lawyer, exasperated at difficulties finding work in her specialty, sold a humorous piece, alleging the job is not worth running the law school gauntlet, to a bar association magazine.

The trick each student mastered sounds easier than it is: *keep the reader in mind*. Whatever issue you're considering, always ask the fundamental question, "What about this would interest another person?"

Hold that thought and stay alert to the things around you, and you'll spot stories everywhere.

HOW STAFF WRITERS DEVELOP IDEAS FOR THEIR EDITORS

Editors and staff writers are expected to present story ideas on a regular basis. Some publications set aside time in weekly editorial meetings to consider new story ideas, when each staff member is asked to provide at least five good ideas. On publications whose atmosphere is more informal, you simply barrage your editor with new ideas as they come.

Ideas come to staffers from several sources:

1. *From free-lance writers.* Most magazine editors have a stable of writers who regularly submit ideas.

2. *From newspapers, magazines, and newsletters.* Most publications receive their state's major urban papers and several of the smaller dailies or weeklies. They take the local magazines, and they often trade out subscriptions to publications of like kinds. Members of the City and Regional Magazine Association, for example, send each other their publications. Staffers make it a habit to review this material regularly, watching for topics that might adapt to their own publication's readers.

3. *From your own sources and contacts.* If you are on the city hall beat, for example, you might attend a city council meeting at which the director of a proposed new shelter for the homeless speaks. Her remarks suggest a feature about the plight of homeless women with children. A local politician tells you that the suburban branch campus of a land-grant university plans to break away from its parent institution and apply for independent accreditation. That's a news story—but from it you derive a feature backgrounding the history and current status of the younger school.

4. *As sidebars to news stories.* Newspapers frequently run features to enlarge or humanize major hard news reports. Virtually every airplane crash, tornado, and earthquake breeds a litter of features looking into the feelings or experiences of survivors. A report on the escalating murder rate in the newspaper's metropolitan area is accompanied by a sadly wry column detailing a writer's response to daily life under the perceived threat of burglary, mugging, auto theft, or assault.

5. *From press releases.* Although these notices from organizations or public relations agents are self-interested, one can often generalize from them to create a larger story. An agency sends you a press kit about a client, a builder who erects extravagantly opulent homes. You decide to do a pictorial on the lifestyles of the rich and locally famous. A museum sends notice of a nationally touring show; you do a piece on how curators lure big names to your city.

6. *From reviews of subjects the magazine has covered before.* The other day, our editor noted that we had run stories on pioneer Jews and on our state's Asian community. He suggested a similar story on prominent Hispanic families.

7. *From contact with other people.* Leads developed through

membership in a humanities council helped sell my editors on three historical stories. One editor's wife met a nun with an unusual hobby, which led to a short piece in the magazine. The executive director of a new cultural center spoke at a luncheon to which my editor and I were invited; we will do a story on the greening of our state's cultural desert. Listen to what people say, and consider who else would be interested.

DEVELOPING AN IDEA INTO A STORY

A story idea is more than just a subject. It's a subject *combined with an approach*, a way of looking at the topic that allows you to focus your reader's attention on a special aspect.

An idea is different from a topic. Anyone can come up with a general subject: "I want to write about quarter horses," says a student. Fine. But what about the beast? She could discuss the breed's development and characteristics—what makes it different from other horses? All fascinating, no doubt, to those who care, but none of it would give her a *story*.

An experienced writer once put it this way: a story is like a clothesline. It has a narrative—a plot line—upon which you hang the facts, much as you pin up your socks and shirts. Put in the conventional language of editors and journalism instructors, you must come up with an angle or slant to an idea that will interest your readers before you try to sell your editor on it.

Let's think, then, about quarter horses. We know they were bred for handling stock—boring stuff to the average reader. Quarter horses are used in rodeos these days. That subject has broader interest: travel editors might go for it. Our student might do a piece on one of the West's major rodeos, trying to get across its excitement, fun, and the emotional weight such events pack for their participants. This would allow her to work in a fair amount of factual information on the horses.

Such a story would still have limited appeal.

Buying and selling horses, we reflect, is an exercise in showmanship. Suppose our student covered a horse auction. Now she has a story! With colorful people, lots of beautiful animals, and plenty of money at stake, it could delight readers across the country.

Her story will cover a single auction. It might be even more tightly focused: she could profile an auctioneer, for example; or follow one buyer through the day, recounting the events from his point of view. But while her narrative focuses on the auction, the factual details can tell her reader everything she ever wanted to say about her favorite breed of horse.

Look ahead to some of the sample articles in part 2, and you will see how often writers use the clothesline principle. Page Stegner's simple narrative (chapter 19) bears a massive weight of historic, geologic, and geographic fact—and even some social commentary. Steve Twomey weaves both sides of a controversy and many facts about aircraft carriers into a narrative describing life aboard the *America* (chapter 21). Barry Bearak says almost as much about stand-up comedy as he does about the man he profiles (chapter 16). In each of these, the *story*—a tale of a couple traveling through some wild country; men at sea; a study of an aging comic—is different from the larger *subject*—the Arizona Strip; military preparedness; the condition of Man.

To determine what approach will work for a given subject, you must know your reader. The market determines how you will tell the story.

GETTING ACQUAINTED WITH A PUBLICATION AND ITS READERS

If you're hired on staff, your editors will explicitly teach you about the readers. But if you're trying land a job on a magazine or sell a story free-lance, you start as an outsider. The way you learn something about the magazine and its readers is to read it carefully.

We cannot emphasize this enough: before you approach an editor, READ THE PUBLICATION. Go to the library and study a half-dozen back issues.

First, read the main features. Observe the language: is it casual or formal? Is the vocabulary sophisticated or simple? Are the writers aiming at an educated reader or one with basic English skills? How long are the paragraphs? The sentences? To write a story for a newspaper or magazine's readers, you must use the language and composition they expect.

Now try to get a feel for the overall tone. Is it light? serious? Politically conservative, liberal, or middle-of-the-road? Stylish or down-home? Does it show a sense of humor? If so, is it sentimental or deadpan, dry or uproarious? Your proposal and your article must fit this style. These elements are more marked in magazine journalism, but they do exist in newspapers, too; compare, for example, the *New York Times* with the *San Francisco Chronicle*.

Look at the stories' length. You should count the words in any article that might be something you could write. Arrive at a rough word count by measuring an inch of one column. Count the words in that space. Then measure the total space the story occupies and multiply by the words-per-inch. If parts of the article are printed in a different typeface or column width, recount the words-per-col-umn-inch in those sections. Remember, there's no point proposing an article longer than the editor can run.

You can learn as much from advertising as from editorial content. Compare, for example, the *New Yorker*'s ads with those in *Reader's Digest*. The length and sophistication of the first magazine's stories tell you the audience is well educated and has plenty of time to read. Niemann-Marcus and Brunschwig & Fils advertisments speak of affluence. The second magazine, full of brief, didactic, sometimes cloying pieces, goes to a middle-class reader with less leisure time or a shorter attention span. Ads for shampoos that wash out the gray and fertilizers guaranteed to save your azaleas tell you this reader is probably middle-aged and can afford neither expensive styling salons nor professional gardeners.

For newspapers especially, consider the obvious facts about cir-culation. Morning papers often address a predominately white-collar audience; afternoon papers may cater to blue-collar readers. Subur-ban papers have a more specialized—and special-interest—reader-ship than large metropolitan papers.

Try to form a mental picture of the people who read the publica-tion. Are they educated? Less educated? How old are they? Are they mostly male? Female? Mixed audience? Are they members of a specific race or religion? Where do they live? Which of their inter-ests does this journal cater to? Do they want to read gossip, or nothing but the facts? Your goal is to satisfy the reader's needs, and to do so, you must know him as you would a friend.

Magazines have some key elements you should systematically note. They help you size up the magazine and its readers.

First, with pen and paper in hand, find the *masthead*. It usually appears near the front, but sometimes it's in the back. The masthead lists the magazine's staff. You're looking for the person who will read your article proposal. Ordinarily, this is the managing editor. Some larger magazines will list an articles editor or features editor; if you see such a title, address your inquiry to that person. Smaller publications may have just one editor. In that case, address yourself to him or her.

Whomever you select, get the person's name and title right. Noth-ing is a faster turn-off than seeing your name misspelled or being demoted from "editor" to "managing editor."

The magazine's address is usually printed on the masthead. If not, look on the contents page. Be sure to get the address for the editorial offices. Sometimes circulation and advertising departments are at a different location.

Newspaper mastheads rarely give the names of subeditors. They do give the paper's telephone number, though. This makes it simple to call and ask for the feature editor's name.

A magazine's *contents page* reveals a lot. It will tell you whether the magazine runs features at all. Compare the by-lines listed on the contents page with the staff names on the masthead. If they're different, the magazine is buying free-lance. If all the writers are on staff, select a different market.

At the contents, look at the kinds of stories that run regularly. Do you find profiles? Reports? Service pieces? How-to-do-its? You will need to cast your material in a form the editors favor. Don't waste your time trying to sell a profile, for example, to a magazine that never uses personality pieces.

Next, look at the *departments*. These are regular sections and columns, often called "front matter" or "back matter." The table of contents should bunch departments separately from feature articles. Sometimes departments are staff-written; sometimes not. A department that runs 150- to 1000-word items may be the best place for a free-lancer to break in: you can show your stuff without asking the editor to bank on an unknown.

How can you tell whether a department accepts free-lance contributions? If the by-line says "edited by . . . ," chances are its compiler farms out some of the copy. If each item is by-lined, clearly they're done by free-lancers. Initials at the department's end, a by-line that reads "by . . . ," or no by-line at all indicates the column is staff-written.

Now take a look at the magazine's *overall appearance*. Would its physical design appeal to sophisticates, like the *GQ* or *Esquire* reader? To down-to-earth types—*Woman's Day* or *Modern Maturity*? Or to people with a given lifestyle—*Mother Earth News* or *Sunset*?

What kind of paper does it use? Slick, shiny paper, because it is costly, suggests the magazine has a decent bankroll. How much color do you see? Is full color used only for advertising, or can you find full-color editorial pages? Full color (called "four-color process") is also expensive. Lots of color may tell you the magazine has enough money to pay writers more than starvation wages. However, a flashy magazine that has been in business only a short time could be overspending on production; in that case, plentiful color is a yellow flag telling you to get your pay up front.

In a year of back issues and you may find a house advertisement announcing the magazine's *demographics*—statistics about readers' ages, education, and income. Magazines gather such information to help sell advertising space, but it's also useful to editors and writers.

INDUSTRY GUIDES TO MAGAZINES

There are other ways to gauge a publication. But before you consider them, brand this on your forehead: *there's no substitute for reading the magazine.*

Try asking the editor directly. Write—getting the person's name off a current masthead and spelling it correctly—and request the magazine's *writer's guidelines*. Enclose a stamped, self-addressed envelope. Sometimes editors will also send you a sample copy of the magazine, if you ask.

Writer's guidelines describe the publication's mission, introduce you to its readership, and outline the editorial requirements. Their completeness, quality, and candor vary from editor to editor. Figure 2.1 is a typical example.

Writer's Market, an annual reference you will find in your library, lists several thousand free-lance magazine markets. Entries give editors' names, addresses, length requirements, pay, rights purchased, and brief synopses of editorial needs. Although it's a handy guide, you should note several caveats:

• *Writer's Market* does not list every free-lance market. Do not assume its categories are comprehensive. Many other magazines will consider your work.

• The editor listed may no longer be with a magazine by the time *Writer's Market* reaches you. Turnover in the magazine industry is very high. Check a current masthead to get the correct reference.

• Payment figures may be misleading. Editors, who are the source of these blurbs, usually list their low-end rates. But sometimes, hoping to attract better writers, they will do the opposite, with no intention of paying the average Joe or Jane that much.

• At the risk of belaboring a point, checking *Writer's Market* is not equivalent to reading the magazine.

Two other guides to periodicals, Ulrich's *International Periodicals Directory* and Gale's *Directory of Publications*, give addresses, editors' names, and other useful information; they list many publications not found in *Writer's Market*. For newspapers, *Editor and Publisher* produces an annual directory called the *Editor and Publisher International Yearbook*, with up-to-date names and titles of departmental editors.

TAILORING YOUR IDEA TO THE READER

As we have noted, a story idea combines a subject with an approach. That approach is tailored to a specific reader, whose char-

Since 1925, *Arizona Highways* has carried out its mandate, "to promote travel to and through the State of Arizona." A state-owned publication, the magazine has a circulation of more than 425,000, of which 80 percent is out-of-state, with subscribers in almost every country in the world. Thus, while we are a premier regional photography and travel magazine, we speak to a national and international audience. We expect top-quality writing on subjects of interest to those who visit and love the American Southwest.

Subject matter: The main editorial thrust is travel in Arizona and its environs. We also buy nature, adventure, history, personality profile, quality arts and crafts, humor, lifestyle, nostalgia, archeology, and Western nonfiction romance.

About travel stories: We are developing a style for travel stories that is distinctively *Arizona Highways*. The style starts with outstanding photographs, which not only depict an area but interpret it and thus become an integral part of the presentation. So our travel stories need not dwell on descriptions of what can be seen.

Concentrate instead on the experience of being there, whether the destination is a hiking trail, a ghost town, a trout stream, a forest, or an urban area. What thoughts and feelings did the experience evoke? What was happening? What were the mood and comportment of the people? What were the sounds and smells? What was the feel of the area? Did bugs get into the sleeping bag? Were the crows curious about the intruders? Could you see to the bottom of the lake, and if so, what was there? We want to know why you went there, what you experienced, and what impressions you came away with.

These experiences and impressions should be focused into a story with a beginning, middle, and end. We do **not** want a rambling series of thoughts or vignettes, diary entries, or a travelogue (a piece that begins in the morning, goes hour-by-hour through the day, and ends in the evening). We want a story: one that opens by introducing us to a story line, then develops the tale, and finally concludes. We want an ending, a logical conclusion to the tale we are telling. Just stopping the story won't do.

The story we are telling should be just that: a story, and it should be as interesting and evocative as you can make it. And since it will not be a general guide to an area, we will need a short sidebar containing the service information.

This sidebar, called "When You Go," should explain how to get to the destination, where to stay, and what to see and do in the area. It also should include places to call for further information.

Approach: Our style is informal yet polished, with a readable, literary quality. We do not want choppy, topical, shallow Sunday supplement treatments. First person is o.k.; present tense, fine. Use strong verbs in the active voice and avoid overuse of the verb "to be" in all its forms.

Length: About 2,000 words or less.

Contract and payment: We buy first North American serial rights, and we expect *original* work. Payment is 35 to 50 cents a word, on acceptance.

Submissions: We prefer one-page written queries to unsolicited manuscripts. Telephone queries out of the blue are difficult for everyone.

2039 West Lewis Avenue • Phoenix, Arizona 85009 • Telephone (602) 258-6641 • Fax (602) 254-4505

Figure 2.1 Typical writer's guidelines.

acter you can deduce by studying the magazine for which you will write. The successful story idea is tightly targeted at a given magazine. It *focuses* on an angle of special interest to that publication's readers.

Suppose, for example, you learn that 27 million Americans cannot read their own language well enough to decipher the label on a medicine bottle. Shocked, you decide to write on illiteracy.

Big topic. You could write a book about it. But to write a feature on the subject, you'll need to ask yourself two questions:

Who cares?

What about illiteracy will you tell them?

To the first question, several answers immediately present themselves. Teachers, parents, employers, psychologists, local citizens concerned about problems facing their city or state, Americans nationwide who care about their country's future.

The second question is partially answered by the first: you want to tell the readers something that will bring the subject home to them.

For an education magazine, you profile a single teacher who has developed a successful program for combatting high school illiteracy. Or you interview several experts who think they can explain why, in a nation that requires universal education, so many people cannot read.

For a magazine aimed at parents, such as *Parenting* or *Family Circle*, you explain how to recognize early whether your child is learning to read properly.

For a local business journal, you explain how the national problem affects local manufacturers and then focus on what a single employer is doing about it. For a national business publication, such as *Barron's*, you tell the story of an entrepreneur who has made a business of teaching adults to read.

For a metropolitan newspaper, you do a series exposing illiteracy as a crisis affecting the reader's city, employer, and schools. It covers the extent of the problem; theories about how it came into existence; the effect on adult illiterates, employers, and taxpayer-supported social service agencies; ways parents can ensure that their children learn to read; and where people can go to get help.

For a city or regional magazine, you report on a local adult literacy program. To present this, you follow a successful student through a week in the program and show how it is affecting his life.

For a national general-interest magazine, you report on the size and seriousness of the problem by generalizing from the experience of a business executive or manager who has to deal with the results of an increasingly illiterate work force. While you're at it, you interview a teacher of adult illiterates and a victim of illiteracy with a particularly heart-wrenching human-interest story.

All these articles weave essentially the same facts into different stories: many intelligent adults cannot read; the problem is large enough to affect the nation's economy; the problem is growing; the reasons are unclear; the government is trying to do something about it; private industry is developing programs to deal with it.

SELLING AN IDEA TO YOUR BOSS

Publications differ in the ways they encourage staff members to submit story ideas to editors. Sometimes proposals are made and accepted quite casually, perhaps in conversation over the water cooler. Normally, however, several editors discuss a suggested feature to decide whether the idea is right for the publication, whether it fits with upcoming editorial mix, how long it should be, how it might be illustrated, and the like. On newspapers, editors normally generate ideas and make assignments to appropriate reporters. A creative city desk may have a suggestion box where reporters can drop tips for stories.

In either case, your editor will need a written proposal describing the subject, the angle you will take, how it fits your publication, the sources available, and the story's length. This proposal must run no longer than one single-spaced page—preferably shorter. Try to keep it to two or three paragraphs.

Some magazines require staff members to produce a quota of story ideas each week or month. You may be asked to present these ideas at regular editorial meetings. If generating ideas is part of your job, remember to put everything in writing and keep copies of the proposals you submit, to ensure that you get credit for your efforts.

FREE-LANCING AN IDEA TO AN EDITOR

Most independent writers restrict themselves to magazines. There's little point in attempting to sell a free-lance story to a large newspaper, because the editors already have plenty of writers on staff. On the rare occasions that papers do buy from independent writers, the pay is too low to justify the work required to produce an acceptable piece. Locally produced Sunday newspaper magazines sometimes buy free-lance contributions, but most have been supplanted by nationally distributed weekend supplements.

However, a few writers do sell to newspapers. It's possible to make a profit at this by self-syndicating; that is, by writing a generic story or column and selling it to papers whose circulation does not overlap. A piece on how to develop one's wine-tasting skills, for example, might succeed here. Some people write book reviews for newspapers, as a sideline to full-time jobs.

Such stories should be offered to the feature editor, or to the editor of the leisure, travel, or arts section. Their names are rarely listed on a newspaper's masthead. You can identify them by looking up the publication in the *Editor and Publisher International Yearbook,* which gives the names of departmental editors. In many large cities, the public relations and advertising industry produces media guides listing editors' names and titles; these are often available in public libraries. Failing a reference work, call the paper and ask for the name of its feature editor.

It is also possible to obtain a kind of part-time job as a newspaper or wire service *stringer,* reporting stories outside bureau cities. These low pay, low prestige positions make it possible for metropolitan papers to develop state-wide or regional networks, and sometimes they lead to full-time jobs on the city staff. If you can't get a job any other way or if circumstances dictate that you live in a rural area, ask the state editor at your region's largest newspaper about openings for part-time correspondents.

Query First

Whether you wish to write for a newspaper or a magazine, your first task is to form a good mental picture of the publication's readers and establish a focus or slant that will interest them in what you have to say. Your next step is to write a query or proposal.

A *query* is a letter that sells your idea. It introduces you, describes what you want to do, and convinces the editor that she needs you more than life.

Always query before writing an article for a magazine.

At this point, half a dozen hands shoot up in the classroom. "Shouldn't we get down to the business of writing the story?" the students chorus. "Isn't it a waste of time to wait around for some editor to read a letter and send an answer?"

No. The way to waste your time is to write a story without knowing whether an editor wants it.

Let's look at the editor's desk. Typically, you can't see the surface for the mound of paper stacked on it. Every day, the mail brings a wad of unsolicited articles, queries, and press releases. In an atmosphere most likely hectic, the editor is fighting several deadlines. He has no time to read an article by an unknown writer who has not even discussed the idea first.

If you are lucky, your unsolicited piece will go to a junior editor whose job is to sort through the slush pile, returning manuscripts with form rejections. Unless your story is incredibly good, she will reject it. Chances that you, as a beginner, will write an "incredibly good" article are nil.

That you sent the article without first querying marks you as a beginner. Professionals land an assignment before they begin to write, because time is money. They cannot afford to write a story without (a) some guarantee that it will be accepted and (b) guidance from the editor about exactly what is wanted.

You might submit a story on a subject that interests the editor, but without that guidance, the approach probably will be wrong. If so, one of two things will happen:

1. The editor will ask you to rewrite it, causing you to spend twice as much time on the story as you should have; or

2. The editor will reject it, because she hasn't time to train an obviously inexperienced writer. Later, she may assign the same topic to someone she knows.

Either way, the unsolicited manuscript represents wasted time and effort.

A query can take the form of a personal letter or of a separate proposal with a cover letter. If you circulate a generic proposal to several similar magazines, don't let it get shopworn. Your best bet is to tailor each query to a specific editor.

It must look professional. Type it, single-spaced, on white bond paper or business stationery, set up as a standard business letter (figure 2.2) or in the format suggested for proposals (figure 2.3). Address yourself to a person, not to "Editor."

A query should run no longer than two pages. Make it long enough to develop your idea, but short enough to read quickly. Many writers feel a snappy title helps, but it's not necessary.

Open with a strong statement, something that would work as a lead for the story. Remember, the editor is busy. You must grab her attention in the first paragraph. If the first few sentences fail to interest her, she'll set your letter aside without finishing it.

Next, state your central idea in a nutshell. Say what specific aspect of the topic you will cover and what angle you will take. Phrase this part of the proposal in the future tense ("I will . . ."), instead of the conditional ("I would like to . . ."). This makes your proposal sound positive, rather than tentative.

Be sure to make your angle clear. Suppose you want to cover the illiteracy question for your city magazine by focusing on a local literacy program's director. State the problem, quickly detailing its nationwide magnitude, and say "someone here in River City is doing something about it." Name the director, briefly say something about her, and specify your approach: a profile of a person involved in an important issue.

Do not write "this story will appeal to your readers because. . . ." The editor knows his readers better than you do; don't presume to tell him how they think. Instead, let your aptly tailored proposal speak for itself.

Your tone should be somewhat formal. This is a business letter, not a note to an old school chum. Address the editor as "Mr." or "Ms."; don't use first names.

Include enough detail to convince the editor that you know what you're talking about. Give enough facts, an anecdote, or some statistics to provide a little background. Name the people you plan to interview. If you will interview recognized experts, identify them and say how you will contact them. If you will use some special sources, say what they are.

If the story has a timely news hook, mention it.

In the second-to-last paragraph, introduce yourself. Explain why you should be assigned to this piece—if you have some expertise in the subject, say so. Describe your writing experience. But if you have none, keep quiet about it. Never say anything like, "this is the first feature I have written, but I just know I can do it. . . ." If your proposal is well written, it will speak for itself.

End with a request for action: "Please let me know if this idea interests you." This is an old salesman's trick. A prospect is more likely to make a move if you tell him what to do next. The query is as much a sales tool as the pitch you hear at the used-car lot.

Always include a self-addressed, stamped envelope (SASE) and, for every new editor, some clips. A clip is a photocopy of a published article you have written. It should include the entire piece, not just the front page. If, however, you want to show book authorship, photocopy the title page.

Letter or Proposal?

Whether you offer your idea in a letter or a proposal depends on the circumstances. Usually, a business letter addressed to the appropriate editor will do the job.

However, if you need to show that you can write in a distinctive style, you might want to present the idea, angle, and details in a separate proposal (figure 2.3) displaying the style you will use for the story. In a more formal cover letter, you can introduce yourself, state your background, and ask for action.

Proposals, sometimes called "article memos," often begin with

```
                                        XXX East Erewhon
                                        Phoenix, Arizona  XXXXX
                                        April 1, 1985


Mr. Craig Boddington
Editor-in-Chief
Petersen's Hunting
8490 Sunset Boulevard
Los Angeles, California  90069

Dear Mr. Boddington:

       A couple of hunting friends have invited me to join
them on an expedition to southern Arizona in search of
Mearn's quail, an elusive game bird that hides instead of
taking flight when approached.  We would go on horseback
into the spectacular hinterlands around Patagonia, taking a
pack of trained hunting dogs.  One of the men, Bob Brannon,
is a professional back-country guide and hunting dog
trainer; the other is a veterinarian who specializes in bird
dogs.
       I would like to do a story for you about hunting
Mearn's quail in southern Arizona.  Photographer John Ormond
will go with us, and we two will work as a team.  The story,
about 2,000 words, will focus on the hunting aspects of the
trip--not as a "me 'n' Joe" piece, but as an outdoor
adventure of special interest to hunters.
       I have been a staff writer for Phoenix Magazine for
about a year.  Before that, I free-lanced successfully for
two years.  My work has appeared in local and regional
publications, including Arizona Highways, as well as in some
national trade magazines.  My first book, a full-length
biography, was just published by Folger Shakespeare Library.
       I enclose some clips and samples of Ormond's work.
Please send me a copy of your writer's guidelines.

                              Sincerely,



                              Vicky Hay
```

Figure 2.2 Typical query letter.

```
Connie Emerson
XXX East Erewhon
Reno, Nevada  89000
(702) 000-0000




Branson, Missouri
COUNTRY MUSIC CHARMER
(article memo)


    Drive along Highway 76 any summer evening with your car
windows down and you'll hear the sound of music--country
western, bluegrass, gospel or old time rock 'n roll.  In
Branson, Missouri, the Ozark's capital of country music, the
number of musical variety shows rivals Nashville.

    Fifteen music theaters, with a total of more than 30,000
seats, provide entertainment with whole-family appeal.  One
club is owned by romance novelest Janet Dailey.  The Sons of
the Pioneers perform regularly at another.  At all of them
you can be assured of toe-tapping music and down-home humor.

*  *  *

    This 800-word piece goes on to tell more about the music
as well as the area's other attractions.  There's the
Shepherd of the Hills Homestead, where visitors can watch a
wheelwright and other craftspeople; milk a cow; savor the
aromas of apple cider, sorghum and woodsmoke.  At a replica
of an Ozark pioneer settlement called Silver Dollar City,
demonstrations of more than 30 pioneer crafts, steam train
excursions and a Tom Sawyer-themed children's playground are
highlights.  Nearby Table Rock Lake, with 857 miles of
shoreline, provides an abundance of recreational
opportunities--nature trails, amphibious vehicle tours,
fishing and water sports.  On the campus of the School of
the Ozarks, the Ralph Foster Museum contains the largest
collection of money in the U.S. and the truck used in
filming the Beverly Hillbillies TV series.  At Wilderness
Safari, roads wind through 325 acres populated by gaurs, emu
and scimitar-horned oryx.  White Water's adventures take the
form of four-foot waves, a body flume, and other water-
related amusements.  A wide range of annual events
(including Kewpiesta, a celebration honoring the creator of
the kewpie doll) are other entertainment options.
```

Figure 2.3   Typical article proposal. This one targeted *Friendly Exchange*.

the lead the author plans to use and then present an outline or summary of the article's contents.

A story idea that could interest more than one magazine—such as women's magazines, regional in-flights, or motoring magazines—might be presented in proposal form. If it is rejected, you needn't retype it before sending it forth again.

Can You Send Queries to More Than One Editor at Once?

Not usually. This is called "simultaneous submission." Editors want to feel they're getting an exclusive story. Sending a story to several markets at once devalues it.

Some writers do send stories to publications whose circulation does not overlap. In other words, you might send a piece on wine-tasting to newspaper lifestyle sections in several states. But woe betide you if the story sells to two editors who see each other as competitors! The publishing world is small, and word gets around very fast. A reputation for this trick can put a writer out of business.

When you make a simultaneous submission, you must tell the editor so and list the markets you are querying.

How long should you wait for an answer before querying another editor? Give the mails at least a week to deliver your letter. Then allow a month for the editors to consider your proposal and reply. If you hear nothing after six weeks, send a follow-up. After another 10 days, you can feel safe taking your business elsewhere.

CASE IN POINT

Let's follow a real story from the idea stage to the sale.

My friend Jerry Jenkins offered an idle suggestion one day when I was visiting his veterinary office. He and several buddies liked to hunt the elusive Mearn's quail. One of his friends, teacher Bob Brannon, was a professional back-country guide. Bob and Jerry planned a horseback expedition into some spectacular upland country in southern Arizona, the only Mearn's quail habitat in the United States. Why didn't I come along and write a story about it?

It looked like a chance to get paid for having fun. I called free-lance photographer John Ormond; would he like to collaborate? "Sure," he said, "but not on spec." If we could get an assignment, he would come along.

Some legwork told me Mearn's, also called "harlequin quail," is a very colorful bird—photo opportunity. Few people know about them; their range is limited to southern Arizona and northern Mexico. Once thought to be an endangered species, they're actually very abundant. They're so elusive, scientists had a difficult time counting them. A recent study showed hunting has no effect on their numbers. Apparently the hunters' victims are weak individuals that would die of cold and thirst in winter. Mearn's is considered great hunting, one of the most delicious game birds. The quail inhabit a gorgeous, sparsely populated area full of exotic birds like the coppery-tailed trogon—birdwatcher's paradise, great camping country, photo opportunities. The region is little known among tourists and hunters.

Ormond and I figured we could come up with either a travel or a sporting piece—or, with any luck, both. We also had an outside chance of selling a nature story. We identified several large markets:

Outdoor and nature magazines
Tourism magazines
Birding publications
Hunting magazines
Regional general-interest magazines

Up front, we discarded *Audubon* and *National Wildlife*, because I knew too little about birding to write authoritatively.

Two in-state hunting magazines paid less than we could afford to work for. *Western Outdoors* offered acceptable pay, but Arizona is outside the 11 states it covers.

We took proposals for tourism stories to *Friendly Exchange, Chevron USA,* and *Outside.* All rejected.

We went to *Gray's Sporting Journal, Field and Stream, Sports Afield,* and *Petersen's Hunting* with hunting proposals. *Gray's* and *Field and Stream* asked to see stories on speculation, but neither John nor I work on spec. *Petersen's Hunting* offered a contract on the basis of the query shown in figure 2.2.

A careful study of the magazine had shown what its features had in common:

They mix anecdotes with how-to-do-it information.
They tend to the macho.
They always focus on people.
They sometimes depict real or implicit danger.
They often have a touch of drama.
They depict hunting as fun.
They're not very deep.

We based our query on these characteristics, and it worked. Editor Craig Boddington wrote back forthwith:

We haven't done anything on Arizona quail—or, more specifically, Mearn's quail—for quite some time, and I am very interested in such a story.

The idea of taking horses in makes it even more interesting. I've always hunted the little so&sos on foot, and it's probably the most difficult bird hunt in this country.

Anyway, I'm interested. I do have a couple of concerns. First, we attempt to take a "how-to" approach to the sport. In other words, a story for us should be interesting, exciting, and perhaps anecdotal, but it should also assist the reader in planning a similar trip, or at least give him the basics of techniques, habitat, etc.

The one thing you didn't mention in your query is your degree of involvement with the sport. Our readers are serious hunters, so articles for this magazine must be from the enthusiast's viewpoint, and the language and such must be correct and the author authoritative on the subject.

Mearn's quail habitat is quite beautiful in a stark way, so I envision good potential for a color layout, particularly if you're able to capture the horses and dogs (and, with luck, perhaps a covey rise!) against some of that scenery. In any case, I'd be looking for some good color, hopefully including some action. Since our four-color usage is limited, I'd also like some black & white of an illustrative nature.

The how-to angle would be built into the trip. The other was more problematic: I had never gone hunting, nor did I grasp the joy in killing. However, Jenkins and Brannon could read the copy for accuracy; my authority would derive from them. As a writer, I had learned to empathize, to see things from others' viewpoints. I wrote back, saying my father and my closest friend's father were avid hunters; so I had grown up around folks who loved hunting. This was true. I did not mention that it never crossed my father's mind to take his daughter hunting, nor that my friend's father, whom I had met twice, lived in another state.

The magazine sent separate contracts to me and Ormond and we were on our way.

–30–

FOR PROJECTS OR DISCUSSION:

Select one or two magazines where you realistically think your talents will sell. Go to the library and study a year's worth of back issues.

From the most recent masthead, note the name, title, and address of an editor to whom you might submit a proposal.

Who reads the magazine? What is their age range? How educated are they? On what do you base these conclusions?

Why do they read this magazine? What specifically does it offer —e.g., how-to tips, consumer information, shop talk, inspiration, intellectual stimulation, humor, etc.?

What is the magazine's overall political, social, or moral orientation?

What is its tone—what attitude does it take toward the reader? Toward its subject matter? Toward life?

What kind of language do the writers use? Is it formal? casual? sophisticated? simple?

What is the average length of a feature?

What themes do they cover regularly? For example, pregnancy, health, personalities, travel, money management, etc.

Do any departments appear to accept free-lance contributions? If so, what is the average length of the items in it? What subject matter is favored?

Ask the editor for the writer's guidelines. Compare what this document says with the conclusions you have drawn.

After—and *only* after—you have done these things, look up your magazine in *Writer's Market*. If it is listed, compare the report with what you have observed so far. Note any additional information you consider useful.

SUGGESTED READING

Lisa Collier Cool. *How to Write Irresistible Query Letters.* Cincinnati, Oh.: Writer's Digest Books, 1987.

Connie Emerson. *Write on Target.* Cincinnati, Oh.: Writers Digest Books, 1981. Extensively revised version due out in 1992.

Herbert J. Gans, *Deciding What's News: A Study of* CBS Evening News, NBC Nightly News, *and* Time. New York: Pantheon Books, 1977. Casts light on where stories come from and how they are selected.

Writer's Digest, a monthly magazine, frequently runs articles and tips on marketing nonfiction stories.

The annual *Writer's Market* (Writer's Digest Books, Cincinnati) includes articles on querying, marketing, bookkeeping, and other information helpful to free-lance writers. See, by the same publisher, another useful annual compendium, the *Writer's Yearbook.*

3

Research for the Feature Story

The first step in research is at once the easiest and the most difficult: Think.

Any information-gathering project, whether it's heavy on interviews and personal observation or whether it requires lots of library work, starts with a systematic, organized approach. Before you begin, you should consider where you will find your material and how you will dig it out.

The basic steps to journalistic research are three: first, gain a broad overview of the subject; second, learn about it in some depth; and third, find and interview knowledgeable people.

Before we begin discussing these techniques, here's a caveat. This chapter reviews important, easily accessible reference works and information sources suitable for most feature-writing, and it tells you how to track down people to interview. But it is not designed for students of investigative journalism. Before you undertake an investigative article, you should take a course in investigative journalism and work on-staff with an experienced editor.

GETTING STARTED

Seasoned reporters will tell you the key to a successful interview is simple: *do your homework first.* Learn enough about your assignment to speak intelligently with your sources. Nothing turns an interviewee off faster than a writer's total ignorance of the subject.

Thus, while the interview is the journalist's most important research tool, it comes last. It's the culmination of your research, undertaken only after considerable reading, legwork, and thought.

Be aware, by the way, that researchers divide sources into two broad types: primary and secondary. A *primary* source is a person who has direct knowlege of an event. Among primary sources are witnesses whom you might interview, letters or reports by people who were on the scene, and depositions or court testimony of witnesses. A *secondary* source is a report from someone knows about the subject or event but who did not actually witness it. Take, for example, an airplane crash. Primary sources are the survivors and the people who saw the crash. Secondary sources are Federal Aviation Authority reports; comments from other aviation experts; writing about air safety in general; interviews with friends and relatives of the victims; and newspaper, television, and magazine accounts.

Does this mean that any one-on-one interview is a primary source? No! You could, for example, talk to someone who speaks from hearsay. If the individual was not at an event, did not witness it firsthand, then he is not a primary source. But if she is an expert on a subject—say, a scientist explaining her experiments in killer bee biology—then she *is* a primary source. So, among interviewees, primary sources include witnesses, participants, and experts directly involved in an action or study. Secondary sources include gossips, people who know someone who was involved in the action, and experts speaking in general about other experts' findings.

Students sometimes jump to the conclusion that anything printed is a secondary source. Again, the distinction depends on whether its writer is "on the scene" of the subject at hand. For example, an article on killer bees written by our entomologist and based on her research would be a primary source. A story written by a reporter, or even by an expert whose article is a reprise of other people's research, would be a secondary source. Diaries, letters, and journals are primary sources. A biography based on those diaries, letters, and journals is a secondary source. An autobiography is a primary source. A witness's statement is a primary source; a report by a police officer who came upon an accident minutes after it occurred may contain primary and secondary material.

Often, you must weigh the credibility of your sources. Let's say you need to understand the latest developments in superconductivity. That has something to do with physics. But because it is a specialized subject with fast-breaking developments, just any physicist won't do. You must be sure your physicist has real expertise in your subject. How do you find out? First, ask him. Then verify his credentials with his colleagues—ask other physicists about his professional reputation. Remember, too, that most people have some ax to grind: try to identify your expert's biases and keep them in mind as you consider his remarks.

Given an assignment about which you know little or nothing, you should first ask yourself a few key questions:

1. Who knows about this subject and cares enough to publish an article or book about it?
2. Where can I find these articles or books?
3. Will this story have a local or a national slant, and how will that affect my choice of sources?

1. Who Knows?

The answer to this question may be less obvious than it looks. Suppose, for example, you're asked to write a story about senior citizens who keep their jobs past the traditional retirement age. Your editor wants you to focus on two or three successful individuals, weaving in lots of solid information about who hires them and why; why seniors continue to work; the issue's political aspects; and the advantages and disadvantages to the worker, the employer, and the larger society. To give the piece some glitz, he expects you to drop names of a few famous older workers, such as Mary Kay Ashe and Col. Harland Sanders, and he asks you to find out what jobs attract older workers, and why.

At the start, all you know about the subject comes from a McDonald's television ad highlighting the company's experiment with senior workers. You make a note to call someone at McDonald's national headquarters, whose telephone number you will obtain from a reference librarian, from the *Standard Directory of Advertisers*, or from the *Million-Dollar Directory*.

First, though, you consider which organizations might be involved with the subject. The American Association of Retired Persons comes immediately to mind. This group concerns itself with anything that affects senior citizens economically. You hazard a guess that something on older workers has already appeared in the AARP organ, *Modern Maturity*.

Your state has a governor's commission on aging; this will be a good source of local information. The National Council on Aging is another likely source, as is the Service Corps of Retired Executives, which has both national and local agencies.

As you think about it, you recall recent legislation eliminating the mandatory retirement age. This means various government agencies have heard testimony on the question of whether older people should be permitted to continue working indefinitely. It also means the subject has some "hot" topics which probably have attracted academic sociologists and psychologists. And it means the subject certainly has been in the news.

If the government is telling business it can't force workers to retire, then various industries will be searching out ways to respond. Good: business and trade publications will report on their solutions.

Older workers may have higher health care costs, because one's health tends to slip as one ages. This means group insurance providers will evince interest in your subject. You make a note to call several major insurers.

Speaking of health, folk wisdom tells you that people who stay active as they age stay healthier and happier. You wonder if there's anything to this, and if so, what are the implications for America's rapidly aging populace, for industry, and for our society in general. This is the meat of sociology and psychology.

Now you have a good idea of where to begin:

1. With national newspapers, such as *The New York Times, The Washington Post,* or *The Christian Science Monitor*
2. With special-interest consumer magazines targeted at older readers
3. With business and trade publications
4. With sociological or psychological journals
5. With government publications

We've arranged these in the order of descending accessibility and ascending difficulty. To gain the quick overview you need before you begin speaking to sources, you should start with the first two or three categories. More detailed familiarity will come from professional journals and congressional testimony. For a light story, you may not have to dig that deep. If you're doing a long, serious piece, you will go to all these sources and more.

Later—after you've done your preliminary reading—you'll search out:

6. Spokesmen for companies that hire older workers, who may refer you to
7. Workers willing to let you highlight their stories;
8. Employment counselors experienced with older workers;
9. Spokesmen for senior citizens' groups, such as AARP;
10. Other experts, academic or otherwise; and
11. Spokesmen for insurance carriers, if you decide that aspect is germane to the story.

Categories one through four bring us to the next question:

2. Where Do I Find Overview Articles?

Magazine, newspaper, and journal articles are indexed in certain standard reference works, listed in this chapter's next section. You'll start with one or two of these indexes—say, the microform *Magazine Index* and *The New York Times Index*, both available in most libraries.

To use these indexes, you'll need a list of logical subject headings that describe your topic, and to arrive at a useful list, you need to think like an indexer; that is, alphabetically, from general to specific. Break the subject down into several main concepts, and then come up with some synonyms for each. For example, "old" means "aged." "Worker" can mean "employee."

For the story on older workers, then, you might come up with these key words:

Age discrimination
Aged, employment of
Employees, aged
Employees, older
Late bloomers
Older workers
Retirement, mandatory
Pension rules
Workers, older

A search of these headings in a magazine index would lead you to articles in *Aging, Science, Modern Maturity, Nation's Business, Time, Ms.,* and *50 Plus* (the latter is now called *New Choices* and at this writing *Ms.* is provisionally defunct, but articles published under a magazine's old title will still be listed that way and your library may carry the back issues). Look up the same topics in a newspaper index and you will find reports about Congressional measures to eliminate mandatory retirement, to require insurers to extend coverage to workers over 70, and to give workers over 65 additional pension credits. You would also find coverage of the opposite trend, in which corporations cut payrolls by urging early retirement, leaving potentially productive workers to face decades of idleness and inflation-driven impoverishment.

If your story is short and simple, a cursory list jotted on scrap paper will serve as an adequate guide.

For more complex projects, you'll find a more systematic approach useful. Write each key word on a separate notecard. Beneath the key word, list the references you intend to search. Check off each as you go, if necessary noting the volume numbers you cover.

If you have to stop in midsearch, you will know where to take up your project, and when you are through, you will have a precise record of where you looked up each item.

3. How Do I Give the Story a Local or National Slant?

With research, as with all aspects of journalism, the writer must keep in mind the audience. Who is going to read this story?

A story of national importance may be written for a local publication. In that case, it needs to say explicitly what the issue means for hometown readers. Show this by finding local authorities to comment on the subject, or by depicting the way the issue affects a resident's life. You may get your facts from national sources, but you must tie them to your reader's immediate concerns.

I once did a story on the big business of telephone soliciting. The article relied on federal government sources, a Wisconsin congressman who lobbied to regulate phone solicitors, a Virginia code of ethics, and spokesmen from California and Michigan public utilities commissions. But to tailor the piece to a city magazine, I led with an anecdote about a local mother denied much-needed rest by the jangling phone and later told of a city family whose telephone was tied up during a medical emergency by an interminable computerized message. Reciting these stories and quoting local telephone company officials, legislators, and Better Business Bureau spokesmen brought the national issue home.

Conversely, a story with local origins may take on a national slant if you focus on the right sources. I learned of an Arizona couple whom the Internal Revenue Service had charged an exorbitant penalty for failing to pay a housekeeper's social security taxes. Casual investigation revealed that the law requires you to pay social security for domestic workers, including housekeepers and, under some circumstances, babysitters and gardeners. Long-distance calls to regional IRS offices and big-city accountants across the nation produced a story that spoke to American taxpayers everywhere. The article went to a magazine for preferred customers of banks and lending institutions.

HOW TO FIND PRINTED INFORMATION

Periodicals

If any aspect of the story has the slightest currency, it's a good idea to start with the newspaper indexes. The *New York Times* index is probably the most comprehensive, followed by the

Washington Post index. Don't neglect the *Wall Street Journal*, which covers subjects extending well beyond business and industry. The *Christian Science Monitor*'s index is also available in most libraries. All these plus the *Los Angeles Times* are collected on Information Access Company's easy-to-use microform, called the *National Newspaper Index*.

This will give you a running head start in the search for recent, easily digested articles to provide background for your own story. Longer, more in-depth stories appear in magazines and professional journals.

If your library has them, begin with Information Access Company's microform *Magazine Index* and *Business Index*. The former is a cumulative index of more than 400 titles; the latter covers 810 periodicals. They also list book reviews.

That old standby, *Reader's Guide to Periodical Literature*, is cumbersome, but it is more comprehensive and dates back to 1905. For nineteenth-century journals, look in *Poole's Index to Periodical Literature*. The *Alternative Press Index* will give you leads to off-beat stories in small publications not listed in the mainstream catalogs.

Specialized indexes survey popular and scholarly publications in specific fields:

Business Periodicals Index (1958 to present) appears monthly except August. It has a cumulative subject index.

Education Index (1929 to present) each month surveys educational periodicals, proceedings, and yearbooks. It also has a cumulative subject index.

Social Science Index (1974 to present) indexes 263 periodicals in anthropology, area studies, economics, environmental science, psychology, public administration, and sociology.

Humanities Index (1974 to present) covers periodicals in archaeology, classics, area studies, folklore, history, language and literature, performing arts, religion, etc.

Essay and General Literature Index (1905 to present) indexes 324 volumes of collected essays and miscellaneous works emphasizing the humanities and social sciences.

Music Index (1949 to present) covers more than 300 music-related periodicals. It includes obituaries, book reviews, and performance and record reviews.

Art Index (1932 to present) indexes periodicals, yearbooks, and museum bulletins by subject and author, and includes entries for art reproductions. It is not cumulative.

Biological and Agricultural Index (1964 to present) is a cumulative subject index to 190 periodicals in biology, agriculture, and related sciences.

Index Medicus, a comprehensive index to world medical literature, exists in three series: 1879–1899, 1879–1927, and 1960–present. The current series, compiled by the National Library of Medicine, is cumulated annually and lists subjects, names, and medical
reviews.

Index to Legal Periodicals (1908 to present) has three-year cumu-
lations of the monthly subject and author indexes, covering about
400 periodicals.

Guide to Theses and Dissertations offers leads to fresh academic
research. This work provides abstracts of each work; University
Microfilms will send the entire study on microfilm for a nominal
cost.

Books

For a quick guide to a library's holdings, go to the subject section
of the card or on-line catalog. Look up "comic strips" in the Phoenix
city library, for example, and you'll find two bibliographies (books
listing printed works on the subject), two encyclopedias of cartoons
and comics, a biographical dictionary of cartoonists, and several
books on the history of comic strips. This was as much as I needed
to sell a proposal to a regional magazine on nationally prominent
comic-strip artists who reside in Arizona.

Some libraries' subject catalogs are more comprehensive than
others. Under "comic strips," the same library's subject catalog
mentions George Herriman's *Krazy Kat* and one book on Bill Mauldin—
but it does not list all the Herriman and Mauldin holdings, nor does
it give the slightest clue to the library's complete collection of Hergé's
Tintin adventures. Expect the subject catalog to provide a thumbnail
guide, useful if you're in a hurry but just a start to a more complete
search.

The subject guide to *Books in Print* is another instant bibliography. It does not list every book published on a topic—only the texts
now in print. It shows you what titles are currently on the market.
Some may not have reached your library; but by the same token, the
library may carry useful books now out of print.

The subject guide to *Forthcoming Books in Print* lists books
scheduled for publication in the next five months.

Most books copyrighted in the United States appear in the *Library
of Congress—National Union Catalog.* This ponderous work lists
Library of Congress holdings by subject, title, and author, plus contents of governmental department libraries and other selected collections. If you can't find a given book in your library, you may
obtain it through interlibrary loan.

Book Review Digest summarizes reviews in a wide range of U.S. and British periodicals. *Book Review Index* lists reviews by the book author's name, without abstracting them, from about 460 magazines and journals. *Index to Book Reviews in the Humanities* catalogs reviews in about 700 scholarly and popular periodicals.

Publisher's Weekly, a publishing industry trade magazine, gives information on recent offerings and announces forthcoming books.

Backgrounding an Individual

Short biographies of the prominent and not-so-prominent can be found in the proliferating Marquis *Who's Who* series. Inspired by the venerable British reference of the same title, Marquis now gives us listings of Americans from four geographic regions and in many special categories. There's a *Who's Who of American Women*, for example, and a *Who's Who in American Law*. To fill all of these volumes, the company includes some obscure folks. You may find a local executive or society matron here. Because each person writes his or her own entry, the information is hardly disinterested, but it gives you something to start with.

For "unauthorized" profiles of people in the news, often including pictures, try *Current Biography* (1940 to present). This monthly compendium uses as sources newspapers, magazines, books, and (sometimes) the biographees.

The *New York Times Biographical Service* compiles offprints of *Times* articles. It contains profiles, obituaries, and pictures, dating from 1970. The *New York Times Personal Name Index* is an alphabetical listing of all personal names that appeared in that newspaper to 1979. And the *New York Times Obituary Index* gives a cumulative list of 353,000 obituaries appearing between 1868 and 1968.

The twenty-volume *Dictionary of American Biography* evaluates prominent intellectual and political leaders who are no longer living. It covers the years 1928–1973, with supplements.

The monumental *Dictionary of National Biography* gives the lives of more than 30,000 British and colonial citizens.

Contemporary Authors, first published in 1962, collects biographies and bibliographies of more than 75,000 twentieth-century authors, with cumulative indexes in alternate volumes. A separate series presents autobiographical essays by many authors.

The *Directory of American Scholars* profiles more than 33,500 U.S. academics. *National Faculty Directory*, while it gives no biographical information, provides institutional affiliations and addresses.

Biography Index directs readers to profiles in books and in 2,600 periodicals. This quarterly begins in 1946.

Webster's New Biographical Dictionary (1983) offers short sketches of 30,000 deceased men and women.

The *National Cyclopedia of American Biography* began in 1882; by 1984, it had collected 66,500 biographies in 74 volumes.

Backgrounding a Business

A good place to start is the *Dun and Bradstreet Million-Dollar Directory*, which lists about 160,000 U.S. companies worth $500,000 or more. A separate directory, *The Top 50,000 Companies*, lists those whose net worth exceeds $1,850,000. Dun and Bradstreet reports each company's state of incorporation, subsidiaries, imports, exports, address, telephone number, Telex or TWX, annual sales, number of employees, principal bank, and titles and functions of officers.

The annual *Dun and Bradstreet Reference Book of Corporate Managements* gives brief biographies of 2,400 companies' officers and directors.

Standard and Poor's Register of Corporations, Directors, and Executives lists 36,000 U.S. and Canadian companies and gives biographies of major business figures.

The *Thomas Register of American Manufacturers* and the *Thomas Catalog File* are more comprehensive than Dun & Bradstreet or Standard and Poor's. The first lists products and services alphabetically and gives short company profiles with addresses, asset ratings, and company officials' names. The latter is exactly what its name implies: a huge collection of wholesale and retail catalogs.

For general business questions, the *Business Periodicals Index* lists about 170 periodicals by subject.

The *Public Affairs Information Service Bulletin* covers current literature on economic and social conditions, indexing books, pamphlets, reports of public and private agencies, periodicals, etc.

The *F & S Index of Corporations and Industries* indexes periodicals and other references on U.S. corporations and on industry as a whole—mergers, new products, technological developments, etc. For foreign companies, try the *F & S Index International*.

Miscellaneous General Information

Beginners often overlook the most obvious source of a quick overview: a good encyclopedia. Most libraries have the *Encyclopaedia Britannica*, *Encyclopedia Americana*, and *Collier's Encyclopedia*. Some regard *Collier's* as less reliable than the others, but it remains popular and accessible. The *Britannica* now contains three sections: a one-volume table of contents, a ten-volume "micropaedia" combining an index with a digest of longer articles in the remaining volumes, and a nineteen-volume "macropaedia" of long, scholarly entries. The one-volume *Columbia Encyclopedia* is a quick, convenient reference.

The annual *Information Please Almanac* is arranged by topic and has a subject index. It offers miscellaneous statistical and historical information on the United States, a chronology of the year's events, statistical and historical descriptions of various countries, etc.

Statistical Abstract of the United States, published by the Treasury Department's Bureau of Statistics since 1879, summarizes figures on the United States' political, social, and economic organization.

World Almanac and Book of Facts, another annual, collects statistics on social, industrial, political, financial, religious, and educational topics, political organizations, societies, and history.

Facts on File is a weekly world news digest with a cumulative index organized under topical headings.

Bartlett's Familiar Quotations is the standard collection of *bons mots*, arranged chronologically by author. The *Oxford Dictionary of Quotations* lists 40,000 quotations, with a concordance-like index.

The *Hammond Ambassador World Atlas* is a convenient book of maps, easy to read and organized in a logical sequence.

The *Columbia Lippincott Gazetteer of the World* lists political and geographical places world-wide, giving variant spellings, pronunciation, location, altitude, history, trade, resources, and other pertinent facts.

A Writer's Six-Foot Shelf

Clearly, nonfiction writers have to do some legwork in a library. But you should keep a select set of reference works at hand, if for no other reason than to check facts. You can often buy excellent references at discount: watch book clubs for special offers, and keep an eye out for sales of remaindered or used books.

Here's a minimal list of books the writer should shelve next to the word processor. If you specialize in a subject, you'll want a few germane sources, too.

Webster's New Unabridged Dictionary
A word speller, such as *Webster's Instant Word Guide*
The compact edition of the *Oxford English Dictionary*
The *Harper Dictionary of Contemporary Usage*
Rodale's Synonym Finder
Roget's Thesaurus
Webster's Biographical Dictionary

Dictionaries of Spanish, French, German, or other languages with which you are familiar

Bartlett's Familiar Quotations or *Oxford Dictionary of Quotations*

The Oxford Companion to American Literature

The Oxford Companion to English Literature

A world atlas

Rand-McNally's *Road Atlas to the United States, Canada, and Mexico*

A road map of your state

Road maps to your state's major cities

U.S. Forest Service maps for your region

William Strunk and E. B. White, *The Elements of Style*

The Associated Press Stylebook and Libel Manual

The University of Chicago Press's *Chicago Manual of Style*

Physician's Desk Reference

Writer's Market

Comprehensive college survey textbooks on U.S., British, European, and world history

A good history of your state or region

The World Almanac

Directory of elected representatives

White and Yellow Pages telephone directories

Telephone directory to your nearest university

City and state government directories

HOW TO FIND EXPERTS

Whatever the story, your key research tool will be the interview. We will discuss interviewing techniques in chapter 4. But before you talk to anyone, you first must find someone qualified to discuss your topic.

Local Sources

A convenient place to start is the Yellow Pages. People love to talk about their work, and officers of small companies can be especially loquacious. If your subject involves a service or a product, somebody no doubt provides it in your area. Look up the topic, call the president of a local firm, and ask for an interview.

Larger companies will probably refer you to their public relations officers. However, it is worth trying to reach the company's executives first—sometimes you can get past a secretary, and occasionally you find executives who feel free to speak to the press.

Although what they say may be self-serving, business men and women or their p.r. agents can provide information about their industry, their customers, and issues that affect them. In-house p.r. agents often will arrange interviews for you with the company's most articulate or expert employees.

Trade groups bring together people with similar concerns. Again using the Yellow Pages, look up "trade associations" or "professional organizations" and you'll often find a lead to your topic. Executive directors of these groups gather much information. They can provide facts and statistics or tell you where to find them. Similar groups may be listed as "associations," "athletic organizations," "business and trade organizations," "political organizations and candidates," "social service organizations," "veterans' and military organizations," "consumer organizations," or "trade unions."

City, county, and state commissions are good local sources of experts on public policy issues. Call the mayor's, county supervisor's, or governor's office for leads.

Elected representatives keep abreast of public issues that affect their constituents. Obtain lists of elected officials from local and state government offices.

State or local governments staff certain departments with experts. Fish and game departments, for example, often hire ecologists knowledgeable in regional conservation issues. The highway department may have an engineer who can talk about safe bridge construction. Experts on corrections, child abuse, the handicapped, real estate, the environment, education, tourism—name a subject, and you'll find someone who knows about it on the public payroll. The telephone book's white pages give a thumbnail guide to government offices. You may obtain more complete directories at city hall or the state capitol. And while you're looking for government experts, check regional offices of federal agencies.

Chambers of commerce collect information on tourism, economic development, and various civic projects. They usually have in-house specialists, or they can refer you to private-sector experts. Here again, watch their comments for bias.

Universities and colleges also are full of people who know what they're talking about. On controversial topics, you may get a straighter story here—scientists and other academics are less likely to speak from pure self-interest than are business executives, p.r. people, and bureaucrats. But bear in mind that academics have their own hobbyhorses, chief among them concerns about promotion and prestige.

Find academic experts by calling the college's press bureau or public information officer. Explain what your story is about, for whom you are writing, and what specific information you need.

One expert is an excellent source of another. Each time you interview someone, ask if he knows anyone else who might help you.

Watch local newspapers and city magazines for clip-and-save listings of consumer advocates, elected representatives, points of interest, etc. Most publications run something of this nature. Local business journals often will run annual lists of the area's largest companies, complete with officers' names and phone numbers. Keep a file of such material.

National Sources

When you are starting cold on a search for sources with national credentials, resort to the library.

Your best friend there is the reference librarian, who will often help you by phone. For a recent wrap-up on inflated health-care costs, a five-minute telephone call yielded addresses and telephone numbers of the American Medical Association, the Federal Health Care Financing Administration, the Health Insurance Association of America, the federal Office of Health Maintenance Organizations, the American Association of Retired Persons, and the American Nursing Association, plus hospital peer review organizations in several states. Spokesmen for these outfits gave me so much information, they practically wrote the story for me.

Most of those references came from Gale's *Encyclopedia of Associations*. It lists more than 16,000 national organizations by category, indexing them alphabetically and by key word. Here you will find addresses and telephone numbers for groups concerned with trade, business, commerce, agriculture, government, public administration, the military, law, science, engineering and technology, public affairs, horticulture, veterans, patriotism, hobbies and avocations, athletics, labor unions, and much more.

National Trade and Professional Associations of the United States, and Labor Unions lists 4,600 national trade associations, professional groups, and learned societies.

For Washington, D.C., sources, the annual *Washington Information Directory* lists more than 5,000 government and private-sector sources there, including phone numbers, addresses, and key officials of all major White House agencies.

No one listens to more expert witnesses than the U.S. Congress. Most of the testimony is public record. If a subject has come up before a house or senate committee, you will find it listed in the *Monthly Catalog of U.S. Government Publications*.

Most libraries should have the *Monthly Catalog*. For copies of the hearings, however, you may have to go to your region's U.S. government repository, often located at the state archives or a major university. Identify the hearing number through the catalog and then go to the transcript. Here you will find witnesses' names, addresses, and telephone numbers, in addition to their testimony.

The press is a wellspring of sources. Check the national newspaper indexes, look up recent articles on your subject, and note the names, expertise, and addresses of the sources they quote. Trace telephone numbers through long-distance information. Don't be shy about calling: a person who has already spoken to one reporter will probably talk to you, too.

The *Research Centers Directory* lists 9,700 university and other nonprofit research organizations in the hard sciences, private and public policies, and social and cultural studies.

The *Consumer Sourcebook* lists several hundred government and private agencies that aid and inform consumers.

HOW TO FIND MANUSCRIPT SOURCES

Much unpublished material rests in state and national archives, university libraries, and various private collections. Historical societies invariably keep documents, letters, and memoires that cast light on modern topics.

The Library of Congress publishes a *National Union Catalog of Manuscript Collections* that indexes 29,350 manuscript collections in about 850 U.S. repositories. Philip Hamer's *Guide to Archives and Manuscripts in the United States* directs readers to useful sources.

If you write regularly about your state or city, make it a point to familiarize yourself with the state's official archives, local museums and historical societies, and university manuscript collections. Introduce yourself to the librarian, and, if you don't have a specific assignment, spend some time browsing.

Public records are by definition just that: "public," meaning you may see them. Official birth and death records, for example, are on file with each state's vital statistics department. Most current criminal and civil court records are available for the asking. Check local and U.S. District Courts, the federal bankruptcy court, and the U.S. tax court. Divorce and probate court records can be enlightening, too.

Sometimes your sources will give you documents such as resumés, in-house memos, correspondence, and unpublished company histories. Ask interview subjects if they have any written material that might help you.

ON-LINE DATABASES

Commercial data banks are technology's boon to the reporter. They cut legwork by a factor of ten, because they let you conduct thorough research without leaving your desk.

They work like this: A company enters indexes, bibliographies, abstracts, and full-text articles into a computer equipped with modems (gadgets that allow computers to talk to each other over the telephone lines). Each reference work, such as the *New York Times Index* or *Standard and Poor's,* forms a single database.

A researcher telephones the service by modem, calls up a database—say, *Magazine Index*—and types a key word or phrase, such as "peer review organization." The distant computer automatically searches the database for every article with those words in the title and every article indexed under that phrase. In a matter of seconds, it disgorges all the references it finds.

Subscribers pay once for a password and identification number that gives access to the service's databases. They also pay a per-minute on-line fee and long-distance phone charges each time they use the service; some services charge by the reference, and some charge a monthly fee.

As you might guess, on-line research is not cheap. However, free-lance writers earn from $20 to $60 an hour. You can accomplish as much in 15 minutes on-line as you would in two hours at the library —not counting commute time. Weigh the value of your time against on-line charges, and you'll often find the computer modem saves you money.

Will a publisher pay a free-lancer's on-line charges? It depends on how technologically liberated the publisher is. If you expect that an assignment will involve an database search, ask to have reasonable on-line costs included in your expenses.

If you work on a publication's staff, chances are your employer will subscribe to one or more databases, such as Nexis, Dialog, or Dow Jones News-Retrieval. In that case, you will be trained to use them.

If you are in charge of a small publication, you can subscribe to one of the less exorbitant services, such as Knowledge Index or CompuServe. To get you started, these firms provide some cursory training in on-line techniques; for more thorough teaching, they charge extra.

And the added help may be worth the cost. On-line searching can be arcane, especially for those accustomed to manual research. None of the serendipity inherent to printed indexes survives on-line: you can't browse the pages here. You must figure what key words will call up the desired references, and know how to combine them so that the concepts are neither too general (yielding hundreds of citations) nor too specific (producing too few).

Easy as this is to learn, it can be tricky. I once searched a magazine database for articles in *Atlantic Monthly* about international law as it extends to outer space, hoping to find none so I could propose such a story. And indeed, I found none. "No need to plow through scores of back issues," thought I, as I typed my query. The reply came by return mail: they would be happy to buy a piece on the subject, if only one hadn't run as the cover story three months before! Because my search concepts had been too specific, they did not elicit the *Atlantic* article.

Too, database searchers are at the mercy of data entry clerks, who are more techie than literary. Key words supposedly reflect an entry's contents, but sometimes there is no evidence an indexer has looked at the content. Dave Foreman and Bill Haywood's *Ecodefense: A Field Guide to Monkeywrenching*, for example, is an eco-raider's handbook prefaced by novelist Edward Abbey. Knowledge Index classifies it as an instruction manual for shop tools.

HOW DO YOU KNOW WHEN YOU'VE FINISHED?

It is possible to get so involved with the research that you never get around to writing the piece; in reporterese jargon, this is called "over-researching the story."

At some point, you'll have to stop, if for no other reason than the editor's snappish reminder that you have twenty minutes to deadline.

When people start repeating things you've heard elsewhere, you usually have done enough. When you've covered all the bases with an interviewee and he answers the final "is-there-more-I-should-know?" question with "no," you're probably safe in quitting.

Think over your angle or focus and ask yourself, "do I have enough material to cover this fairly? If the issue is controversial, have I investigated all sides? Do I know the most current developments?" If the answer is yes, you might as well stop.

You should finish with several times more material than you can use. Before you begin writing, you will sift and organize your notes, picking out the most germane points, while the rest serves as the background that makes you an informed speaker.

–30–

FOR PROJECTS OR DISCUSSION

1. Select one of these topics. Find six printed sources about it and names, addresses, and telephone numbers for six people who can speak about it. Tell how you found this information.

The effect of a woman's imprisonment on her children
Where and how to obtain services available to telephone consumers
"Water marketing" as a device to alleviate water shortages in the West
How outpatient surgery can save you money
Teenage unemployment
Fear of flying
Drug abuse among children under 12
The downside of coronary bypass surgery
Use of robots in American manufacturing plants
How lead birdshot is poisoning wild eagles
Densa, the organization for the five billion folks not bright enough to belong to Mensa
Freeze-drying your pet
Airport helicopter services—rent-a-copter
The Nature Conservancy

2. Select one or more of these individuals. For each, find three biographical articles and the person's address. If you can't find an address, at least produce a lead to finding him or her (an agent or place of employment, for example). Cite your sources.

Hugh Downs
Leslie Marmon Silko (poet)
Paul Berg (biochemist)
Dianne Feinstein
Woody Allen
Andrew A. Rooney
Mike Bossy
Bella Abzug
Max Frankel
Arthur Ashe
Harold Stassen
Byron White
Patty Duke
Craig Claiborne
Michael Graves (architect)
Arthur Mitchell (Dance Theater of Harlem)

Judith Richards Hope
Bobby Knight
Arieh Neier (author; civil libertarian)
Floretta Dukes McKenzie (public school administrator)

SUGGESTED READING

Philip C. Brooks. *Research in Archives: The Use of Unpublished Primary Sources*, 1969. Reprint. Chicago: University of Chicago Press, 1982.

Robert B. Downs and Clara D. Keller. *How to Do Library Research*. 2d ed. Ann Arbor, Mich.: University Microfilms International, Books on Demand.

Philip M. Hamer, ed. *A Guide to Archives and Mss in the United States*. New Haven: Yale University Press, 1961.

4

Interviewing

HOW DO YOU GET AN INTERVIEW?

Simple: call the person and ask.

Telephone your interview subject; explain who you are, what you are doing, and how he or she can help you. Identify your publication, and make it clear up front that you are not selling advertising. It's usually best to open with something like "I'm a writer [or assistant editor or whatever your position is] with *The Daily Clarion* and I'm doing a story about. . . ." If you got the person's name from a mutual acquaintance, say so.

"Call the person" sounds easier than it is. Executives and politicians usually put a phalanx of underlings between themselves and the press. You can expect to repeat your spiel several times to telephone operators, secretaries, and public relations officers before you reach your man or woman.

First call the person's office (or home, if you can get the number) and ask to speak to Mr. So-and-so. You just might get through.

But chances are you'll be routed to the p.r. (public relations) department. This can be boon or disaster, depending on the p.r. person and your purpose.

When you're writing something upbeat, p.r. officers can help you a lot. They'll give you more puffy information than you can use, and, if they have any competence, they'll set up appointments with key people. If you're doing something tougher, they should at least give you their employer's official stance. They may arrange an interview, depending on the p.r. department's philosophy. Some public relations experts believe in meeting controversy head-on. Others will try to shield their client behind a stone wall.

If you can't get past the p.r. department or other barriers, try writing a letter to your subject. Explain that your publication is doing an article about thus-and-such, and you think she may be able to help you. Specify how much time you'll need, and note that there's no cost to her and no advertising tie. Include your telephone number and ask her to call you. If you have a clip similar to the story you're writing, send it.

Be kind to secretaries and receptionists. Learn their names and show some interest in them. A cooperative secretary can be most helpful. Once I had to profile a man I thought was a colorless bureaucrat. While I was waiting in his outer office for him to get off the phone, his secretary struck up a conversation. By the time he was ready to see me, she had told me all about his passion for glider flying, his treatment of the hired help, and his open affection for his wife and kids. These details helped me focus the interview on his character, rather than restricting it to his drab occupation.

Expect to fit your schedule to the interviewee's. Often, busy executives or public figures have little time to spare. Yes, you're busy too—but your business is to get the story.

By the way, the days of getting the story at any cost, including subterfuge, are past. Don't misrepresent yourself over the telephone, and don't fib about what subject you're covering in order to prompt an unsuspecting comment. You might not openly admit that you're digging for dirt—if that's what you're doing—but neither should you allow someone to believe you're going to write a puff piece.

It is unethical to say you are someone other than who you are. Do not, for example, call your subject's wife and tell her you're a co-worker or member of his club in order to gain her confidence and extract information.

What if the person demands to be paid for the interview? When someone asks "what's in it for me," you can point out that he's getting free publicity of a much more credible variety than his advertising dollar could buy. If the person openly asks to be paid, explain that such a decision is not yours to make, and then tell your editor. Usually, the answer is "no." In any case, cashbox journalism takes place on the publisher's dime, not yours.

THIS BEARS REPEATING

Although we said it in the last chapter, we'll say it again here: *do your homework before you go into an interview*. Read some background material about the topics you and the interviewee will discuss. If the interviewee is the subject, look him or her up in *Who's Who* or another biographical resource. If you're interviewing a celebrity who has had a lot of press, check past reports and try not to ask the person questions that have been asked many times before. And if the person has written anything, for heaven's sake read his stuff.

A writer once profiled Mark Harris, author of *Bang the Drum Slowly* and a slew of other novels, plays, essays, and nonfiction. Confronted with Harris's plans to leave town, she scheduled an interview before she had time to familiarize herself with his work.

Harris, she said, was "evasive" throughout the meeting. At one point, she asked what his next book would be.

"I think my next book will be called *Why Am I in the English Department?*" he returned.

This prompted no more response than a polite "how interesting."

Why Am I in the English Department? is a fictional book written by the protagonist of two of Harris's novels. The title figures prominently in both. No wonder the interview fizzled!

AN INTERVIEW IS MORE THAN TALK

It's also *observing*. Readers want to know more than just what was said. They want to hear the nuances, note the subtle pauses and modulations of tone. And they want to see what's going on. Part of your job is to show how the speakers look, how they behave, and how they fit into their settings.

Watch for what Tom Wolfe calls symbols of a person's *status life* —the pattern of behavior through which people express their position in the world. These may be subtle—the way he gestures, the way she applies her eye makeup. Or they can be very obvious: dialect, clothing, the quality of the furniture, the presence of servants. These are tags that readers who share your cultural background will recognize and mentally enlarge into an interpretation of the subject's character.

When you go into the interview, take notes on the subject's appearance—his clothing, hairstyle, coloring, mannerisms, and anything else that strikes you. Look closely at the surroundings, and make specific, detailed notes.

And "specific" means just that. A forest, for example, is more than "a glade of trees and underbrush." The writer must say what kind of trees, what sort of ground cover, how thick it is, what time of day it is, how the light falls through the leaves. A misty redwood grove with bracken undercover is quite a different place from a pine and aspen forest.

Weaving closely observed details into a story works to wondrous effect. Take, for example, a piece in the "Talk of the Town" department of *The New Yorker* of March 21, 1988. The writer introduces us to a sound effects artist named Arthur Miller, whom we meet in a recording studio. The story opens with Miller saying many book publishers are making audiocassettes of their books. Then we see the man: "a shock of frizzy gray hair . . . a loud blue Hawaiian shirt." Another quote is followed by a look around the studio: "a cluttered table of props in front of him, a fake red door to his right, more clutter on the floor behind him (miniature bedsprings, bundles of clothes, several pairs of shoes), and a selection of stones and wooden boards next to his feet." Not just "clutter," but *what kind* of clutter and *where*.

But wait; Miller does more than stand around and chat.

He took a pair of children's shoes and walked them through a shallow box of gravel on the table. "Footsteps in gravel," he said. "Here's earth." He tromped the shoes through a box filled with kitty litter. He turned abruptly and opened the fake door, which had a good, slow squeak, and then pointed to his feet. "See, I have a microphone down there. I can use my feet *and* hands to walk." He pranced the shoes on the table while walking in place. Then he picked up a piece of slate and slid it over a wooden board while he sprayed an aerosol can toward it. "Air locks! You know when you open a spaceship?" He held up a sturdy balloon with ball bearings inside. "A small explosion." He shook the balloon slightly but steadily, and sure enough, we heard a distant blast.

Note how the writer combines sights, sounds, and motion with conversation. The copy relies on verbs to communicate these things: Miller *walks* the shoes and *prances* them, he tromps and turns and points and slides and sprays and shakes. The language places us at the writer's side, watching the action.

DURING THE INTERVIEW

Try to arrange the meeting in a relatively private setting, preferably where the interviewee works or lives. Women, unfortunately, should not go alone to a strange man's home nor to an out-of-the-way place. If there is no alternative, arrange to meet in a quiet restaurant.

Dress appropriately. This means office attire, not your favorite bohemian outfit. Men should usually wear a jacket and tie; women a skirt or good pair of slacks. But do use some common sense. If you're going to interview a mountain-climber on location, you should dress accordingly.

Don't chew gum, and don't smoke without permission. Avoid drinking—if you're meeting the person in a bar, you needn't feel required to keep up with your companion, shot for shot. If someone offers you coffee, turn it down gracefully. It's hard to balance a notepad, tape recorder, and coffee cup with just two hands.

Now that you're dressed up and appropriately forewarned, relax.

An interview is like a dinner-party conversation. As a polite conversationalist, you want to keep the talk going without focusing on yourself. The idea is to put the other person at ease while you discuss what interests him: his work, his life, and himself.

Small talk will usually break the ice. Establishing good rapport at the outset is especially important with someone who seems ill at ease. I often begin by explaining briefly where my story is going, what I have already learned, and how I hope the person can help. This directs the conversation toward our subject without springing any blunt questions.

Start out on a slightly formal footing—address the person as Mr., Ms., Mrs., or Miss. Many people, especially in the East, dislike having strangers use their first names. Try to empathize with the person, putting yourself in her place. Even if you feel skeptical or antagonistic, come across as sympathetic.

This, however, does not mean you have to be obsequious. Show some self-confidence—treat the person as worthy of respect but not adoration.

Follow the person's lead at first. You may have a series of questions you want answered, but there's no hurry. Remember, your interviewee probably knows more about the subject than you. If she wants to tackle an aspect you hadn't thought of, let her do so. Later, you can bring the conversation around to your original concerns.

She may, however, start by giving you a fishy look and a peremptory "what do you want to know?" Do *not* respond to this with a reprise of everything you plan to ask. Dumping a list of questions on a person may unnerve her or make her suspect you come with preconceived notions. Start with a single question and build the interview from there.

Once you get the conversation rolling, *listen*, don't talk. Veteran reporter Tom Kuhn has remarked that the worst noise on a tape recording is the sound of one's own voice. Resist the temptation to share your opinions and experiences; instead, let the other person do the talking.

Several devices encourage talk. One is liberal use of neutral expressions like "uh-huh," "yes," and "I see." You should also cultivate the habit of nodding your head agreeably now and then, as though you're raptly taking in the person's words.

One researcher discovered that an interviewer who murmurs "mm-hmm" now and then gets responses up to twice as long as one who sits like a lump. Plenty of eye contact helps, too. Other research has shown that women and minorities tend to look down or away from conversation partners, while white males look each other in the eye. You will find that looking the person in the face elicits confidence in your ability, franker answers, and greater detail.

Sometimes a follow-up question or remark will encourage an interviewee to elaborate on a detail: "That must have been fun," or "You feel that was a turning point, don't you?" A remark that shows empathy can break the dike: "It must have been tough, driving that taxi while you were training for the Olympics."

Expectant silence also works to bring out added comments. Empty spaces in conversation beg to be filled, and if you don't do it, your interviewee will. Pause a few seconds after she finishes an answer, as though you were giving her time to think. She'll begin to feel uncomfortable with the hiatus, and to fill it she'll keep talking.

Also, you may spur the person to say more with respectful, low-key disagreement. Taking this approach to an expert who knows more than you requires some tact, but you can usually pull it off by feigning surprise and saying "Oh, I thought it was the other way around. . . ." The person will then elaborate on her point to answer your objections.

If you miss a detail or don't understand something, ask the inter-viewee to repeat or explain it. Don't be shy about this; you'll sound less foolish getting it straight during the interview than telephoning later, which may reveal that half the exchange went over your head.

It's a good idea to wrap up the interview by asking if you've missed anything or if there is anything else the subject would like to add. Sometimes the person will give you new leads or, by taking time to think over what he has said, make some highly quotable reflection.

SHOULD YOU WRITE OUT YOUR INTERVIEW QUESTIONS BEFOREHAND?

You certainly should have some plan in mind before you go into an interview. Whether it's a detailed set of questions or just a mental list of the general topics you want to discuss depends on your ability, skill, and personal style.

One item you must always determine in every interview: the

correct spelling of the subject's name. Ask, even if you think you already know. I usually do so at the outset; if the interview is rushed or interrupted, you may forget before the finish. While you're asking how she spells her name, double-check her title, company name, and similar details.

Before you start, decide what you want to learn from the interview. Your story's angle will help focus the exchange. Ask yourself what is the point of the interview and why you want to know. Beware, however, a pitfall that traps even experienced reporters: assuming in advance that the interview will confirm some thesis you've concocted. Keep an open mind, *listen*, and be prepared to punt if the interview undermines your basic theory.

Some writers like to prepare a complete list of specific questions, arranged in a careful order. They feel this rigid organization keeps the interview on track while it insures that no important issues are forgotten.

Others see the interview as an organic entity, something that grows from one point to the next like a cascading vine. They may jot down important questions that they don't want to forget, but otherwise plan to guide the conversation through its topics in the order that seems most comfortable.

Either way, most interviews go in one of two directions: from specifics to generalities, or from generalities to specifics. Sometimes, it is in your interest to deliberately lay out the interview one way or the other.

Unsophisticated subjects—children, less educated speakers, and those inexperienced in dealing with the press—do better when you start with concrete questions. Not, for example, "Do you enjoy your job as a clam-digger, Mr. Boxankle," but "What do you like most about clam-digging?" In *Shoah: An Oral History of the Holocaust*, interviewer Claude Lanzmann almost never asks a general question; his thrust is confined to specifics:

So you were in the "castle detail"?
Can you describe what you saw?
Was the castle big?
Then what happened?
How long did the Jews stay there?
Did the Jews enter the van willingly?
Describe the gas vans.
What system was used? How did they kill them?
Yes, but how?
Yes, but through what?
It was just exhaust gas?

Who were the drivers?
Were there many of these drivers?

For those who are more comfortable with words and ideas, you may come at the subject in broad terms and work toward specifics. *Paris Review* interviewers begin an exchange with John Hollander by asking, "Is poetry a way of thinking for you?" Then, more specifically, "What's the genesis of a poem? What comes first to you?" A lengthy foray results, and the interviewer follows with "for example?"

Keep your questions short, and don't preface them with a long-winded background. You want to hear the interviewee's voice on your tape recording, not yours.

In any interview, we all hope to dig out some entertaining anecdotes. If your interviewee is a natural storyteller, you're in luck. Not everyone, though, expresses himself in little tales. You can prompt even the most reticent speaker to spin a story by asking Five-W questions:

Who first encouraged you to become a playwright?
What made you realize you wanted a career in clam-digging?
When did you have your first paranormal experience?
Where were you when Pearl Harbor was bombed?
Why did you decide to tour Tibet in disguise?

Another way to elicit anecdotes is to ask the person to help you understand by clarifying a point with an example. In the same *Paris Review* interview, Hollander remarks of his education that "there were my teachers-at-a-distance, so to speak, the voices of instruction that came to me from the rustling leaves of books." The interviewer's simple follow-up—"such as?"—yields a story about what certain authors mean to Hollander and why.

ASKING TOUGH QUESTIONS

Most reporters like to hold the rough stuff until the end. They believe a cordial chat loosens up the interviewee, leaving him more open to answering hard questions. On the other hand, when time is short and the subject hardened, it may be better to get right down to business.

A courteous, fair-minded approach is always to be preferred. And while you certainly should examine the tough issues, avoid taking cheap shots. Asking the governor to comment on the dowdy clothes his wife wore on a goodwill trip to Guatemala is a cheap shot.

Always stay polite—keep your wits about you and your tongue reined in, even if your subject loses his temper.

There are several ways to soften unpleasant questions. You can open with praise: "Mike Royko says your political cartoons are 'wonderful,' Mr. Benson, but. . . ." You can pose the question as hypothetical: "It might be possible to conclude from your 'Torah Torah Torah' cartoon that you are anti-Semitic. . . ." Or you can put the onus on someone else: "The Girl Scouts of America say your cartoons are un-American. . . ."

If the person refuses to talk or says "no comment," explain that a gap in the story can make him look bad or lead to untrue speculation. In his own interest, he may change his mind. By the way, if no comment from a subject appears in your story, you must explain why: "Mr. Boxankle declined comment," "Boxankle did not return *Infamous* Magazine's calls," or whatever.

"OFF THE RECORD" AND "NOT FOR ATTRIBUTION"

Should a subject ask to speak off the record, agree on the ground rules before you go any further. Establish whether you may use the remarks as background without attributing them to her, whether you may quote them as coming from an unnamed source, or whether they are not for print. "Off the record" means you will not include the remarks in your story; "not for attribution" means you can use the information provided you don't say where it came from.

Some editors would have you be tough about off-the-record status. An interviewee should know the reporter is there to quote him, the theory goes. If he's foolish enough to say something he doesn't want printed, that's his problem. Thus, you should decline to listen to any off-the-record talk, and refuse to honor requests to quash careless remarks.

There are several reasons for this. If a speaker is unwilling to accept responsibility for what he says, his words are no more reliable than gossip. And, by agreeing to accept anonymous information, the unwary reporter may trap herself into hiding sources that should be identified.

Still, off-the-record commentary can provide valuable insight. And you may be able to get someone else to confirm it on the record. Author John Brady suggests writers can use anonymous information in either of two ways:

• Quote it directly but attribute to a "reliable source." Most good editors will no longer accept this ploy.

• Paraphrase it, without attribution, and accept responsibility for its accuracy.

In the end, it's a judgment call. How you handle the problem will depend on the circumstances, the interviewee, and your editor.

TAKING NOTES

An old school of thought advises reporters to train themselves for total recall. Just listen and observe, they say. Make mental notes and write them down immediately after the encounter.

This is risky to the point of absurdity. It invites misquotation, and I have yet to meet an editor who will take a writer's unsubstantiated word for accuracy.

Keep some ongoing record during your interview. On what doesn't matter—the back of an envelope, a pocket notebook, a steno pad, or one of those ubiquitous yellow legal pads. Write it down, even if you are also tape-recording—tape recorders die when you most need them.

Unless you're a stenographer, you can't expect to write as fast as your interviewee speaks. So, you need to develop the art of editing as you listen. Don't try to take down every word the person says. Train yourself instead to listen for the high points, to recognize when a remark is important and when it's peripheral.

You also should develop your own shorthand system. The inventors of Speedwriting ("f u cn rd ths, u cn gt a gd jb") noticed that most English words are intelligible if you leave out the vowels. Try it—you'll be surprised at how much faster you can write.

Many words and syllables can be reduced to a single letter or symbol. Here are a few that work well:

v	of; have; very
t	it; to; their; there
n	in; on; not; no
N	nothing; none
E	ever; everything
tg	thing
l	will
k	can; con-; com-
kn	can't; cannot
U	under; under-
O	over; over-
u	you
r	our; are
+	more; most
−	less; least
<	according to; comes from; is less than; was told by

```
>      goes to; becomes; is more than; told or said [to]
//     like; is similar to; parallels
/      or
=      means; equals
```

Context determines the sense of those with multiple meanings.

Combine these with short forms of your own and practice your technique in your college lectures.

USING A TAPE RECORDER

A tape recording provides proof that you quoted your interviewee correctly. And, by capturing long passages verbatim, it gives you a better feel for the way the person talks, the color and flavor of his speech.

Some people are put off by tape recorders and notepads. You can usually disarm them, however, by explaining that you want to be sure to quote them accurately.

It's wise to take notes even when you're taping an interview. Recorders run out of juice, run out of tape, and jam; sometimes, too, background noise overrides the speakers.

Taking handwritten notes forces you to concentrate on the story's ultimate organization and, as the interview proceeds, to make choices about what information is important and what can be ignored. The practice keeps you, as a reporter, from allowing the exchange to shift from interview to casual chat.

Why do both? No matter how fast you take notes, a recording is always more likely to get everything. Compare, for example, these handwritten notes from an interview with two small-town Chamber of Commerce types (designated BB and BH) with a transcript of the taped version:

Shorthand Notes

BB: We can take credit for bringing a lot of manufacturers.

The program builds momentum. One of the keys is that this program emphasizes developing a better place for existing businesses.

It works from the inside out rather than the outside in.

If it's not a good climate for people already there, it's not for people to come in.
BH: Tourism is big in Arizona. But I think our emphasis should be to develop the business that provides services and products for the people who live here.

You cannot focus your town on tourism.

The place would be alive only a few months a year.
BB: We're not in the professional ghost town business.

Tape Transcript

BB: Like Bob brings out, that's one of the keys to the success of this program. It builds momentum and it keeps the momentum going. I think one of the keys, too, is that it doesn't depend, its emphasis is not on bringing in new business. It's on making this a better place for existing businesses to operate. It works from the inside out, rather than trying to work from the outside in. That's usually a losing proposition, when you have to go in that direction, from what I've seen out-of-state. The communities that put all their eggs in this recruiting basket, seein' what they can bring in from the outside, are beating their heads up against the wall. Because if it's not a good climate for the people to do business that are already there, it's not a good climate for people to come into.

BH: I think it's important, too, that there's a lot of talk about tourism in Arizona in general. And a lot of the smaller communities are looking to that either [pauses] as a savior type of thing. I think our emphasis here—my own personal emphasis has been that what we need to do in this downtown first is develop the business that provides the services and products to the people that live here. Once you do that, then you basically create some place that tourists like to come to, anyway—because it's a comfortable, neat, interesting place to be. You can't focus your downtown on tourism and survive. There's towns in different places that are only open three months a year. The rest of the year, that town is a dead place, because they don't have any tourists. That's no good here.

Interviewer: That's right. You think of Silverton [Colorado].

BB: It's a professional ghost town.

Interviewer: Right.

BB: That's what you have. But we're not in the ghost town business around here.

While paraphrasing and taking down the high points spare you plowing through pages of irrelevant chatter, you can lose the context. BB meant something quite different from what the handwritten notes had him say: the "ghost town" comment was about Silverton, not about the tourism industry in general.

TAPE RECORDING HARDWARE

Portable cassette recorders come in the standard size, as microcassette recorders, and in a tiny minicassette version. The microcassette is probably most convenient; it will fit in a pocket or purse, and the tapes are widely available. Minicassette tapes are hard to find, and standard recorders are large and obtrusive.

When you buy a recorder, be sure it has a pause button—this is indispensable for transcribing notes. You should also be able to adjust the tape speed; recording at half-speed allows you to wring 120 minutes out of a 60-minute tape. Some recorders come with an optional voice actuation feature, which stops the tape when no sound enters the microphone. These unreliable devices are not worth the extra cost; they may truncate words or whole sentences.

Portable recorders have built-in condenser microphones sensitive enough to pick up conversation at a table or in a normal room. However, condenser mikes don't filter out background noise—they pick up everything in range and record it at about the same volume. An interview in a restaurant, then, may be drowned out by conversations at adjacent tables or the clatter of dinnerware. In a car, road noise can overwhelm.

An inexpensive jack microphone, which you plug into the recorder, will correct this. Some makers include one with the recorder.

Another convenient plug-in device is earphones. Of course, you will use them when you have to transcribe a tape in an office. Sometimes, too, they help you make out an unclear passage when you can't understand it through the speaker.

You also should have a telephone pickup. This consists of a suction cup, which you attach to the telephone handset, and a wire that you plug into the recorder's microphone jack. They are cheap, and they allow you to record both ends of a telephone conversation.

That's *if* they work ideally. Some telephones block half of a phone pickup, usually the incoming half. Test the gadget by calling a toll number without dialing "1." Speak into the telephone before or after the phone company's recorded message, and when you play it back, you will know what your mike is picking up.

This brings us to the subject of . . .

TELEPHONE INTERVIEWS

A telephone interview puts you at a disadvantage because you and the subject can't see each other. Body language counts a lot, and we have seen the importance of noting visual details. Still, the phone interview is indispensable to short, workaday pieces. Even for more important articles, the telephone may be the only feasible way to reach a distant subject.

Interviewees often talk faster over the telephone than in person, because they don't see you trying to take notes. If you can't follow a statement, ask the person to repeat it. Ask, too, how things look—what color they are, how they operate, etc.

Should you mention that you're recording the conversation? Yes. It's common courtesy.

Often, you don't have to. The business about the beep every 15 seconds is a telephone company regulation, not a law, and many states do not ban recording people without their knowledge. Some states do, however; so, even if yours does not, whenever you call across state lines, always ask, "do you mind if I record this interview?"

Save your interview tapes at least six months after publication. If any question arises, you'll need them to prove your accuracy.

Questions do arise, even in the most benign circumstances. I once interviewed a California real estate broker, long-distance, for a frothy trade journal piece on married agents who work together. When my editor called to arrange a photography session, the broker said she never heard of me and did not know what he was talking about.

Luckily, I still had the tape, on which she had identified herself by name. Confronted with this, she relented and allowed herself to be photographed.

TRANSCRIBING TAPED INTERVIEWS

Typing up a tape takes about half again as long as the interview, because you have to back up to catch missed passages and ponder garbled words. Working against a deadline, you may not have time for that.

In that case, many reporters simply play the tape and make notes on the high points, transcribing attractive quotes verbatim. They summarize the gist of the conversation and edit as they go.

For an important story where accuracy is paramount, you probably should transcribe the entire tape. If you're going to build a piece to be proud of, don't cut corners in the foundations.

−30−

FOR PROJECTS OR DISCUSSION

1. Many people in the news claim they are misquoted. Why do you think this is?

2. Bring an interview from *Paris Review, Interview*, or *Playboy*. Bearing in mind that these interviews are carefully edited, study their technique and effectiveness.

SUGGESTED READING

Shirley Biagi. *Interviews That Work: A Practical Guide for Journalists.* Belmont, Calif.: Wadsworth Publishing, 1986.

John Brady. *The Craft of Interviewing.* New York: Random House Vintage Books, 1977.

Interview, a magazine founded by Andy Warhol, is filled with glitzy interviews of people in the news.

Claude Lanzmann. *Shoah: An Oral History of the Holocaust.* New York: Pantheon Books, 1985.

Paris Review, a little literary magazine, runs interviews of renowned authors. Periodically, this journal collects these interviews into books; the series is called *Writers at Work*.

5

Organizing Your Research

You've done all your research and interviews and now you have a giant mound of notes. How do you put them together to form a story?

It depends on your style. Some people use elaborate systems involving file folders and notecards; others highlight important points in their notes with color-coded markers and then follow the yellow (and red and green and purple) brick roads as they write up each topic.

This chapter will suggest two methods, one for complicated, long stories and one for short, easy pieces. They are not the only ways—every writer has individual habits. But they will give you some direction. As you become more practiced, you will develop an approach that works for you.

Try to keep notes in one consistent form, whether it's 8 1/2 x 11-inch paper, steno-pad sheets, or notecards. Juggling notes is much easier if they all come in the same size, rather than on miscellaneous scraps.

EXTENSIVE NOTES FOR A LONG ARTICLE

A complex project with many interviews, photocopied background articles, and scribbled personal observations, thoughts, and insights may net several hundred pages of notes. The sheer size of this paper monster can bring on acute writer's block, especially when the you realize it all must boil down to two or three thousand words.

Here's what you'll need to bring the beast under control:

Your notes, written on or glued to 8 1/2 by 11-inch paper
A large three-ring binder
A paper punch
Divider sheets
A package of 3 x 5-inch notecards or small pad of scratch paper
A pen with ink in a color different from your notes
A highlighting marker (optional)

Organize Notes

Perforate each sheet of notes and file it in the binder roughly by the story's main subtopics.

Suppose, for example, you are doing a story on your state's Main Street Historic Preservation Program, a federally sponsored economic redevelopment plan. You have interviewed local potentates, developers, and volunteers in nine small cities, plus the state program director, the state historic architect, an architectural historian, and several federal bureaucrats. In addition, you located a half-dozen articles on the national program, eight or ten government publications, and a videotape (from which you took written notes). You attended two conferences, where you spoke with nationally prominent historic preservation mavens. And of course, you went to each town, scouted redevelopment, and took careful notes on what you saw.

So, you might organize your binder under these rubrics:

Federal program
State program
Headings for each of the nine towns

Punch holes in each sheet and file your notes under the headings you have established. Use the divider sheets to separate the headings. Prominently number each page in the binder.

Review and Outline

Once you have divided your notes into manageable segments, you should sit down and read the notebook, cover to cover. As you do so, think about the shape your story will take. If you haven't already found a lead, look for a good opener. Decide on the main points you will make, and watch for anecdotes and a strong wrap-up. As ideas, insights, or further questions come to you, write them down.

When you've finished, rough out a story outline. Show the lead, the transition to the story's body, the order in which you will develop the body, and the wrap-up. To sharpen your focus, write a one- or two-sentence statement defining exactly what the story is about (see figure 5.1).

If you discovered any blank spots in your research, now is the time to fill them in. Add this follow-up material to the binder in the appropriate places.

Review and Highlight

With pen in hand, read the notes again. This time, mark topic headings in the margins, roughly keyed to your preliminary outline. Highlight or underscore don't-miss passages, and put stars or exclamation points next to especially urgent items. If any new insights come to you, revise your outline accordingly.

Prepare Notecards and Polish Outline

Go through the notes once again. This time, write each topic heading and its page number on a separate note card (figure 5.2). Add reminders or comments to highlight a particular passage's importance or show how it fits the narrative.

Collate the stack by topic (figure 5.3). Now you have a rough guide to your notes which can be shuffled and reorganized any way you choose.

Because you have now read your notes several times, you should have a clear idea of the story's organization. Rewrite your rough outline to crystallize your thoughts and provide firm direction (figure 5.4).

Organize Notecards According to Outline

Clear your desk or a space on the floor. Deal the notecards, by topic and subtopic, into piles arranged according to the headings in your final outline. When everything is in its proper place, neatly stack the cards in the order in which you will use them.

Rough Outline

Lyrical opening, vividly evocative of AZ small-town life
    PROBLEM: small towns decaying. Growing interest nationwide
    in historic preservation as solution.
One successful answer: Federal Main Street Program
    define
    scope
    tax incentives
Focus on AZ Main Street Program
Quickly hit five towns—2 or 3 grafs each
    show how program works in each
Work in:
    economics
    safety
    tax incentives
    political controversy
Pan back out with a lyrical windup

THESIS: The Main Street Program, using historic preservation as its thrust, plans to revive 15 decaying Arizona small-town commercial districts. The program helps property owners with expert advisers, guidelines, & tax breaks.

Figure 5.1. Rough outline and thesis statement.

Draft the Article

Now all you have to do is put your stacks next to your word processor and start writing. The outline and corresponding note cards will guide you through the story in an orderly, coherent way (figure 5.5).

QUICK, SHORT STORIES

The method described above is organized, thorough, and professional. And time-consuming. We all have to write squat-and-run stories on short deadlines, whose significance will scarcely ring through the ages. Indeed, for many of us such pieces form the bulk of our work.

Even if you had several weeks to collect three or four hundred pages of notes for these stories—which you won't—you certainly will have no time to mull over them, write two outlines, and compile stacks of notecards.

For quick, lightweight stories, there's an easier way. This method dispenses with notecards (and sometimes, unfortunately, with carful thought).

Take your notes on 8 1/2 x 11-inch legal pads. Type your interview transcripts on the same size paper. Stash it all in a manila file folder. Record the names, addresses, and phone numbers of your contacts on the inside cover of the file folder; this makes it easy to type up a list of sources for your editor.

Review, Highlight, and Outline

Before you start writing, read your notes once, scribbling topic headings in the margins and highlighting strong quotes and important points.

Make a quick, informal outline showing the direction you plan to take the story. This may be a list of topics, or it may be more elaborate—either way, expect it to change as you move forward.

Write the lead.

Write the Story

Now leaf through your notes, following your outline. Look for the marginal notes that fit your topics as the outline tells you to deal with them, and write them up briefly and coherently. Fit them together with logical transitions, and wrap it up with a choice quote, anecdote, or observation.

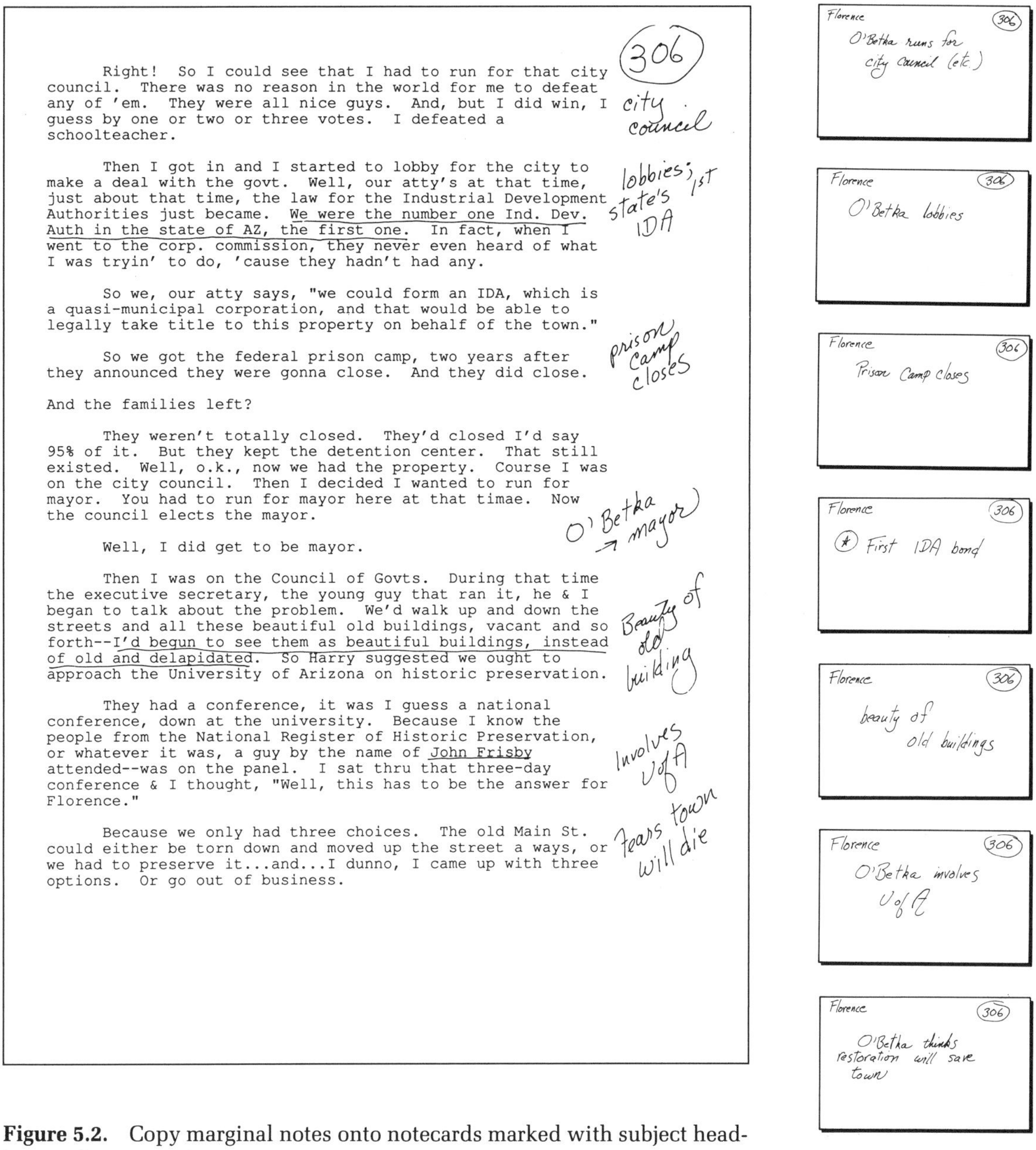

Right! So I could see that I had to run for that city
council. There was no reason in the world for me to defeat
any of 'em. They were all nice guys. And, but I did win, I
guess by one or two or three votes. I defeated a
schoolteacher.

Then I got in and I started to lobby for the city to
make a deal with the govt. Well, our atty's at that time,
just about that time, the law for the Industrial Development
Authorities just became. We were the number one Ind. Dev.
Auth in the state of AZ, the first one. In fact, when I
went to the corp. commission, they never even heard of what
I was tryin' to do, 'cause they hadn't had any.

So we, our atty says, "we could form an IDA, which is
a quasi-municipal corporation, and that would be able to
legally take title to this property on behalf of the town."

So we got the federal prison camp, two years after
they announced they were gonna close. And they did close.

And the families left?

They weren't totally closed. They'd closed I'd say
95% of it. But they kept the detention center. That still
existed. Well, o.k., now we had the property. Course I was
on the city council. Then I decided I wanted to run for
mayor. You had to run for mayor here at that timae. Now
the council elects the mayor.

Well, I did get to be mayor.

Then I was on the Council of Govts. During that time
the executive secretary, the young guy that ran it, he & I
began to talk about the problem. We'd walk up and down the
streets and all these beautiful old buildings, vacant and so
forth--I'd begun to see them as beautiful buildings, instead
of old and delapidated. So Harry suggested we ought to
approach the University of Arizona on historic preservation.

They had a conference, it was I guess a national
conference, down at the university. Because I know the
people from the National Register of Historic Preservation,
or whatever it was, a guy by the name of John Frisby
attended--was on the panel. I sat thru that three-day
conference & I thought, "Well, this has to be the answer for
Florence."

Because we only had three choices. The old Main St.
could either be torn down and moved up the street a ways, or
we had to preserve it...and...I dunno, I came up with three
options. Or go out of business.

marginal notes: 306 · city council · lobbies; 1st state's IDA · prison camp closes · O'Betka → mayor · Beauty of old building · Involves U of A · fears town will die

Notecards (right margin):

Florence — 306
O'Betka runs for city council (etc)

Florence — 306
O'Betka lobbies

Florence — 306
Prison Camp closes

Florence — 306
(*) First IDA bond

Florence — 306
beauty of old buildings

Florence — 306
O'Betka involves U of A

Florence — 306
O'Betka thinks restoration will save town

Figure 5.2. Copy marginal notes onto notecards marked with subject headings and page numbers.

Figure 5.3.   Collate notecards into stacks, by topic.

Final Outline

Willcox: Mary and Charles Leighton outraged at demolition of high
    school. "To know where we're going, we have to know where
    we're coming from."
Mary learns of Main Street
    identify, define
Main Street Program's background—Kate Singleton
    begins 1977
    250 towns, 25 states
    85% to 90% success rate
    enters AZ, 1986
Leightons, Bette Ruffner lobby to introduce it here
How it works in AZ
Florence
    describe; famous natives
    Sobin—quote
    survey historic buildings
Bisbee
    town's character, politics
        Hort, Miller, Tinkers
    survey buildings, Brewery Gulch, OK Street
    events
    stumbling blocks; transition to
Kingman
    similar problems
    describe
    Beale; Tedi Ronchetti
Controversy
    Bisbee—Hort
    Prescott—Kimsey
    Florence—O'Betka, Sobin
    what historic zoning means to property owners
Wrapup: Willcox—Main Street Kids
    Quote Eileen Tucker: "Why Main Street works."

Figure 5.4. Write a final outline.

Please note that this can lead to a sloppy product *unless* you have a strong grasp of your subject and a good feel for the final shape you want the story to take. You must spend some time—ideally, a day or more—thinking about what you have learned and what you want to say. The story's organization should be clear in your mind before you start writing.

A CAVEAT

A writer free-lancing for a trade magazine quoted a highly placed Coldwell-Banker executive, commenting on a technical aspect of industry practices. The remarks seemed to make sense, at least to the layman. When the story hit print, the executive hit the ceiling: he told the editor he had been misquoted and had never said anything like what appeared in the story.

The writer insisted she was right, and she read parts of her transcript to the editor over the phone to confirm that indeed she had quoted those words accurately. The editor accepted this and refused to run a correction.

Later, a nationally respected corporate attorney, who knew all the principals interviewed for the story, read the passage. "So-and-so couldn't have said this," he observed. "Although the facts are essentially accurate, stated in this context, they don't make sense. The quote makes the man sound like a fool."

The facts were right; the source said what was written; but the quote was wrong. What happened?

During their meeting, the writer and the executive had touched on a single topic twice. When the writer went back over her notes, she found one remark on the subject near the top, and another about two-thirds through the interview. Reasoning that the widely separated comments after all concerned the same issue, she ran them together into a single quote. Because she understood less about corporate finance and organization than she imagined, she failed to see that the two remarks really didn't work together.

This is a common practice. We cannot tell you not to indulge in it, because conversations are often circular. In most cases, you're safe in joining remarks on a single topic into one quote. But you must be very sure of what you're doing.

WHY ARE WE TELLING YOU ALL THIS?

This book has devoted three chapters to the art of gathering and organizing information. There's a reason.

The key to nonfiction writing is research. Readers can spot hot air

Adobe homes and shops with original <u>viga</u> and <u>savina</u> roofs
(fashioned of cottonwood beams and saguaro ribs) line
adjacent streets.   The town's sunbaked Hispanic feel reminds
you of Gus Arriola's popular comic strip, <u>Gordo</u>--and indeed,
Florence was the cartoonist's hometown.

Florence has preserved more early buildings and styles
than any other Arizona small town, according to Harris J.
Sobin, an architect and University of Arizona professor who
prepared an extensive historic study in 1977.   "The entire
history of Territorial architecture can be seen along the
streets of Florence," he writes.   "Phoenix grew out of a
community exactly like this one," says Florence Main Street
Manager Rod Keeling.   "When you look at the old pictures,
you see Phoenix looked just like this."

Florence recently increased revenues by annexing the
prison, which allowed street paving, improved services, and
automated trash pickup.

Figure 5.5.   Use the notecards to help construct your narrative. This page
from a manuscript is based on notes whose location in my transcripts and
notes is marked on notecards. When I was ready to speak of the Hispanic
influence on Florence's historic architecture, a card told me to turn to page
98 in my binder. The allusion to Gus Arriola was on page 312; the business
about the town's diversity and extensive preservation, on page 23. Thus my
notecards (shown in the margin) allowed me to keep track of a large volume
of scattered information and write it up coherently.

faster than you can blow it. And—given a writer's basic literacy most editors value strong research skills more than flashy writing style.

Good writers know how to find the facts and use them.

—30—

FOR PROJECTS OR DISCUSSION

1. How did you research your most recent article or term paper? Would you do it differently in light of chapters 3, 4, and 5? What would you change?

2. How important do you think it is to outline your story before you begin writing? Why?

3. Are you familiar with organizing techniques different from those presented here? If so, explain them to the class and discuss their relative merits.

SUGGESTED READING

Jacques Barzun and Henry F. Graff. *The Modern Researcher.* New York: Harcourt Brace Jovanovich, 1977. Strictly speaking a book for historians, this readable work offers a helpful chapter titled "The ABC of Technique," another on "The Arts of Quoting and Translating," and much sensible advice on writing.

6

The Feature Story's Structure

An article, like a work of fiction, has a beginning, a middle, and an end. Accomplished writers organize their material up front. Before they sit down at the keyboard, they know how the story will begin, how it will finish, and what path it will take to reach the end.

If you look closely at published feature stories, you'll see they follow a fairly standard format.

• *The lead,* which opens the story with a person, an anecdote, a set scene, or—rarely—dialogue.

• *The transition,* often called the *capsule statement, bridge, nut paragraph,* or *"nut graf."* It tells the reader why you're writing about this subject. The nut graf has its equivalent in the "thesis sentence" of freshman composition.

• *Development* of the issue in a series of logical, well-connected paragraphs.

• *A strong ending,* a real gem saved for the last paragraph.

The way the writer develops these elements depends on his purpose and his material. An effective story is shaped logically to fit its substance.

THE STORY'S ARCHITECTURE

We have seen the typical news story's structure, the venerable inverted pyramid:

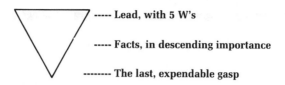

----- Lead, with 5 W's

----- Facts, in descending importance

-------- The last, expendable gasp

Figure 6.1. The "Inverted Pyramid"

The feature story may take any of several shapes. The basic structure described above looks like a paper doll:

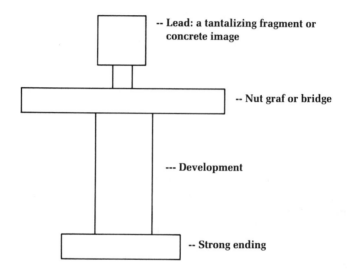

-- Lead: a tantalizing fragment or concrete image

-- Nut graf or bridge

--- Development

-- Strong ending

Figure 6.2. The "Paper Doll"

Without the transitional plateau of the nut paragraph, you get a footed bowl, also a usable structure:

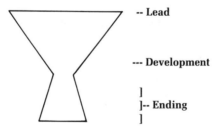

-- Lead

--- Development

]
]-- Ending
]

Figure 6.3. The "Footed Bowl"

Some feature stories are circular: the ending brings the reader back to the lead.

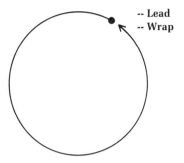

-- Lead
-- Wrap

Figure 6.4. Circular

Others may be Y- or menorah-shaped, braiding several strands or parallel sub-stories together in a rousing conclusion:

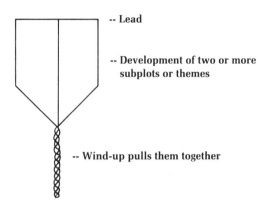

-- Lead

-- Development of two or more
   subplots or themes

-- Wind-up pulls them together

Figure 6.5. The "Menorah"

The best writers understand the importance of structure. William Howarth, in his introduction to *The John McPhee Reader*, notes that McPhee, a master craftsman, seeks "to create a form [for a given story] that is logical but so unobtrusive that judgments of its content will seem to arise only in the reader's mind." In designing a structure, Howarth observes, McPhee may "either find an idea for order *in* the material or impose one *upon* it, selecting what Coleridge called the 'organic' or 'mechanic' principles of structure." *Levels of the Game*, a study of Arthur Ashe and Clarke Graebner's September

8, 1968, Forest Hills semi-finals match, takes up the back-and-forth action of a tennis game, deriving its form from the material at hand.

The structure you choose for your story must give it unity, balance, and coherence. You can point out the facts' meaning simply by the order in which you present them, sometimes by setting two telling items side-by-side without editorial comment. While no one expects a beginner to write another *Levels of the Game*, you should search for a structure that complements your story's theme. You might, for example, write a human-interest piece about someone caught in a bureaucratic runaround: the story could have a circular structure, taking your subject from Point A right back to Point A. You would thus effectively underscore theme with structure, conveying the victim's frustration or bemusement without ever preaching or explicitly criticizing.

WRITING LEADS

The lead's purpose is to grab the reader's attention, give him the central idea, and persuade him to read on. It need not state the story's point or most important facts. Feature leads are less formulaic than hard news leads; they give you more room to be creative.

Feature leads for newspapers are necessarily short and to the point. Newspaper editors invariably prefer a punchy opening over the impressionistic lead that appeals to magazine editors. Try a magazine lead on a newspaper editor and he'll accuse you of "backing into the story."

Bear in mind that the lead's information must be related to the story's main point. Don't open a piece with a colorful descriptive passage that has little to do with your message. If a catchy anecdote illuminates the story's point, fine—use it. Otherwise, find a better lead.

Many writers will start a story by *focusing on a person* whose experience underscores what the story is about, and they will try to get a good quote near the top. *Wall Street Journal* reporter Francine Schwadel does exactly that in this lead, which opens an August 22, 1986, story on AT&T's continued dominance of the long-distance market:

When Paul C. Seitz was asked to pick a long-distance phone company last year, the 36-year-old acccountant from Wilmington, Del., spent "all of about a minute" pondering his options. Then he chose American Telephone & Telegraph Co., the carrier he had always used. With AT&T, he explains, "I knew what I had. The other companies were question marks."

This approach humanizes what might otherwise be a dry topic. As the story proceeds, Schwadel must present soporific figures such as the market shares held by AT&T, MCI, US Sprint, GTE Corp., and United Telecommunications, Inc.; the percentages of users for whom quality of service, cost, convenience, and company size are deciding factors; consumer demographics; and telephone bill costs. But she keeps the reader awake—and indeed writes an interesting piece— by consistently translating the numbers and facts into human terms, enriching the story with quotations and anecdotes from consumers, phone company executives, and market analysts.

Some of the most effective leads are *anecdotal*. An anecdote is a mini-story with its own opening, middle and end. When you use it as a lead, its ending should tie the lead into the rest of the story by making a transition into the capsule statement or body of the story, by making a strong point that underscores your story's subject, or by serving as a capsule statement itself. Marcia Stamell opened a service piece for *Savvy* about negotiating for a severance package with the following tale:

Late one Friday afternoon in 1982, Ellen G., an advertising account manager with seven years' experience at a New York agency, was told by her boss that her services would no longer be needed. He gave her a check for two weeks' severance and asked her to clean out her office. Ellen spent Friday evening commiserating with friends. She spent the weekend planning. On Monday morning, she returned to the company to present to the personnel office, in writing, a request for office space and six months' pay. "My rationale was that two weeks was nowhere near the time I needed to find a new job," she says. "I also wrote that after seven years, I deserved a better break."

She got the office space, but it took some negotiation with the personnel officer before arriving at a financial settlement of one week's pay for each year of service, accrued vacation pay, and a specialized payment schedule of half-time salary over 14 weeks. The package was less than Ellen had hoped for, but it prolonged the steady flow of income and gave her a tax advantage. And it was a good deal more generous than two weeks' pay.

This anecdote leads into the nut paragraph, which explains that a growing number of nonunion workers are asking for and receiving sweetened severance packages when they are discharged from their jobs. From there, the story explains how to get one for yourself.

Similar to the anecdote is the *single example or series of briefly stated examples*. These often are short case histories illustrating a problem the story will address. They are very popular in women's magazines, especially for health-oriented stories. A typical such lead appeared in the December 28, 1987, *Insight*, opening Daniel Holzman's report on long-term health care costs, "Endless Care with Costs to Match."

"Pop had to be put in a nursing home at a cost to my mother of about $2,400 per month," a man from Cicero, Ill., wrote to the National Committee to Preserve Social Security and Medicare, "and neither Medicare nor Medicaid could help because my parents had a nest egg. The law is without pity. Had my father lived for just 2 more years in a nursing home, my mother would have had to spend the rest of her life in poverty, but God called Pop to his eternal rest in 1 year, instead of 2. My mother and I can never forget the terrible feeling of relief we had when Pop died. We can only live with it in shame. We loved him."

This lead, which appeared in a newspaper's magazine, begins with a *quote*. Many editors, particularly those with newspaper experience, dislike a lead that opens with dialogue. Although they sometimes go with it if the lead works exceptionally well, beginning writers should avoid leading with a quote.

Similarly, many editors disapprove of leading with a *rhetorical question*. This approach is becoming more common, though. The problem with the rhetorical question—posed so the writer can provide the answer—is that it may appear patronizing. If you can avoid this, you may be able to make it work as a lead. This one appeared at the top of Homer Circle's "Skamania: Indiana's Super Steelhead," in the January, 1985, *Sports Afield*:

Which freshwater fish weighs an average of between 12 and 20 pounds, slams your lure with a hair-raising jolt, screams line off your reel with alarming speed, splits the air with slashing, leaping runs, and shucks free about three out of five times to leave you with nothing but a memory of it?

The answer is Skamania, a very special steelhead found almost exclusively in Indiana.

The *narrative lead* opens the story with a chain of events unfolded in a dramatic, chronological way. First this happened, then this, then . . . we get to the substance of the story. Narrative leads often appear in *Reader's Digest* "Drama in Real Life" stories. One such piece, "Falling From Mt. Garfield," by Emily and Per Ola d'Aulaire (*Reader's Digest*, May 1986), begins with this sequence:

It was 3 a.m. when Florian Ioan Wells arrived at the Parsley house in Seattle, Wash. The 33-year-old aerospace engineer had driven from across town, where his wife and daughter still slept peacefully. Craig Parsley, a 25-year-old environmental technician, had been careful not to disturb his wife when he blinked himself awake.

Over breakfast the two men discussed their plan for that day, May 14, 1983. They were going to climb one of Mt. Garfield's western peaks, a minor if perilous crag in the Cascade Range east of Seattle. For them it was a routine climb, and neither had bothered to pinpoint for his wife where he would be.

As they headed in Craig's truck toward the mountains, the two men talked about the importance of physical and mental conditioning. Both had years of climbing experience. Before fleeing to the United States with his family in 1979 to escape the confines of a Communist regime, Florian had been a member of Romania's Mountain Rescue Team. Craig, a native Californian, had taken up the sport in the ninth grade.

When they reached the mountain, the sky was cloudy and the temperature was 34 degrees Fahrenheit. Conditions weren't ideal, but the men decided to continue on, hoping the weather would hold. Scrambling over rocks and through gullies, they hiked two miles to the climbing area. It was 8 a.m. when they roped up and started climbing the half-mile-high granite face that led to the 4,896-foot-high summit.

Setting the scene is also effective. To do this, the writer establishes the story's locale or circumstances and puts the players in place. *The New York Times Magazine* writer Stephen G. Michaud takes us to the office of forensic experts dedicated to recovering and identifying victims of Argentine terrorism ("Identifying Argentina's 'Disappeared,'" December 7, 1987):

On a warm November afternoon, four friends gather to talk in a windowless upper room of an old office complex in downtown Buenos Aires. One is a medical student; two have undergraduate degrees in anthropology and another is working toward one. Although they speak with measured dispassion, their subject is death, violent death—the kind only state terrorism can produce.

"Generally, we find the victims' skulls exploded and the bullets still inside them," says Mercedes Doretti. As she sips her coffee, Alejandro Inchaurregui elaborates: "They used cheap coffins which quickly rot away. Also, sometimes we find their hands have been chopped off and mixed up with others."

"At first we were very scared, and this has been a very emotional experience for us all," Patricia Bernardi says. "We knew as soon as we started, we would be marked. The police are always there, and I remember a day when one of them turned to a police doctor at one grave site and said, 'If we had done it right 10 years ago, these people wouldn't be here now.'"

"They asked us all the time, 'Why are you doing this? What kind of ideology do you have?'" adds Luis Fondebrider.

Note the length of this lead and the one that precedes it: four paragraphs. Compare that with Schwadel's lead for the *Wall Street Journal*. Magazine leads may run longer than the one- or two-paragraph lead you see in newspaper features. Some *New Yorker* leads, for example, go on at substantial length—John McPhee's "Rising from the Plains" is a case in point.

Sometimes you can lead with a bit of *striking, well-written description:*

Before me is what looks like a small, serene idol. It is in fact a beautiful child, eyes outlined in black ointments, dark hair gleaming with mustard oil, relieving herself in the street. I try to move left but bump into a businessman's briefcase. Nudging right, I'm nudged back by a bull wearing a necklace of marigolds. Pressed from behind by a piping flute seller, I step over the child as a bus blares up the narrow brick canyon, missing us all by inches. Within its coils of exhaust a man painted orange, carrying a snake-headed staff, takes form, nods at me, then vanishes behind a jostle of teenagers with stereo headphones working out their rock 'n' roll moves. Pagodas that writhe with erotic carvings thrust roof upon roof above the trees, where big bats hang like fruit. And above the rooftops pure white snow peaks reach upward toward the stratosphere. At the moment all I'm looking for is the local computer club—somewhere in the magic confusion of modern Kathmandu.

With this tapestry-like imagery, *National Geographic* writer Douglas H. Chadwick introduces us to the sights, sounds, smells, and people of an almost unimaginably exotic locale. ("New Forces Challenge the Gods at the Crossroads of Kathmandu," July 1987.)

Occasionally, you can use some *odd, unusual,* or *outrageous statement:*

HENDRICKS COUNTY, Ind.—Detective Michael Nelson is walking a beat with one foot in the Twilight Zone.

So *Wall Street Journal* reporter Alex Kotlowitz launched a story about a cop who covers the witchcraft beat (January 7, 1988).

Related to outrageous statement is the *surprising contrast:* things look this way, but they're actually that way. Donna Fenn set an old chestnut against reality to open a story for *Inc.* (March 1985) on mousetraps through the ages:

"If a man can write a better book, preach a better sermon, or make a better mousetrap than his neighbor, though he builds his house in the woods the world will make a beaten path to his door."—*Ralph Waldo Emerson, as reported by Mrs. Sarah S. B. Yule*

Emerson had it all wrong. If you make a better mousetrap, chances are you will be completely ignored by the public at large and destined to labor in obscurity. Such, at least, was the fate of many a hopeful inventor who took the philosopher's advice literally.

Some magazines like to *address the reader as "you" in the first few sentences.* This is a common, easy, and effective device. Diane Hales uses it to open a *McCall's* story on "How to Say You're Sorry" (October 1987):

You snapped at your husband, kept a friend waiting for an hour, forgot your sister's birthday, wounded a co-worker's feelings. Now you're sorry but don't know how to express your regrets. And you're wondering why making up is so hard to do.

Sometimes you can simply *open with your capsule statement,* as Gary Graf does in an *Air & Space* story, "Putting Mars on the Map" (November 1987):

Through the 1960s and '70s, a series of space probes took off from Cape Canaveral on picture taking expeditions to Mars. Today the pictures are yielding information that will end up on maps of the planet's surface. In the 21st century, Earthlings landing on Mars won't worry about getting lost; they'll arrive with maps of the sort familiar to legions of Earthbound backpackers, maps with "U.S. Geological Survey" printed at the bottom.

Then there's the *opinion lead.* Journalists are rarely asked to express their opinion in a story's lead, unless they are writing a review or op-ed article. Even in those cases, unless one is a recognized authority on the subject, one should avoid opening with an opinion. In an instance that works, two publishing industry consultants, DeWitt Baker and Jim Hileman, excerpt their report on "College Publishers and Used Books" for *Publishers Weekly* (December 11, 1987):

The world of college text publishing is populated by many highly dedicated and talented people. The difficulty is that in important respects the whole does not seem to equal the sum of the parts.

Many other kinds of leads are possible. You could elect to open with a *direct statement,* if it's not witheringly obvious. You might ask your reader a *"what-if" question:* "imagine if the world were this way." You might describe some societal predicament and ask how we can get out of it. Study your target magazine for some idea of the editor's taste in leads. If one kind appears frequently, you might be wise to open your article along those lines. If some varieties of leads are conspicuously absent—particularly the rhetorical question and the quote—don't use them for that editor.

But whatever you choose, remember, the lead sets the tone. If you're going to be informal, your lead should start informally and you should keep up that style throughout the piece. If you start outraged, stay indignant all the way to the last word. A funny, mellow, serious, or dramatic lead should open a story that is funny, mellow, serious, or dramatic, respectively. Above all, *the lead must be concrete, never vague or fuzzy.* Always start with something the reader can visualize.

NUT PARAGRAPHS

The nut graf or transitional capsule statement (often called the "bridge" by newspaper writers) moves the reader smoothly from the lead, which may be rather startling, into the body of the story. It explains what this piece is to be about and how the opening ties into the subject.

Many writers compose a one- or two-sentence thesis statement before they begin the story. Some version of this can often fit into the nut graf, but whether or not it does, the habit helps organize and focus one's thoughts.

Let's return to Francine Schwadel's *Wall Street Journal* piece about AT&T. After she introduces Paul Seitz in the lead, telling us how quickly he decided to go with AT&T as a long-distance carrier, she continues:

Millions of Americans have made the same call. In the big wave of balloting that started two years ago and ends Sept. 1, roughly 75% of the voters so far have chosen AT&T to provide long-distance service to their home or business. And a recent Wall Street Journal/NBC News poll indicates that feelings like Mr. Seitz's are largely responsible for the outcome: Half of the 1,565 respondents who expressed a preference for one of the phone firms cited familiarity with AT&T as the most influential element in their choice.

The next paragraph notes that the firm's competition has made some inroads, but the gist of the story is summarized above: AT&T is beating the dickens out of its rivals.

In Michaud's story about the Argentine terror victims, the paragraph that follows the introduction succinctly summarizes what is to come:

The four are unlikely forensic sleuths, specializing in scientific evidence that will be admissible in courts of law. In 1983, they were college students in a nation newly released from seven years of military rule—seven long years during which at least 9,000 *desaparacidos*, or "disappeared ones," were eliminated by Government death squads. Last year, these young men and women—together with two others—established themselves as Equipo Argentino de Antropologia Forense (the Argentine Forensic Anthropology Team). Now court-certified experts, they lead the wrenching effort to recover and identify the victims of state-sanctioned terror.

Note that this goes beyond the traditional "who, what, when, where, why" you would find in a newspaper lead, which is also expected to summarize the story's contents. Those elements are there, but as an entity Michaud's capsule statement leads us in the direction he will take as his story progresses: investigation into government-sanctioned murder, using forensic and archaeological techniques. It puts the story's theme and content in a nutshell.

DEVELOPMENT

In the body of the story, you make your points or discuss the issues at hand. These details must come in a logical order, one leading sensibly to the next. Most writers accomplish this by outlining the information they wish to present, either on paper or mentally.

A newspaper or magazine story may be organized along any of the standard lines you should have learned in freshman composition. You may compare and contrast issues. You may develop an argument inductively (working from particular facts to a general conclusion) or deductively (reasoning from the general to the specific, or from a familiar principle to the unfamiliar). You can build a chronological narrative, presenting events in the order they occurred. You can show cause and effect, or write a story that is an extended definition of some abstract concept.

Your approach to your story's organization should fit your purpose. Chronological ordering works effectively with how-to-do-it stories and straight reports. Deduction—leading the reader from something familiar to new, unfamiliar concepts—is especially useful in science writing, where you may have to present bizarre, difficult ideas. Induction—drawing general conclusions from specific, concrete facts—helps clarify economics, sociology, and business issues, and it also works well in writing profiles. Cause-and-effect and comparison-and-contrast are useful approaches to the report.

One dramatic variety of development involves abutting a series of peaceful or pleasing events against an ironic fact or a stunning change in fortune. A writer discussing feral horses, for example, described the beauty and grace of a wild stallion that eluded capture for many years. She wrapped up this idyllic passage with a bald statement: "The next year, the big black and five of his mares were gutshot in cold blood by vandals and left to die in a meadow where once they peacefully grazed." This can be a forceful way to make a point.

However you decide to develop your facts, they should hang together coherently. Short but smooth transitions should tie each paragraph with the ones that come before and after it. You can accomplish this by repeating key words and phrases and by using transitional words like *but, and, however, so,* or *nevertheless.* Schwadel leads almost every paragraph in her story's body with some transitional device. The story's second developmental paragraph begins, "AT&T's success in the balloting," echoing "impressive victory" in a preceding paragraph. This paragraph ends with "The theory was that people would desert AT&T in droves once federally mandated 'equal access' enabled them to enjoy cheaper service without having to dial extra digits."

Next graf begins, "*But* the results indicate. . . ." Now we see a steady progression of transitional function words heading paragraph after paragraph:

"*Another reason* for AT&T's strong showing. . . ."
"*But* AT&T didn't succeed solely. . . ."
"AT&T's efforts, *however,* were clearly the most extensive. . . ."
"*Still,* some people didn't buy. . . ."
"AT&T describes *such* defectors. . . ."
"AT&T's competitors *also* attract. . . ."
"*Indeed,* of the customers that AT&T's rivals are *attracting.* . . ."
"In some parts of the country, *meanwhile.* . . ."

"*Many* [customers, mentioned in preceding paragraph] figure they don't spend enough to justify. . . ."

"*Still,* AT&T did win some talkative customers. . . ."

Although this approach seems mechanical when shown out of context, it demonstrates the importance of everyday transition words. They help your reader follow your train of thought.

Careful, logical ordering of your points so that the reader's thought moves easily from one paragraph to the next will do the job, although you'll need an occasional assist from those mechanical transition words. To succeed with this, you lay out a meticulously organized outline *before* you start to write. If the outline flows logically and the writing is coherent, the article should move logically, too.

THE LAST WORD

Save a strong quote or a striking observation for the ending. It may or may not hark back directly to the lead, but it should summarize what you've said in a powerful, colorful, or succinct way. Sometimes you can use an ironic or telling quote for this purpose.

To wind up the Argentine story, Michaud comes back to one of the speakers he introduced in the lead.

"We all have other ambitions," says Mercedes Doretti [speaking of the future], "ideas more connected to life." But for now, she and her colleagues recognize a responsibility as scientists to give their country's desaparecidos their names and to tell their stories.

"It's too easy to let them become paper people," she says. "We can't let that happen."

As a prosodic note, some writers try to end a story on an accented beat. That is, the last syllable in the last sentence is stressed, rather than unstressed. About Indiana's steelheads, Homer Circle concludes,

The dictionary defines mania as "a form of insanity characterized by great excitement." After you do battle with your first one, win or lose, you'll see why Skamaniacs are well named.

Because English usually stresses the first syllable, this reversal subtly catches the reader's attention and, like the final flourish in a song, it ends the piece on an emphatic note. It's not necessary to do this—it's not always possible—but it's a nice touch.

–30–

FOR PROJECTS OR DISCUSSION

1. As a class, write a lead for a story on one of the following topics:

How to travel comfortably on airplanes with small children.

A survey of the most popular watering holes (or sushi bars, or doughnut shops, or whatever) in your town.

An exposé about air and water contamination emanating from industrial plants near a low-income residential neighborhood, where 15 cases of childhood cancer have occurred within a 6-block area over the past two years.

A report about several local companies that sell their services as handwriting analysts to businesses, for use in hiring and personnel evaluation.

A profile of your school's football coach.

Read several of these efforts in class and discuss their merits.

2. Select a magazine that most people in the class enjoy reading. Bring the current copy to class and analyze the structure of the longest story it contains. How does the structure support the subject matter? Is it effective? Why or why not?

3. Go through this magazine and observe the final paragraphs of each story. What do they have in common?

4. Now study the transitional devices that link paragraphs together. Do any stand out as especially common? Do any work better than others? Why?

SUGGESTED READING

Art Kleiner and Stewart Brand. *Ten Years of CoEvolution Quarterly: News that Stayed News.* San Francisco: North Point Press, 1986. Innovative pieces that show nonfiction writing can be creative.

John McPhee. *The John McPhee Reader,* ed. William L. Howarth. New York: Farrar, Straus and Giroux, 1965. You can't go wrong following John McPhee's example.

Norman Sims. *The Literary Journalists.* New York: Ballantine Books, 1984. A collection of well-crafted stories by master writers.

The Wall Street Journal runs classically organized feature articles every day on the front page.

7

The Journalist as Storyteller

The other day Dick Stahl, my managing editor at *Arizona Highways*, was grumbling over an article that had been submitted on assignment. When he handed it to me, I thought it seemed competent enough: the language was clear and literate, the facts were well organized, and the writer had covered the subject comprehensively.

"This story looks all right, Dick," I said. "What's wrong with it?"

"It *is* all right," he returned. "That's what's wrong with it. I don't want a story that's just 'all right.' I want a piece that makes me sit up and shout *Wow!*"

What makes an editor sit up and shout "Wow"? One sure bet is a nonfiction piece that shares some attributes with good fiction.

An accomplished storyteller never bores the listener by unloading the bare facts, by divulging the punch line before the joke is over, or by revealing the key to the plot before the story's climax. Instead, he unveils the story a piece at a time, by drawing a series of word pictures full of engaging details. He introduces people, makes them seem real, and involves them in emotions and predicaments that move the listeners. A strong nonfiction writer uses fictional techniques for the same purpose: to hold the reader's interest.

The elements of fiction are plot, point of view, characterization, theme, and setting. Each corresponds to a nonfictional technique.

Plot is roughly the same as structure, discussed in Chapter 6. You will recall the feature article's classic architecture: a lead, often containing a capsule statement or nut paragraph; development of the facts; and a wrap-up.

Most fictional plots have a similar shape. Think of a movie or half-hour television show: if the story hasn't caught your interest within the first five or ten minutes, you'll probably leave the theater or turn off the television. A piece of short fiction must win over the reader in the first third of the story. After this equivalent of the lead, the fiction builds toward a climax or resolution of its problem and then falls off in a dénouement, the counterpart of the journalist's wrap-up.

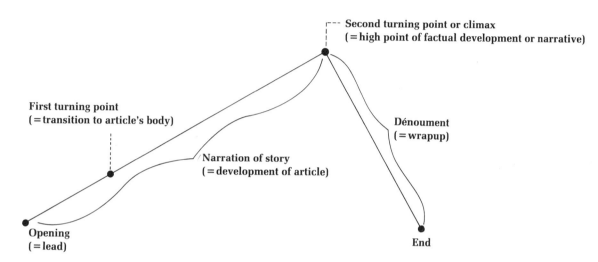

Figure 7.1. Fiction and feature compared

Plot involves conflict. Not all nonfiction stories lend themselves to this—the only conflict in a new-product roundup, for example, may take place between the editorial and advertising departments. But many articles do contain this element. Conflict may occur between human beings, between a person and an obstacle or handicap, between an individual and Nature or an animal, between large groups, or within a single person's mind. Anyone who faces a problem is engaged in a conflict.

You often can set up a kind of opposition within a nonfiction piece that will move the action forward to a resolution, just as a fictional story builds toward a climax that resolves the plot's conflict.

For example, you might write about a coalition of your city's small neighborhood homeowners' associations. Such groups usually form to fight city hall. Leaders may say they exist for local beautification or to sponsor block parties. But sooner or later, they involve themselves in zoning questions, highway development, taxation, crime-stopping programs, or whatever. Knowing this, you would focus on some problem the local groups took on, and you would use that conflict to show members in action. The story's body would move toward the disposition of the issue, and, in doing so, cover the coalition's history, function, and methods. For a "dénouement," the story might wind up with a quote or two on the group's effectiveness or a mention of future plans. Such an approach allows you to hold forth on the issues while you *show* how they affect real people.

Even when no conflict is inherent in your story, you should present your facts so that they build to a logical, satisfying conclusion. In other words, you should avoid either dumping all your information in a single pile or stringing the facts out at random so they go nowhere. The story should open on a captivating note, move toward some meaningful high point, and leave its readers feeling they have caught its significance.

Point of view, in nonfiction as in fiction, has to do with the perspective from which the story is told. The most obvious approach to nonfiction is to report the facts from the journalist's equivalent of the omniscient point of view. But that's not always the most desirable choice. Sometimes it's better to tell the story through the eyes of one of the people involved, even if that person is yourself.

The trick to relating a story from a specific point of view is to maintain the same perspective. Once you have begun to narrate the story from one person's viewpoint, do not waver by inserting another character's observations or your own comments.

Note the difference between *point of view* and the grammatical term *person*. By *first person*, we mean the subject of a verb is "I" or "we." In the *second person*, the verb's subject is "you;" and in the *third person*, "he," "she," or "they." Narrative may be written in the first or the third person.

Marguerite Reiss, in "Nightmare Hunt" (see chapter 17), reports a bear attack from the victim's point of view. She writes Rollin Braden's story in the third person: "Rollin didn't relish crossing tracks with [an Alaskan brown bear]. . . . The only sound he heard. . . . He knew . . . ." Although she does not use the first-person "I," the story is still told from a single perspective. Everything that takes place is experienced through Rollin: we hear, see, and feel what Rollin hears, sees, and feels, as the events happen to him. We never see any part of the story from the bear's viewpoint, nor through the eyes of Rollin's brother, father, or buddy. Had Reiss allowed this focus to slip, the story would have lost its impact.

A caveat about person and point of view: beginning writers are often wont to put themselves in stories where they don't belong. How do you know whether to write a story in the first person? If a narrator's presence helps, then by all means use the first person. In a Bob Greene or Hunter Thompson story, for example, a first-person narrator serves as a character—he performs a function, often as a foil to the other characters. This is most likely to work if the narrator took a leading part in the action—as, for example, Norman Mailer did in *Armies of the Night*. But if you were present only as a reporter, the first person will add nothing except to draw the reader's attention unnecessarily—tediously—to you. Then you should use the third person.

Good *characterization* presents a believable word picture of a human being. As soon as you introduce an individual into a story, you should immediately describe and characterize him.

Whether the person is real or imaginary, any ink-on-paper portrait is an abstraction. You never can present another human being as he or she actually is; the best you can do is show how you perceive someone. For this reason, John McPhee's Thomas Hoving is as much a literary character as John Updike's Roger Lambert. The fiction writer must provide enough detail to convince readers that the characters act as they do for believable reasons. As a nonfiction writer you have an added problem: you cannot manipulate or re-imagine a real person's motives or words to make them fit the story.

We perceive a person on several levels. One is superficial: we see her clothes, her physique, the color of her hair and eyes; we observe her mannerisms and hear the cadence of her speech; we sense the mood of the moment. As we come to know her better, we discover a second level of her reality: what she does for a living; where she grew up; how she was educated; what her parents, spouse, and children are like. The deepest level is psychological. She feels; she thinks; she responds to her environment in special ways. Key factors in her life have changed her: divorced parents, perhaps; or an accident, an abortion, a lost lover. These elements need not be dark—they might include a chance to study art coming at a moment of indecision, a special teacher, or a meeting with an admired role model.

Writers draw people just so. A *one-dimensional character* is lightly sketched—usually with one or two physical characteristics or an allusion to some habit. In describing a courtroom scene, for example, you would fill the spectators' gallery with one-dimensional characters. The danger in picking out a single trait, of course, is the lurking cliché. Try not to populate your stories with good-old-boy businessmen, liberated grandmothers, macho truck drivers, Valley girls, and similar stage figures.

Two-dimensional characters are more carefully drawn, with allusions to their personal background, tastes, and aspirations. You often find them in the standard 1,000- to 1,500-word magazine profile. We meet a young tycoon who at the age of 17 decided he could buy fast cars sooner by selling houses than by attending college, and voilà! Now he heads a three-state commercial realty empire. The story may interest the reader in passing, but it offers little insight into the subject's personality.

Three-dimensional characters are fleshed-out, fully rounded portraits. They happen when a writer knows a subject intimately, the result of long conversations and much time spent together. This picture tells us what the person looks like, where he grew up and went to school, who are the most important people in his life, and whether in an Italian restaurant he'll choose spaghetti over veal saltimbocca—and then it tells us why. *New Yorker* profiles are classic examples of fully drawn nonfictional characterization.

A story's *theme* is its sense of meaning: why do the things you're saying matter? An article, like a novel, story, or play, expresses its author's perception of life. In rare cases, you may communicate your view of the facts explicitly, through direct comment. Usually, you work it into the story through allusion and symbol, and by showing believable characters in meaningful action.

Barry Bearak, in his profile of comedian Sonny Sands (chapter 16), uses a sophisticated literary device to let us know why his subject matters. He manages, through the use of language, allusion, and subtle comparison, to make Sonny a kind of symbol. More than an aging comic, Sonny represents the decrepitude that all of us face, and at the same time he stands for an entertainment era that has passed. Bearak suggests this in his choice of quotes ("Life is like a composition. . . ."; "How much time you think you got in this world?"); by placing Sonny in a historic context; by suggesting that most of Sonny's audience now live in condominiums for the elderly; and by contrasting the old pro with a young part-timer whose life is radically different from Sonny's early life. In the stratospheric realms of literary criticism, this technique is called *iconography*. To find it in journalism is so rare as to be startling—but Bearak almost won a Pulitzer with it.

Setting reveals the story's time, place, and social milieu. Drawing a setting requires skill, both as observer and as writer. Description may be vivid, but it must never be purple—that is, florid, overblown, or gaudy.

It is vital to let the reader understand early on where the story takes place and how the surroundings look. In establishing the setting for "The Big Dry," *Time*'s July 4, 1988, cover story, Hugh

Sidey provides an excellent example of the show-don't-tell principle:

Leon Malard sat at his small kitchen table, covered with a blue plastic cloth, and with strong, thick fingers stroked the stubble on his chin. His black hair was cropped to its roots, his glasses coated at the edges with the grit from a morning of tilling in his stunted cornfield, which hugs a bluff above the Missouri River between Bismarck and Cannon Ball, N. Dak.

The 93° F wind scoured the boards of his tiny home, gusting and swirling up to 30 m.p.h., drying, loosening, lofting, trying again to blow him away. The big prairie sun, without a wisp of cloud to soften it, hammered the land as far as a squinted eye could see, which is a long way out there.

Rather than flatly saying Malard is a farmer, Sidey shows us a man who tills a cornfield. In this lead to a story about a drought, Sidey does not use the word "drought." Instead, he draws a picture: grit, stunted corn, 93° winds, the sun, the squinted eye.

Note, too, how specific the details are and how they add up. We see Malard, who is immediately named. His *small* kitchen table covered with a *blue plastic* cloth tells us he is a man of modest means with middle-class, pragmatic tastes. His *black* hair is *cropped* to its roots, suggesting middle- or working-class conservatism—he wears his hair like a U.S. Marine's. The word "roots" is connotative. He has *strong, thick* fingers: a working man's hands. The *stubble on his chin* says he didn't stop to primp on the way to a hard morning in the fields. That he has been *tilling* tells us he farms. He raises not just any crop, but corn, the quintessential American grain, and the cornfield is *stunted*, a signal that something is wrong.

In the second paragraph, Sidey uses a literary device known as "pathetic fallacy," in which Nature is imagined to reflect, sympathize with, or be capable of human actions. The 30-mile-an-hour winds try to blow Malard away—of course, the wind has no motive, nor can the sun consciously hammer the land like the Norse god Thor. Other verbs also carry faint suggestions of human behavior: *scoured, lofting.*

The entire setting is allusive. A man speaking from his small kitchen table in a tiny house hugging a bluff in the harsh vastness of the North Dakota prairie evokes a favorite American folk image: the little guy who stands up against massive, primal forces.

The strength of this passage lies in its restraint. Add any elaboration at all—one more windy verb, an extra adjective about the sun, a whiff of pity for Malard—and the writing would turn mauve. But because the details are carefully chosen, very specific, and concise, they paint an effective, convincing picture.

Another literary technique commonly used in nonfiction is *dialogue*, or, in the language of journalism, *quotes*. Direct quotation gives life and spirit to a narrative—but only when handled with some grace.

Quotes can serve several purposes. In exposition—where you are explaining a subject—quotes allow voices other than the writer's to comment. This adds interest or authority to what is being said. You might use an expert's remarks to support a generalization, or have a witness to some event speak about what she saw, heard, or thought.

Expository quotes should do more than simply repeat the author's assertion. They must add some fact or give insight into the characters' emotions. Try to avoid constructions of this nature, for example:

> Fitts, however, [said] he had reservations of his own regarding a constitutional challenge to his indictment because he wanted the opportunity to prove in court that what he wrote about the two politicians is true.
>
> "I want to prove my case," he [said]. "If this motion is accepted, the case probably will not go to court. I need to go to court."

Redundant and boring—the writer has Fitts say the same thing three times. By contrast, a quote in Ralph Backlund's July 1988 *Smithsonian* story about the Dance Theater of Harlem works well:

> People contrasted the energy of the company with the lethargy that sometimes overtakes performances of the Bolshoi Ballet. At a dress rehearsal the afternoon of opening night, there were many dance students. They said that not only could they not maintain the speed and precision demanded by the company, they never imagined anyone else could. Julia Kazlova, a student at the Moscow School of Ballet, said, "These are techniques and talents we have never seen."

That quote emphasizes the point without repeating it, and it adds a fact. Another quote in the same story demonstrates a different use of quotation: to characterize.

> Rabovsky shouts, stamps, and gives a convincing display of what we think of as Hungarian temperament. He scolds the boys for landing too audibly. "Do I hear noise? Oh, the noise is killing me! You are landing with *thuds*." Then he laughs and everyone relaxes.

Novice writers often stumble over attributions, those words that tell who said what. In " 'I find Paul appealing and Peale appalling,' said Adlai Stevenson," the word *said* is an attribution.

Speakers utter their words in many ways: they may *say, remark, observe, explain, reflect, ask,* or *tell.* Sometimes they may *whisper, mumble, murmur, exclaim, scream, yell, cry,* or *shriek.* But never do they *smile* their words, *laugh* them, *sigh* them, *think* them, or anything else of the sort. Do not write, " 'I just love pizza,' she grinned." Pick the most unobtrusive attribution that makes sense in your context: the point is to draw attention to the speaker, not to your writing. Usually a form of *say* suffices.

Ordinarily, you should start a new paragraph for each new quote, unless the quote supports a point you are making within a paragraph. When two or more people converse, begin a new paragraph with each change of speaker. Attribute as often as is necessary for clarity; you need not attribute every utterance, as long as the speaker is clear to the reader.

Attributions normally fall at the end or in the middle of a quote. If the quote is several lines long, place the attribution where a comma would naturally occur. If it is short, place the attribution at the end. Only when you wish to emphasize the speaker should you begin with the attribution: "John Kennedy said, 'Ask not what your country can do for you. . . .' "

Newspapers often invert the normal word order in attributions: "said Adlai Stevenson," rather than "Adlai Stevenson said." Some editors dislike this style. Do not feel you *must* use one or the other. Listen to the rhythm of the prose and use the order that best pleases the ear.

On most newspapers, too, reporters put attributions in the past tense. This does not hold true for magazines, or, on some papers, for the feature pages. If a speaker says something that he clearly means as generally true—that is, he'd repeat it right now if asked—use the present tense: " 'I personally despise them,' he says." But if the remark applies only to something that took place once, use the past tense: " 'Hey,' " Darrel said quietly, 'It's your moose.' "

For many kinds of nonfiction, mastery of the techniques of *suspense* and *foreshadowing* is vital. In learning to write for *Reader's Digest*, for example, Marguerite Reiss was taught "to get the reader on the edge of his chair." The magazine's editors call this "nail-biting," she reports. "You have to hold him there until he can hardly stand it, and at the very last minute, you give him a little relief."

Several expedients can help bring the reader to the edge of the chair. Most obvious is withholding information until the end of the story. We know, for example, that Rollin Braden will survive the bear attack—otherwise the story wouldn't appear in *Reader's Digest*. But we don't know how he will escape or what will happen to him before he does.

In "Nightmare Hunt," Reiss builds suspense by dropping hints in the first few paragraphs:

"Thought you told me I'd see some bears," Darrel chided his friend. . . . Alaskan brown bears forage intensely before holing up for the winter. Rollin didn't relish crossing tracks with one. . . . Suddenly Rollin sensed something . . . there was a rustle. . . . Before long he was 300 yards into the woods, then 400 yards. A chill rippled through his body. He knew that whatever animal he had heard was probably watching him right now. . . . A branch snapped . . . .

All these details foreshadow something ominous. Later in the piece, the suspense resumes when the enraged animals back off momentarily during their attack.

Rollin could hear the bears nearby ... the seconds ticked by ... the heavy panting subsided. ...

Telling the story from Rollin's point of view also helps create a sense of tension in this story, because it builds empathy. "I learned to put myself in the person's shoes, in interviewing as well as writing," Reiss says. "Rather than being objective and standing away, like I used to do in newspaper work, you have to actually get in and almost hurt with the guy.

"You look for tiny bits of suspense, and then some little flavors that aren't so openly suspenseful," she adds. Reiss once interviewed a young Air Force sergeant who was accidentally caught on a helicopter's basket litter above the Bering Sea. He assumed a macho pose about the incident. "I asked him, 'did you look down?' He was being sort of light about it. But when I asked him that, he said, 'No, I didn't look down. Once I glanced a little bit, but I didn't want to look down.' So he was giving me just a little tincture of what I would call fear. But of course, he wouldn't call it that."

Details like this make the story.

A fiction writer may invent details. In nonfiction, you must be absolutely factual. But there's a reason articles are called stories: that's what any good writer tells.

–30–

FOR PROJECTS OR DISCUSSION

1. Scan a Sunday newspaper for leads to potential magazine stories. What conflicts are inherent in each? Remember, these oppositions may be subtle.

2. By now, you probably have watched your instructor for several weeks; perhaps you even took notes. Write a 500- to 1,000-word characterization of this person; use quotes, description, point-of-view, and narrative to show something of his or her personality. Is the result one-, two-, or three-dimensional? What would you need to make your portrait more true to life?

3. Obtain several back issues of *Reader's Digest* and study the "Drama in Real Life" departments. Outline the structure of each story, and compare it to what you know of fictional plot.

4. If you have recently written a story that involves people in action, rewrite it to relate the events from one participant's point of view.

SUGGESTED READING

Syd Field. *Screenplay: The Foundations of Screenwriting*. New York: Dell Trade Paperbacks, 1982. The chapters on characterization and plot structure apply to all fictional genres and extend to nonfiction.

John Gardner. *The Art of Fiction: Notes on Craft for Young Writers*. New York: Knopf, 1983. See the chapter titled "Plotting."

Norman Sims, ed. *The Literary Journalists*. New York: Ballantine Books, 1984. Contains a revealing introduction and useful examples of work by journalists who enhance their styles with fictional techniques.

Joseph J. Trimmer and C. Wade Jennings, "Introduction." *Fictions*. New York: Harcourt Brace Jovanovich, 1985. The first section of this essay contains an excellent summary of the elements of fiction.

Tom Wolfe. *The New Journalism*. New York: Harper and Row, 1973. The classic statement on this approach to nonfiction.

8

The Language of Magazines and Newspapers

The late Joe Spring, a veteran newspaperman, wound up his long career as director of a university news bureau. One day a dew-eared young fellow applied for a job as a copy writer.

"What makes you think you're qualified to write copy?" Joe demanded. He had a dyspeptic way of glaring at those who aroused his skepticism.

"I can write a simple sentence," the young man said.

Joe hired him on the spot.

Why? Because the kid hit on the key to good journalistic writing: clarity.

CULTIVATING CLARITY

Reading levels in this country, already low, continue to sink. *USA Today* bases its staccato, skim-the-top-of-the-news approach on the theory that the average American's attention span maxes out at the length of time between television commercials. Even the *Wall Street Journal* is written at an eleventh-grade reading level. Sophisticated readers as well as those who read only when driven to it expect writers to keep it simple.

This does not mean your writing should be simple-minded. People who avoid reading are not necessarily stupid; they know when someone is talking down to them. Nor should your style be choppy. Vary the length and structure of your sentences, but keep them crisp and uncluttered.

To help develop a clear style, keep in mind the following principles.

Avoid the Passive Voice

Verbs come in two voices: "active" and "passive." The active voice moves the action directly from the subject to the object.

Jerry shot the bear.

When the voice is passive, the action moves in the opposite direction, back toward the subject. The verb's subject becomes the "passive" receiver of the action. You can recognize a passive voice because the prepositional phrase "by [the doer of the action]" is either explicit or implicit.

The bear was shot [by Jerry].

This is a mealy-mouthed way of speaking, much favored by bureaucrats and the military because it passes the buck. Suppose a game warden came along shortly after the bear's out-of-season demise. We could expect Jerry to describe the animal's mishap in the passive voice.

In most circumstances, prefer the active over the passive voice. It is more direct and less verbose.

Use Verbs that Convey Action, Instead of Verbs of Being

Here are the verbs of being:

am, is, are, was, were, be, being, been.

There's nothing wrong with these words, per se. But they do lack interest. Good writers let their verbs carry the weight of a sentence's meaning, and a verb of being just doesn't bear much weight.

Sometimes replacing weak "being" verbs with stronger language entails more than erasing one word and dropping in another. You may have to recast a sentence completely.

Consider this:

Energetic and stimulating, Ríos is a favorite among students.

We could rewrite it to say

Students love the energetic and stimulating Ríos.

But the result would be as clumsy as it is dull. Let's get rid of the tedious word "stimulating" (what *does* that mean?) and put our man into action:

Ríos projects a sense of excitement and energy that charms his students.

Not perfect, but it's better. It says something about Ríos: as a teacher, he "projects" like an actor. It replaces the invisible word "is" with "charms," a more descriptive and suggestive term. And it shows Ríos acting on his students, rather than as a passive object of their favor.

Write in Complete Sentences

Most of the time. As a teacher, I sometimes feel at a loss with journalism and communications majors who cannot or will not put their thoughts in sentences, complete with subject and verb. As an editor, I know exactly what to do with such stuff: reject it or rewrite it.

Sentence fragments are like exclamation points. They're emphatic. Good writers use them as they use exclamation points— sparingly. To pepper a story with either fragments or exclamation points is bad style.

Use Anglo-Saxon Instead of Latinate words

Prefer the short word to the long. It is not true that the more syllables a word has, the more important it sounds. Consider the alternatives to a few mouth-fillers:

numerous: many
donation: gift
illustrate: show
accountability: duty
merchandise: stock
to merchandise: to sell
acquiesce: agree
communicate: say
conference: meeting
indicate: say; imply
knowledgeable: trained
optimal: best
restructure: change
institute: start

Delete the Jargon

Of AIDS, a high-ranking bureaucrat once said, "The disease has heterosexualized, proletarianized, and ruralized." So, apparently, has the gobbledygook plague.

Jargon is mishmash that tends to obscure meaning while it suggests the speaker is an insider. Almost any word that ends in -ize or -ate is probably jargon:

capacitize
prioritize
collateralize
maximize and minimize
originate
administrate
facilitate
medicate

Nouns and adjectives almost always convert to jargon when they pop up as brand-new verbs:

to author
to office
to parent
to network
to obsolete

Some words come into the language from various baleful sources —shop talk, admanese, educationese, political doublethink. They have an alluring buzz but little meaning. Their sound presumably triggers some impulse in like-minded speakers, the way small electric shocks signal experimental rats to push buttons. These terms usually fade; the good writer helps usher them out by shunning them. Let us mention a few once and never again:

upscale
downscale
Smokestack America
fast track
dog-and-pony show
hands-on
world class
downside
charisma
meaningful dialogue
relevant
revolution ("a marketing revolution")
communications (for *journalism, public relations,* or *English*)

A few survive from that "world-class" political debacle, Watergate: stonewall, at this point in time, go public. Some slop over from computerese: input, output, to keyboard, interface, parameter. Pop psychology and sociology are rich lodes of jargon: generation gap, peer group, inner-directed, identity crisis.

William and Mary Morris, in the *Harper Dictionary of Contemporary Usage*, call these "vogue words," which "brighten our prose for a moment and then . . . bore us until they drop entirely out of sight." Just so: jargon bores. Whatever you do, don't bore your reader.

Avoid Clichés . . .

. . . like the plague. A cliché is an aging quip, once original and smart, that has worn thin with overuse.

How can you tell if some gilded phrase is hackneyed? Say the first few words; if the last few follow automatically, it's a cliché:

It's raining cats and _____
It's so hot you could fry ____ _____ on the _____
filled to the _____
full _____ ahead
fit as a _____
sell like _____

There are larger forms of clichés, platitudes people accept without thinking them through:

Sugar makes children hyperactive
Overweight people are unhappy
To succeed, you must dress for success
The generation of the eighties was preoccupied with material goods
Insurance rates have skyrocketed because courts award outrageously high damages to people who file frivolous lawsuits
Newspapers are afraid to address certain topics for fear of offending advertisers, potential litigators, or community leaders

Beware any blanket generalization, broad statement, or popular theory, especially if it's one you or your friends accept on faith.

Use Specific Terms, Not Mush-Words

Certain mush-words, devoid of solid meaning, often crop up in student writing. "Area" and "field" are ubiquitous: "that's not my area"; "an expert in the field." What do you suppose the speaker means? Discipline? Concern? Job? Meadow? *Say* what you mean.

Watch out for vague words, like *thing, idea, situation, experience* (as in "a dining experience"), and *group* (meaning anything from the Boy Scouts to a witches' coven).

One word in this category has become singularly offensive: *unique*. The word "unique" means there is nothing anywhere—nay, not in the whole universe—exactly like it. If an object is the only one in existence, by all means call it "unique." Otherwise, try "rare," "different," "unusual," or "special." Uniqueness, like pregnancy, is an absolute condition. A product (advertising copywriters love the word) cannot be "very," "completely," "more," or "the most" unique.

Use the Right Word

"When a person has a poor ear for music," wrote Mark Twain, "he will flat and sharp right along without knowing it. He keeps near the tune, but it is *not* the tune. When a person has a poor ear for words, the result is a literary flatting and sharping; you perceive what he is intending to say, but you also perceive that he doesn't *say* it."

Twain then listed almost three dozen false notes from six pages of James Fenimore Cooper. Some are still in use:

"verbal" for *oral*
"unsophisticated" for *primitive*
"dependent on" for *resulting from*
"fact" for *condition* or *conjecture*
"precaution" for *caution*
"mortified" for *disappointed*
"situation" for *condition*
"treacherous" for *hostile*

Some words sound, to the untrained ear, as though they should mean what they don't. *Fortuitous*, for example, does not mean *fortunate*. *Appraised* is not *apprised*, to *revenge* is not *to avenge*, *nauseated* is not *nauseous*. If you feel even faintly vague about a word's meaning, look it up.

Shun Euphemisms

Euphemism is prettified speech that supposedly softens blunt reality ("she passed away") or replaces frank words with ostensibly more acceptable language ("little girls' room"). No one wants you to be crude, but neither must the writer be nicey-nice. An environmental engineer in education is still a school janitor, a task force is a committee, a recreation facility a gym, and a one-man excavation implement a spade.

Cut Redundancies

Any unnecessary word is redundant. In the patter of everyday speech, we habitually repeat ourselves. For example:

close proximity
more and more
one and only
free gift
sworn affidavit
single most
component parts
completely surrounded
future plans
returned again
completely unable
totally unique
time and again

People who talk this way may have an excuse—you don't edit the spoken word after it has been uttered. But writers can't get away with it.

Keep It Short

No one has expressed this principle better than William Strunk and E. B. White. Under Rule 17, "Omit needless words":

Vigorous writing is concise. A sentence should contain no unnecessary words, a paragraph no unnecessary sentences, for the same reason that a drawing should have no unnecessary lines and a machine no unnecessary parts. This requires not that the writer make all his sentences short, or that he avoid all detail and treat his subjects only in outline, but that every word tell.

Certain mechanical tricks, although no substitute for thoughtful composition, will help. Start by cutting adverbs and adjectives, especially *very, rather, quite, a little, a bit, somewhat,* and *really.*

Ask yourself if you need that adverb, or if you can find a verb that carries the meaning with it. Instead of "he walked slowly," try "he ambled," "plodded," "strolled," or "shuffled." Never use two words when one will serve better.

Watch for wordy constructions. They're everywhere:

has the capability to; is capable of *(can)*
is able to *(can)*
is similar to *(resembles)*

can be compared to *(is like; resembles)*
are forced to *(must)*
is a product of Japan *(comes from Japan)*
has a great influence on *(influences)*
in the majority of cases *(usually)*
considered to be *(considered; thought)*
in order to *(to)*

Often you can delete the coordinating conjunction *that:* "foods that healthy people eat" becomes "foods healthy people eat," Similarly, *who* and *which* may be superfluous:

Sgt. Preston, who is a Vietnam veteran, said . . .
Sgt. Preston, a Vietnam veteran, said . . .

The canyon, which is a wildlife sanctuary, runs north . . .
The canyon, a wildlife sanctuary, runs north . . .

Another device: replace prepositional phrases with possessives or noun phrases.

The laughter of the children
The children's laughter

A spokesman for Honeywell
Honeywell spokesman

Take care, though. You can get as tangled up in noun phrases as a puppy in its own feet. Don't stumble into monstrosities like "violent crime victims." *Victims of violent crime,* even if it does have more words, makes better sense.

Avoid Double Meanings

"Since"—does it mean *because* or *after?* It could mean either in a sentence like "Since he lost his wife, he would not leave town."

"While" may mean *during the time* or *although:* "While he was a trucker, he preferred not to drive a car."

"Last" implies finality, although some people use it to mean "most recent." Was "her last book" the final one she ever wrote, or just her latest work?

The careful writer chooses words that leave no doubt to the meaning.

Avoid Portmanteau Sentences

James Kilpatrick coined that term with the help of Lewis Carroll. It aptly compares the overburdened sentence to a stuffed suitcase, ready to fly apart at the hinges. Don't pack your sentence with more than it can hold. Consider this horrendous example from *Editor and Publisher*:

Achorn suggested that women set the ground rules early and stick to them, not underestimate themselves or set their goals too low, be prepared for a certain amount of loneliness as they get to the top (it goes with the job), not carry a chip on their shoulders, take advantage of every educational and training opportunity, make sure their company has a sound policy against sexual harassment, not assume all women working with them are for them, be optimistic and not expect the workplace to solve all the problems and change cultural attitudes that have built up over the centuries.

The writer need not have recited every hackneyed aphorism the speaker uttered. But were the advice not trite, the sentence still would look overstuffed.

Learn to Use Metaphor and Simile Correctly

Metaphors and similes are figurative ways of speaking that describe one thing in terms of something else. A simile is a comparison that uses "like" or "as":

She looks as clear as morning roses newly washed with dew
A merry heart doeth good like a medicine
Flying a helicopter is like trying to balance on a beach ball

A metaphor, instead of saying "like" or "as," makes an implicit comparison:

A peaches-and-cream complexion
The Lord is my shepherd
Home is the girl's prison and the woman's workhouse
He sows hurry and reaps indigestion

The soul of simile and metaphor is brevity. You should keep figures of speech short, hard-hitting, and to the point. When you let them ramble on, you risk falling into purple prose. One writer hit upon the conceit that thunderheads look like meringue. Before she finished, the sky, the mountains, and the fruited plain sounded like a bakery showcase.

A more common abuse, however, is the mixed metaphor. Erik Larson, writing in *Harper's* ("Brave New Foods," May 1988), unearthed a classic when he quoted a Campbell's Soup Company executive: "If you don't get on the bandwagon, you're going to miss the boat."

Use Correct Punctuation

It's the little things, they say, that ultimately get you down. For editors, one of life's most wearing irritants is their writers' ignorance of punctuation. More than once I have felt the urge to wring necks over incorrectly placed apostrophes (*its* does not mean *it's*, and there is no such animal as *its'*), commas between subjects and verbs, separate sentences slopped together with a comma, and ludicrous hyphenation (*psyc-hology*). Bad punctuation makes a writer look like a fool. The stuff is not hard to learn. Read Appendix A, commit it to memory, and apply it to your work.

Keep It Simple

The best journalistic writing sounds like conversation because it uses unaffected language. But clear writing has an advantage over speech. Because you rework your words before others receive them, you can free your style of conversation's redundancy, illogic, and ambiguity. William Zinsser said it well: "The secret of good writing is to strip every sentence to its cleanest components."

–30–

FOR PROJECTS OR DISCUSSION

1. Here's an exercise you can continue for the rest of your career. It will help you develop a sensitive ear ("sensitize" you) for the uses and misuses of English:

Start a collection of jargon words, the more outrageous the better. Whenever you hear a new one, make a mental note of it (if you have a strong memory) or keep it in a notebook or file. Between your classmates and your teacher, you can round up a healthy starter set in a few minutes of brainstorming. Here are a few to begin with:

"The ensemble has *concertized* and taught each summer."
"No one else can fit in here. We have *capacitized* the room."
"The principal is *conferencing* with the teachers."
A school library is a *media center*
A low-paid university public relations writer is an *information specialist II*

2. Bring to class some likely sources of poor writing—newsletters for state employees, education bulletins, in-house memos, and trade magazines are rich lodes—and analyze the language. Could they be improved? How?

SUGGESTED READING

Robert Graves and Alan Hodge. *The Reader over Your Shoulder.* New York: Random House, 1971.

James J. Kilpatrick. *The Writer's Art*. Kansas City: Andrews, McMeel and Parker, 1984.

William Lutz. *Doublespeak*. New York: Harper and Row, 1990.

Benton Rain Patterson. *Write to Be Read*. Ames, Iowa: Iowa State University Press, 1986.

Mark Twain. "Fenimore Cooper's Literary Offenses." In Lawrence Teacher, ed., *The Unabridged Mark Twain*, pp. 1241–1250. Philadelphia: Running Press, 1976.

E. B. White and William Strunk. *The Elements of Style*. New York: Macmillan, 1979.

William Zinsser. *On Writing Well*. New York: Harper and Row, 1985.

9

Once More Through the Typewriter

Getting the facts on paper brings such relief that you sometimes forget you've just begun.

Experienced writers understand, however, that a first draft represents just another step toward the end of the project. The piece will require still more work before it is ready for an editor's eyes.

It's a good idea to let your freshly completed story "cool" for a while before you begin editing, tightening, and revising. Then, take your time and do a thorough, thoughtful job. "Many a gifted piece of writing," noted Jacques Barzun, "has been lost in the flood of print because it was hastily revised and hence bore the marks of an imperfection at once pitiable and insulting."

Try to build enough time into your schedule to allow 12 to 24 hours between the first draft and your revision. If your deadline is too tight to permit that, at least set the story aside and work on some other project for an hour or two before coming back to it.

Your goal in polishing a story is to produce a final draft that requires minimal revision by the editor. This means the story's content, organization, style, and mechanics must be as good as you can make them. To accomplish that, review the story twice: once for content and style, and once again for mechanics.

CONTENT OR SUBSTANTIVE EDITING

When you pick up your story for revision and polishing, bear in mind this fact: *it is not carved in granite*. Brilliant as your prose certainly is, most first and second drafts are helped by pruning, reorganizing, and rewriting.

You might as well start with your most difficult task. Read the story coolly and ask yourself whether, if you did not know its writer, you would find this article so interesting you would stick with it to the end. Do you *care* enough to read it? The way to persuade people to read your work is to convince them that your topic matters—that the characters act for some significant reason, or the facts are worth knowing. Often your own enthusiasm for a subject comes through strongly enough to influence the reader. Sometimes not. In that case, you must state explicitly why this story is important.

What if—as sometimes happens—you are simply not interested in the subject you have been assigned to cover? Then you must try to empathize with those who do feel some passion about it and communicate their reasons or feeling to the reader. Empathy, like skepticism, goes with the writer's job.

Review the mechanical devices you have used to maintain interest. Be sure you spaced the facts through the story in a readable way, rather than dumping them all at the beginning or end. Ask yourself if you have used enough metaphor and simile, dialogue, and detailed description to give the reader a clear picture of what is happening. See that the story builds to a logical or dramatic climax and ends with a satisfying conclusion.

If your story fails in any of these ways, you must rewrite. Boldly recast passages so that they say, whether through metaphor and symbol or by explicit statement, why the story matters. Be sure the entire story follows this line of thought or emotion—that your facts support the central argument.

Once you feel sure your approach will hold the reader's attention, you should review the story's organization. Each point must follow logically from the one that precedes it. Again, look at the copy through the readers' eyes. They don't know as much as you do about the subject—connections that seem obvious to you may not be so for them.

Here again, you may have to rewrite. Cut and paste so the paragraphs hang together in a sensible way. Add understandable transitions so the reader can quickly grasp how the facts relate to each other. Where necessary, recast paragraphs or longer passages so they fit logically with the new organization.

My first draft of the story on cartoonists mentioned in Chapter 3 was organized like this:

Lead: Anecdote in which Bil Keane gets an idea for adding a character to *Family Circus*
Bridge: Popularity of comics and cartoons; historically many well-known

cartoonists have lived in our state. (List about a half-dozen old-time stars, among them J. R. Williams, Walt Ditzen, Virgil Partch.) These prominent cartoonists are associated with the state: Bil Keane, Gus Arriola, Nick Dallis, Bill Mauldin, Reg Manning, Jerry Scott, Steve Benson.

Transition: They have in common strongly felt personal emotion that shows in their work

Bil Keane
  Characterize
  Development of *Family Circus*
  Quote: cartoon based on real life
Gus Arriola
  Gordo influenced by Sonoran ambience of hometown
  Development & nature of strip
Reg Manning
  Character & career at local paper
  Wins Pulitzer Prize
Steve Benson
  Characterize
  Describe recent controversial cartoon
  Quotes on how it exemplifies his philosophy of political cartooning
Bill Mauldin
  Characterize; protégé of Manning
  Wins Pulitzer Prizes
  Other activities
  Quote: re Dukakis
Transition: Controversy in comic strips
Jerry Scott
  The new *Nancy*
  Talk show incident
  Letters
Nick Dallis
  Local paper drops *Judge Parker* cocaine sequence, which later wins award
  Quotes on other controversies
Wrap: Quote Benson on moving West from Washington, D.C.: "Thought I'd died and gone to cartoonist's heaven."

The resulting story was loose and unfocused near the top. The development was adequate; pacing the story from mild or nostalgic cartoons to the increasingly vociferous political opinions of Benson and Mauldin and then moving into the strange nonpolitical controversies around the likes of *Nancy, Rex Morgan, M.D.,* and *Judge Parker* sustained interest. The lead, which involved a gently ribald exchange between Keane and his wife, was charming and effective. The problem was in the bridge or "nut paragraph" linking the lead to the story's body. After some give-and-take with my editor, the new version looked like this:

Lead: Same
Bridge: Keane is the state's most prominent cartoonist today, but others have rivaled his renown.

List old-timers; briefly introduce the people this story will cover.
Transitional paragraph: popularity of comics and editorial cartoons:
Focus on Keane as one who enjoys extreme popularity.
　Development of *Family Circus*
　[The rest is identical]

This reorganization required more than simply cutting and pasting; some rewriting took place, too.

Next, consider whether the story is complete. Have you covered all the bases? Have you presented all sides of the issue? In covering an innovative city park, an architectural writer opened a story by reporting on the outrage the unusual design had engendered. But he also was careful to include remarks from the park's admirers. Commenting on plans to install laser beams aimed at the night sky which, when members of the public are allowed to play with them, will be visible for miles around, he made it clear that he doubted this would be environmentally pleasing—but explained why supporters liked the idea.

On the other hand, you can in a sense be "too complete." Make sure you have not thrown in so much that your story loses focus. When I interviewed Bill Mauldin for the cartoonists piece, he had plenty to say about the Pulitzer Prize committee—two transcript pages full of juicy remarks. But because my angle had nothing to do with the controversy over the Pulitzers, I left all that tempting stuff out. Never forget the purpose of your story, which should be clear in the nut graf or lead; restrict the body of your story to material that supports it. That is, *keep to the point.*

When you are dealing with a complex subject, you must place current facts in context. Sometimes what is happening now makes little sense unless it is seen in the light of what has happened in the past or what is happening elsewhere. For example, a young writer covered a months-long mining strike, which took an ugly turn when a small child was shot in the head. After working very hard on the story, she fastidiously presented the union's and management's sides. However, she knew next to nothing about labor history or about the background of the state's right-to-work law. The piece came off as naive and shallow. To rework it, she needed to discuss past regional labor-management relations and set the current events off against earlier injustices.

Next, check your story for economy. Is the copy free of redundancy? Normally, you need say things just once; be sure you have not unwittingly repeated yourself. Cut all fat and puffery—see that you express yourself without wasting words. Ask if parts of the story can be removed without harm; passages that do nothing to support your point or that do not carry their weight in fact should go.

Be sure, too, that you have not contradicted yourself. Writing about a copper mining community, a reporter mentioned that Mexican-Americans were banned from the lucrative underground jobs until World War II diminished Anglo manpower enough to overcome discrimination. Later, he quoted a fellow with a Hispanic surname saying he'd started to work in the mines in 1939. Pay attention!

Next, review the story's overall tone. Is it appropriate to your purpose and consistent with the tone you set in the lead? Is it fair? Humor can be particularly devastating, because there is no answer to laughter. Ask yourself, too, whether your tone fits your publication. You might describe the city council's latest action in a sardonic vein for an alternative paper—but not for a daily. Some magazines never print anything negative; even subjects such as pollution and crime are approached as minor problems with feasible solutions. Others take an unflinching stand on news and issues. Your attitude should fit your story's lead, your publisher's agenda—and ultimately what you know to be true.

The flaw most difficult to spot in your own work is what we must frankly call "stupid stuff." By that I mean unintelligible copy, purple prose, clichés, ridiculous statements, and downright clumsy writing. Here, for example, is a paragraph submitted by an honest-to-goodness published magazine writer:

Sea storms may have been common in Arizona 350 million years ago. Fossils tell you that much of the state was once lapped by the ocean's comforting infinity; waves rose and fell like the chest of a sleeping giant. Then the beaches could have been immense wide swaths, surrounded by jutting semicircles of shifting dunes.

Heaven help us. Let's start with the most outrageous gaffe and move downward.

No ocean is infinite. To the contrary, the oceans in question were shallow seas, far from *infinite*, which means "without end." Some of us do not regard infinity as a "comforting" concept. But picture that warm, fuzzy infinity lapping the state, like a big slobbering dog! Given that oceans did exist 350 million years ago, it's safe to say sea storms *were* common, rather than hedging with the wimpy "may have been." Instead of "waves," the writer meant "tides." "Immense wide": redundant. "Surrounded by" means "enclosed" or "encircled"—we're talking about an ocean here, not Walden Pond. Semicircles do not "jut."

The revised version, in my opinion, is just marginally acceptable:

Sea storms were common in Arizona 350 million years ago. Fossils tell us that much of the state was once covered by oceans. Tides rose and fell like the chest of a sleeping giant. Then the beaches may have been immense swaths bordered by semicircles of shifting dunes.

Don't write like this. As you can see, there's little an editor can do with such drivel. Hold the heavy breathing and substitute some facts (What kind of oceans? Where were these oceans? How deep and extensive were they? Where did they come from and where did they go? What was the climate like? The geology? How do we know —by what sort of fossils?). Choose your words carefully and be sure you know what they mean.

Double-check every fact and assertion, especially if you think you know it as you do your own name.

Pop quiz: Thomas Hardy derived the title of his 1876 novel, *Far from the Madding Crowd*, from a line in Shakespeare's *Twelfth Night*. Right?

No, certainly not. In the *Oxford Dictionary of Quotations*, you easily discover the title's source: Thomas Gray's "Elegy Written in a Country Churchyard." Good. But did you check that date?

Back to the story: read it aloud. Does it sound like plain English? The language should roll smoothly from the tongue in clear, idiomatic phrases. Rewrite clumsy, ambiguous, or verbose passages until their style is graceful, their meaning unmistakable, and their economy tight. Are there any infelicitous rhymes or rhythms? If so, recast the passage to eliminate them.

The writing should be clear and conversational; it should favor the active over the passive voice and shun verbosity. It should be concrete, specific (not abstract), and free of jargon. Action verbs should predominate over verbs of being, and vivid nouns should draw a picture for the reader.

Here's a checklist of the things you should watch for in content editing:

1. Factual completeness
2. Logical organization and development of the facts
3. Perfect clarity
4. Accuracy
5. Consistency
6. Freshness; freedom from jargon and hackneyed thought
7. Pleasing language
8. An appealing lead
9. Lively, interesting presentation
10. A satisfying wrap-up

LINE EDITING FOR MECHANICS

Once you feel satisfied with the story's overall style and content, you must go over the copy line by line to see that your grammar and spelling are correct, your punctuation accurate, your syntax irreproachable, and your manuscript properly typed.

Use a dictionary or speller such as *Webster's Instant Word Guide* to double-check hyphenation, spelling, and capitalization.

Does spelling matter? Recently, I attended a board meeting of a state arm of the National Endowment for the Humanities, a group that grants money to people who present cultural programs. Among the grant proposals we reviewed was a plan to offer a summer seminar to inner-city schoolteachers at a cool vacation getaway. The grant writer proposed to teach *The Milagro Beanfield War* during this event. At stake were a chance to be paid for spending a couple of weeks in a resort community, points toward a promotion, and no doubt a substantial investment of time and ego. Unfortunately, the writer spelled the word *milagro* "malagra" throughout her copy. (The Spanish term means "miracle.") Board members suspected that a person who could not spell the title of a readily available paperback might lack the skill to teach it; for that and similar reasons, the request was denied.

Be sure you have capitalized all proper names and trademarks. Words such as "Realtor," "Xerox," and "Kleenex" should be used accurately and upper-cased. Confirm and re-confirm the spellings of personal and place names and the accuracy of dates, telephone numbers, addresses, and other figures.

Check all your punctuation. Have you linked any sentences with commas? Express them as two sentences, or (if you must) join them with semicolons. Spare your editor the aggravating "it's" when you mean "belonging to it," and "its" when you mean "it is." Be sure quotation marks and parentheses are closed and possessives are correctly marked.

Check your grammar. Do all your verbs agree with their subjects? Be especially careful of clauses in which a prepositional phrase surfaces between the subject and the verb. Which is correct?

The group of girls have . . .

or

The group of girls has . . .

The object of a prepositional phrase can never be the subject of a verb. *Group,* a singular noun, is the subject of this verb, whose correct American form is *has.*

Know when to use *which* and when *that.* The following two sentences have different meanings:

The ideals, which we love, are in danger.
The ideals that we love are in danger.

In the first, the phrase "which we love" is *non-restrictive*; that is, it does nothing to define or change the endangered ideals. In the second, the *restrictive* phrase "that we love" tells us that *only* the ideals we love are in danger; the rest, presumably, are safe. As a rule of thumb, if you could eliminate the subordinating conjunction ("that" or "which") without changing the meaning, use *that* instead of *which*.

Do you find any dangling modifiers, any cryptic pronouns that could refer to more than one noun? Recast the language to eliminate these ambiguities.

If your copy contains incomplete sentences, have you used them sparingly and only for good cause? Recast fragments into whole sentences unless you are absolutely sure of what you are doing.

Type numbers, dates, and addresses in the style your publication uses. If the editor hasn't explained the house style, examine a back issue to see whether these items are spelled out or expressed in numerals. If numbers larger than nine are set as numerals, the editors probably use the Associated Press or *New York Times* stylebook. If numbers larger than nine are spelled out, they're probably using the *Chicago Manual of Style*. Proof your copy accordingly.

Check your language for economy. Have you expressed everything in the sparest possible way? In doing so, have you introduced any barbarisms (such as "rehabilitation foundation")?

Examine the language, too, for simplicity. Have you used a sesquipedalian word where a term like "sixteen-syllable" would do?

Now be sure your typing conforms to a consistent manuscript style. You should double-space the copy and top each page with a running head and page number. Place your name and address on the first page, and mark the end of the manuscript with number symbols (###) or –30–.

Here's a list of items you should check in mechanical editing:

1. Spelling
2. Punctuation
3. Grammar
4. Freedom from verbosity
5. Consistent use of numerals, dates, and addresses
6. Correct manuscript style

GIMMICKS AND ELECTRONIC DOODADS

Catering to those who seem unable to learn the principles of clarity, some theoreticians have contrived formulae that guarantee clear writing intelligible to the lowest common reader. Among the best known are Gunning's "Fog Index" and Rudolf Flesch's "Readability Formula." These schemes calculate a passage's academic grade level by comparing syllable counts with total words and sentences. Some computer programs will automatically make such calculations and tell you whether your writing measures up (or down).

Although such formulae have something to recommend them, like any mechanical device they can fail when applied to an endeavor as wholly human as writing. Consider, for example, this passage:

> Dapping from an eyot in the bight, his cade ascob at his side, a snod wight dropped his brills, stotted on his gamp, and enewed into the letch. Anon came a simous cuddy, and at his side marched a dicty young aulete, her brees all limned in kohl—indeed, she liked to fard her face. The wight lirped at his leal tyke and hirred it off across the brumous croft to fetch the other two. "Hent that besom, if you will," he asked them as they reached the marge, "and pull me out." But the lass began to fyke and affied, "The sight of water makes me hilo."*

According to the Flesch formula, that incomprehensible paragraph reads at the sixth-grade level.

Now consider this:

> In "I Live on Your Visits," an adolescent boy observes with chagrin and precision the drunken mannerisms of a woman who, from her high-toned and arch way of talking, exactly matches what we know of Dorothy Parker. The consolations and detachment of art remained inviolable to her, and it might also be said in admiration that neither alcoholic haze nor romantic distress cut her off from the pleasures of reading. She was, as her column for this magazine proclaimed long ago (1927–33), a Constant Reader, and the book reviews she procrastinatingly executed for *Esquire* toward the end of her life show the same enthusiasm for the written word that lighted up her girlhood as a mock orphan. (John Updike, reviewing Marion Meade's *Dorothy Parker: What Hell is This?* In *The New Yorker*, April 25, 1988)

Lucid and charming, no? And according to the formula, inaccessible: its "grade level" is almost off the scale, way into the college years.

Computerized spelling and grammar checkers suffer from similar defects. Their most telling fault is that they do not recognize homonyms and wrong word choices because they can't understand con-

---

*Translation: Fishing from an islet in the bay, his pampered cocker spaniel at his side, a smooth, well-trimmed fellow dropped his glasses, stumbled on his umbrella, and fell into the muddy ditch. Soon a snub-nosed rustic came along, and at his side marched a classy young flute player, her eyelashes all outlined in black eye shadow —indeed, she liked to make up her face. The fellow snapped his fingers at his faithful dog and ordered it off across the foggy meadow to fetch the other two. "Grab that broom, if you will," he asked them as they reached the bank, "and pull me out." But the girl began to fidget and confided, "The sight of water makes me seasick."

text. When, for example, I run my SpellStar and XyWrite dictionaries on this sentence:

To boys wrote two many letters too their fiends,

both programs accept it without pause. Our human editor, however, is probably apoplectic.

Spelling and grammar are part of the creative process. They are the writer's tools. Learn how to use them. Don't rely on a machine to use them for you. And never take leave of your common sense.

—30—

FOR PROJECTS OR DISCUSSION

1. Find a paper you have recently written—an article, a term paper, or an essay. It should be at least 1,000 words long, preferably more (1,000 words is about four double-spaced pages). Bearing in mind the things you have learned in this chapter, cut the length in half. Use every technique you know to accomplish this, including reorganizing material, if necessary. Improve your use of verbs and nouns, wherever possible, and cut all superfluous adverbs. Double-check all your facts and assertions for accuracy and freshness. Polish the prose so it reads conversationally. When you're finished, set both manuscripts aside for a day or two. Then compare them. Which do you think is better? In what specific ways?

SUGGESTED READING

Jan Veniola, *Rewrite Right!* Berkeley, Calif.: Ten Speed Press, Periwinkle, 1987.

Rather than plowing through manuals on how to revise and edit, read for pleasure. When you do, take note of the author's craft, and consider carefully what effort went into the work before you. Some of the most finely crafted writing of the twentieth century is to be found in E. B. White's essays. Search out others whose styles are distinctive: among them are Mark Twain, Ernest Hemingway, John Updike, Garrison Keillor, Joyce Carol Oates, N. Scott Momaday, Lillian Hellman, Calvin Trillin, Ian Frazier, Sara Davidson, Ursula K. LeGuin, Tom Wolfe, Hunter Thompson. Pay as much attention to how they write as to what they say.

10

Packaging the Manuscript

Let's start this chapter with its most basic premise: anything you submit for publication must be typed. That should go without saying. Yet some editors still get handwritten copy—and reject it. If your typewriter breaks on deadline, borrow or rent one. Or use the coin-operated typewriters at your college or public library.

All manuscript copy to be typeset should be double-spaced. This is true whether you send your article to a magazine, a newspaper, or a book publisher. Double-spacing allows the editor to make changes and write legible instructions to the typesetter.

Use 8 1/2 by 11-inch bond paper. It needn't be the heaviest stock, but don't use onionskin. Never type a story on erasable (sometimes called "corrasible") paper: ink deposited on this paper will rub off during the dozen or more readings your story gets as it passes from editor to editor and from editor to typesetter. Also, erasable paper has a waxy coating that resists the editor's ball-point ink.

Your copy should as neat as you can make it, but unless you're using a word processor, you needn't worry about typing perfectly. Two or three errors on a page, *if they are corrected neatly and legibly,* are acceptable. Don't turn in smudged or messy copy or pages with long interlineal corrections. By all means, try to produce clean copy: it looks more professional and may help the editor forgive any small flaws in your writing.

Paperclip the pages together—never staple them. If you're using accordion-fold computer paper, remove the perforated border and break the pages apart.

TYPING A MAGAZINE ARTICLE

The first line of your article should start about halfway or two-thirds down the first page. This gives your editor plenty of room to make notes for the typesetter or other editors. Margins should be at least an inch wide all the way around.

In the upper left corner of page one, you should type your name and (unless you're a staff member) your address and telephone number. In the upper right, type a one- or two-word "slug" to serve as a shorthand working title. Beneath that, type the approximate number of words in the story. You arrive at this figure by averaging the number of words in several lines and multiplying this average by the total number of lines in the manuscript. One full double-spaced page usually has 26 lines. Cite the actual word count of the finished copy—not the approximate length your editor assigned.

Space slightly more than halfway down the page. If you are using a title, type it in capital and lower-case letters, flush left. Double space and type your by-line, also flush left. If you're not offering a title, skip these two steps. If you don't have a title but your by-line is a pseudonym, type your by-line here, flush left.

Triple space below your by-line and begin typing your copy. If you don't provide a title and by-line, start typing the story at about line 35.

Indent the first line of each new paragraph five spaces. Do not triple-space between paragraphs.

For magazines (unless the writer's guidelines instruct you differently), you may let a paragraph run over onto the next page. Do not type MORE at the bottom of the pages.

Type a running head at the top of each page. It should include your last name, the page number, and the story's slug. *Be sure to number each page.* Manuscripts have been known to fall off editors' desks and scatter all over the floor; so your small courtesy may save someone a big headache. Number the pages consecutively, counting your first page as page 1. For magazines, do not count subsequent pages as "add 1, add 2," etc.

Type subheads flush left. If you want them set in bold face, use a pencil to draw a wavy line beneath the words to be boldfaced. Then mark "bf" over the first or last word in the bold face passage.

Mark the end of your story with a centered −30− or three centered number symbols (they're sometimes called "pound" symbols), ###

(See figure 10.1). If your story has several discrete sections which a layout artist or typesetter needs to recognize as separate entities, mark the end of each section with a single centered number symbol

TYPING A NEWSPAPER STORY

If you are a free-lance writer, you should put your name, address, and phone number on the first page, preferably in the upper left corner. In the upper right, type the slug and page number.

Staff writers usually put their name, the slug, and the page number at the top of the story:

Smith—Birdwatchers—1

If you are asked to do so, include in your heading the story's approximate length in column inches. To arrive at this figure, count the number of manuscript lines (including one-word lines) and divide by four.

Begin typing the story about a third of the way down the first page.

In newspaper jargon, pages following the first page are called "adds." The second page is "add 1," the third is "add 2," and so on. For this reason, the running head for a newspaper story looks different from a magazine manuscript's. In the upper left corner, type either your name and the add number or the slug and add number:

Smith—Add 1

or

Birdwatchers—Add 1

When you prepare a story for a newspaper, do not run a paragraph over onto a subsequent page. If you can't fit the whole paragraph above the bottom of a page, start it on the following page. Type MORE at the bottom of each page except the final page. Mark the end of your story by typing –30– or ### after the last word, and circle this final symbol in pencil (see figure 10.2).

PULL QUOTES AND TEASERS

If your publication uses pull quotes or teasers—short passages from the copy set in bold face to catch the reader's attention—you might suggest a few as a courtesy to the editor. Type them, double-spaced, on a separate page headed "Suggestions for Pull Quotes."

```
Vicky Hay                                    Donald Locke
000 East Erewhon                             About 2055 words
Phoenix, Arizona   85000
(602) 000-0000
```

```
     Donald Locke lives with his wife, Brenda, in a midtown

Phoenix bungalow.  Bright spring flowers surround a shaded

wooden porch where, materializing from the cool depths within,

Locke greets a visitor and invites her indoors.  A comfortable

living room furnished with massive, handcrafted chairs flows

inward toward the back of the house through a small, modern

kitchen and into a spacious two-room studio.  Shelves laden with

good books and art objects line the walls, and atop a six-foot-

long work table in the studio lies an unfinished bronze nude,

part of its surface rough and part chased to a smooth burnished

glow.
```

Figure 10.1. Manuscript format for magazine articles (first and last pages).

glide above the form's surface, tracing the ideal shape.   "I may

leave the navel out, and I may leave this [the nipples] out,

just give it a gentle swelling where she sort of sweeps up."

Locke's sculptures--the fruitful <u>Pomona</u> and all her related

Venus figures, the eggs and the phallic lingam shields--speak of

their maker's self-confident maturity.   "The full-time artist is

not an artist who does art full time," he reflects.   "Being an

artist is a state of mind, not a state of profession.   So that

now I could go teach two days a week.   But when I'm teaching two

days a week, I'm an artist teaching two days a week, as against

a teacher trying to be an artist three days a week.

"This is definitely a state of mind."

                              ###

```
                              Hay--Lawyers
                              18 col. in




          Photographer Tom Gerczynski is a small-business owner with a

     typical fear--that when he needs a lawyer he'll choose badly.

          "I wish there were a way to see what kind of work a lawyer

     does and how well he does it, some sort of publicized track

     record," he says.

          "What do you have to go by?  Can you ask him how many cases

     he's won?  What if you ask him about other clients--he's not

     going to give out the names of people whose cases he's messed

     up.  And is it ethical to ask how much he charges?  How do I

     know I'm getting my money's worth?"


                              MORE
```

Figure 10.2. Manuscript format for newspaper articles, (first and last pages)

If, after repeated inquiries, you don't understand what your lawyer is doing or you think he is doing something wrong, do not hesitate to get a second opinion. Good lawyers are not threatened by this and many like to have confirmation from another attorney.

"Remember," Bacon says, "the lawyer doesn't own you. If you don't like your lawyer, don't go to him."

-30-

LIST OF SOURCES

Always provide your editor with the names, titles, addresses, and phone numbers of everyone you interviewed. List any printed or manuscript sources you used, too. Since this page is not to be typeset, you may single-space it.

STYLE SHEETS AND MANUALS

Some publications use their own in-house style sheet, a guide to manuscript preparation. These are called "writer's guidelines," and some are better than others. Ask your editor for a copy. If the magazine does not have one, ask which style manual he prefers.

Of course you will own and regularly reread William Strunk and E. B. White's *The Elements of Style*. This is the classic style guide, and editors expect you to know it by heart.

In addition, most publications use the AP Stylebook. Officially titled *The Associated Press Stylebook and Libel Manual*, it is available in paperback through bookstores or from The Associated Press, 50 Rockefeller Plaza, New York, N.Y. 10020. It explains such details as how to express street addresses, what are the correct abbreviations for states, how to handle quotations, possessives, plurals, capitalization, and the like.

A few high-brow magazines use the University of Chicago's *Chicago Manual of Style*, familiarly known as the "Chicago Style Manual." Although primarily a stylebook for book authors and editors, it's a useful guide for any writer.

WRITING HEADS AND SUBHEADS

A title or "head" should capture your story's essence in a succinct, catchy way while it fits the space available. Writing titles can be an art—some publications relegate the task to a single editor who shows a flair for it. Indeed, I know of one magazine whose management hired a free-lance title writer at an exorbitant rate, hoping to spice up the book.

Should a free-lance contributer even bother to title a story? Some do, because they feel a catchy title is a selling point. It really isn't necessary. Editors usually have to discard such titles or rewrite them, because they don't fit the space allotted.

If you are asked to write a title, first find out how much room you have to fill: how many characters. Try to come as close as you can to this character count—don't exceed it. Read the titles in a few back issues to get a feel for their style. Titles may be dramatic or bright, but not cute. They should summarize the story's contents without giving away the writer's best lines. If you see a particularly striking phrase in the first few paragraphs, refrain from lifting it for the title.

Subheads serve as a guide to the story's practical information. They are often set in boldface or italic and emphasized with bullets, but the writer need not mark these typesetting instructions in the copy. Beware of using subheads strictly as an organizing device; your copy should flow logically without any gimmicks. As with titles, study and follow your publication's style.

WRITING CAPTIONS

This is another minor art sometimes assigned to a single staff member.

A good caption (or "cutline") adds to the story: it says more about the picture than one could glean from the article. For that reason, you should avoid the habit of pulling a sentence or phrase out of the copy and pasting it under the picture. Find out who is in the photograph, where, when, and what is going on. Then write some short, descriptive copy that goes beyond the obvious. "Spectators watch burning warehouse" beneath a picture of a crowd watching a warehouse fire, for example, will not suffice. Tell whose warehouse it was, where it was located, when the fire took place, how much damage was estimated, or how large the crowd was. If you've done a decent job of research, you will have some material that did not fit into the story. Be alert for opportunities to work this into the cutlines.

Be sure you correctly identify the people in the photo and spell their names right. Captions usually name the people pictured in a photograph from left to right. *Never* write a caption without seeing the picture! At blueline, check that the printer has not flopped the photo, which will reverse the left-to-right appearance of the people in it.

The writing in cutlines should be even tighter than the body of your story, if possible. Eliminate as many adjectives as you can. Use strong verbs and nouns, and shun the passive voice. Identify the scene fully, and be sure your copy reads smoothly and clearly.

Here's a simple method to help editors and layout artists match the captions with the correct photographs:

Number the photographs to be used in the story. Mark the number of each slide on its cardboard holder. For transparencies, place a gummed label with the appropriate number on the plastic sleeve in which you store the photo. Label black-and-white glossies with stickers on the back. Then type the captions on a separate sheet of paper, and number them to correspond with the numbered photographs.

PREPARING PHOTOGRAPHS

For color photos, most publications require transparencies or slides. Place transparencies in a plastic sleeve made for the purpose. Submit originals only, not duplicates. On the outside of the sleeve (*not* on the photograph), affix a gummed sticker with your name, address, and telephone number. Slides also should be placed in special plastic sleeves. Write your name and address on each slide's cardboard holder.

Black-and-white pictures should be printed as 8 1/2 x 11-inch or 5 x 7-inch glossies. Do not write on the back of black-and-white pictures with a ball-point pen or pencil, which can mar the photograph. If you use a felt-tip pen, remember that sometimes felt-tip ink does not dry properly on photographic paper, so it may rub off on another picture if several are stacked together. It's safest to type or write on gummed stickers. Affix a sticker with the subject's name, and one with your name, address, and telephone number. If someone other than you took the picture, credit the photographer here.

Never use paperclips on photographs.

If you are selling one-time rights to your pictures, or if someone else owns the copyright, you should place a copyright notice on the back of a black-and-white print, on the sleeve of a transparency, on the cardboard border of a slide, and on the sheet bearing the cutlines.

SUPPLYING OR OBTAINING PICTURES

Most publications hire professional photographers to take pictures. If you are an accomplished photographer, you may be able to sell pictures to accompany your article. In that case, ask your editor for her photographer's guidelines.

Magazine-quality pictures are of high caliber, with bright colors, clear contrast, and perfect focus. Each photo should have a single point of interest, and no bizarre background details should distract from the subject—no television antennae protruding from people's heads.

Writers sometimes team up with photographers for free-lance assignments. Usually, the writer sells himself, the photographer, and their idea to the editors. Most often, the magazine offers separate contracts to the photographer and the writer. If you and a photographer are given a joint contract, the two of you should work out a written agreement which says what each party will provide, sets a deadline, and establishes each party's share of the fee.

Many photographers are happy to work with free-lance writers, despite the relatively low pay, because publication in a good magazine is a nice credit. How do you find a partner? Note the photographers' credits in recent issues of local and regional magazines. When you see work you admire, look up the photographer in the telephone book, call, and suggest collaborating. Another possibility: contact a local photography school or the art department at a nearby college or university.

If you are covering a story in your region for a national magazine, telephone local editors and ask them for the names of free-lance photographers who might work with you. Keep a permanent list, so you can refer out-of-state editors to reliable artists.

Sometimes you can obtain pictures that will fit your story, either free or for a nominal price. Does anything you are covering tie in with an organization that has a public relations department? P.R. people often have photographs you can use. Sometimes you can obtain press photos of interview subjects through their employers. These are scarcely studio portraits, but for some trade magazines, they'll do. Don't forget government public information offices— tourism and fish-and-game departments often keep photos in stock, as do universities, school districts, mayors' and governors' offices, and state and national parks.

Some professional photographers build files of stock photos, which they sell to magazines and newspapers. They may have scenics, cityscapes, pictures of annual civic events, photos of tourist attractions, and the like. Also check with your librarian for local sources of wire photos.

Stock photos work only when you can use a generic picture. Readers will recognize that you haven't taken the picture expressly for the given story, and so you should avoid trying to give them that impression in the cutline.

If a photographer gives you a stock photo that pictures any identifiable person, be sure he or she has obtained a model's release. Send a copy with the photograph to your editor. Don't skip this important detail, even if your editor inclines to. Recently, a private individual sued a book publisher, photographer, and author when her likeness appeared without her permission. The writer was eventually dismissed from the suit, but at great cost in lawyers' fees, time, and worry.

PUTTING THE PACKAGE IN THE MAIL

Mail your manuscript flat, in a large manila envelope. Always keep a copy of anything you send through the mails. If you're submitting a story over the transom (unsolicited, without an assignment), remember to include a stamped, self-addressed envelope.

To mail photographs, cut a sheet of corrugated cardboard into two pieces as large as the sheet of photos you're sending. Sandwich the pictures between them, and tape the back and front together so the photos can't slide out. In large, clear letters, mark the envelope "Photos—Do Not Bend."

When you submit copy on disk, you should place the disk in a padded envelope designed for the purpose. Mark the envelope "Magnetic Media—Handle with Care" and pray. Keep a back-up copy, and if you have to mail that, make another copy.

If you use the U.S. mail, send the package first-class. A fourth-class manuscript rate is available, but delivery can be slow. Sending your story by private carrier seems to have only one advantage: if it is lost, private carriers will start searching for it sooner than the post office will. Otherwise, their delivery is not much faster, and they take no more care with your package than first-class mail handling.

—30—

FOR PROJECTS OR DISCUSSION

1. Does your college provide typewriters or word processors for student use? Find out where they are, when you can use them, and how much they cost.

2. Compose a checklist, based on what you've read in this chapter, of everything that should go into a package containing a manuscript story and five photos.

3. Bring several photos to class. For each one, make up a story and then write an informative, clear, concise caption.

4. Have your teacher or a class member obtain writer's and photographer's guidelines from several publications in your state. What do they have in common? How do they differ from each other?

SUGGESTED READING

The Associated Press Stylebook and Libel Manual. New York: The Associated Press, 1977. A standard reference for newspaper and magazine journalists.

Chicago Manual of Style. 13th ed. Chicago: University of Chicago Press, 1982. The standard for book editors and authors.

Arthur Plotnik. *The Elements of Editing: A Modern Guide for Editors and Journalists.*, New York: Macmillan, 1982. Chapter 10, "Basic Photography for Editors," provides a thumbnail guide to photojournalism.

Marjorie E. Skillin. *Words into Type.* 3rd ed. Englewood Cliffs, N.J.: Prentice-Hall, 1974. Another favorite with editors; an important guide for staff writers.

William Strunk, Jr., and E. B. White. *The Elements of Style.* 3rd Ed. New York: Macmillan, 1978. Indispensable. Read it; know it; use it.

The annual *Writer's Market* (Cincinnati, Ohio: Writer's Digest Books) has a section on manuscript mechanics and appendices showing how to estimate postage by the number of pages in a manuscript.

11

Law, Conscience, and the Writer

Ethics has to do with how we treat the people we write about and the people we work with. Ethical behavior extends beyond mere good will or malice; it also takes in vaguer issues of propriety and intent. Sometimes it concerns the way things seem as much as the way they really are.

To behave in an ethical manner means to conduct oneself in a way that never compromises one's own or one's employer's honesty or credibility. If you have taken many journalism courses, you have undoubtedly heard several lectures on ethics. But it is such an urgent subject—one too often underplayed—that we should take some time here to review the industry's standards.

CODES OF ETHICS

We will review two ethical guides here: the Society of Professional Journalists Code of Ethics, and the American Society of Journalists and Authors' Code of Ethics and Fair Practices. The first primarily addresses issues of integrity, accuracy, and fairness; the second deals with ethics between writers and editors.

Let us consider the issues that especially apply to feature writers.

The Society of Professional Journalists Code of Ethics

The SPJ Code of Ethics opens with the organization's credo and salutes the ideals of free speech, the public's right to know, and freedom of the press—good words and true. Seven paragraphs down, under "Ethics," the code has this to say:

1. Gifts, favors, free travel, special treatment, or privileges can compromise the integrity of journalists and their employers. Nothing of value should be accepted.

This sounds straightforward. But from your first day on the job you'll be faced with questions that challenge it.

What does "of value" mean? Does anyone really believe that you'll write a puff piece because a developer gives you a glass of champagne and some canapes during the grand opening of his monster office building, from the top floor of which you can see the ruins of the formerly charming neighborhood he bulldozed? And what's "special treatment"? Does that include press passes to conferences? To athletic events?

As I write this, I have on my desk a press packet containing an invitation to a reception for the general manager of a new Ritz-Carlton Hotel. The bash will take place at an elegant, snobbish boutique. And there's more: they want me to spend a weekend at the Ritz-Carlton in Laguna Niguel, on the coast of southern California. Accommodations, sightseeing, and meals are complimentary.

My publication does not plug resorts. Even if I were inclined to do so, I would never have an opportunity to gush for the Ritz-Carlton. Should I grab what I can get?

Travel writers often accept these perks. Sometimes they take free accommodations and air fare from the very resorts they are covering. Such hospitality casts a rosy glow over the whole junket. This is why tourists' experiences so often differ from the reports sent back by travel writers. Writers do their readers a disservice when they compromise their objectivity in this way.

2. Secondary employment, political involvement, holding public office, and service in community organizations should be avoided if it compromises the integrity of journalists and their employers. Journalists and their employers should conduct their personal lives in a manner that protects them from conflict of interest, real or apparent.

Reporters have no business, for example, speaking out at a public meeting they're covering. Nor should they involve themselves actively in political parties or campaigns.

"Secondary employment" has special meaning for free-lance writers. Few writers earn enough at free-lance journalism to support themselves. So, most free-lancers do public relations. And therein lies enormous potential for conflict.

If you are writing public relations material, you should not attempt to sell journalistic pieces at all. If you want to be a free-lance journalist, you must avoid any encumbering p.r. clients. All p.r. clients are potential encumbrances. No matter what you cover, sooner or later you'll have a client whose interests extend to that subject. Then you will be faced with the temptation to feature the people you know, who will be pleased with the coverage; or else to overlook a client in an exposé.

One free-lance writer worked for a local business journal. She was a competent writer; the editor was happy to have her copy. What he didn't know was this:

Whenever she covered a story, she made it a point to interview subjects in person, even when the comments she needed were brief enough to obtain by telephone. She would turn on the charm, and after the interview she would hand the person her business card and mention in passing that she also did public relations.

In her first six months at this, she earned more than $20,000 from p.r. fees.

Do you believe she ever wrote an honest word for that business journal?

Even if you manage to separate public relations from journalism —and few people can—handling both can still create the *appearance* of conflict. This is also to be avoided.

A newspaper editor quit his job to set up a small public relations shop. His first love, however, was journalism. When he learned that a celebrity living in his city was starting an unusual business venture, he sold the story to a local magazine.

During interviews and conversations, he impressed the fledgling entrepreneur. After the story came out, the celebrity asked him to handle the business's p.r., which he agreed to do. The writer then arranged for the magazine to send a stack of issues containing the story to his new client. Hearing this, the editor assumed the writer had been the other's agent from the start. She vowed never to hire him again, and she made no secret of her reason.

3. So-called news communications from private sources should not be published or broadcast without substantiation of their claims to news value.

By "so-called news communications" they mean press releases and canned video "news" stories.

It should go without saying that any information coming from someone who is paid to give it to you is tainted. Yet writers and broadcast news directors persist in using the self-interested utterances of advertisers and public-relations agents.

On my desk, next to the Ritz-Carlton press packet, is a stack of clips from the local newspaper. One hard news report raves about a newly opened motel and all its sparkling amenities—nine-foot ceilings, wet bar, microwave, refrigerator, stereo, tape deck, cable t.v., and even a cooked-to-order breakfast of eggs, hash browns, bacon, sausage, juice, pastries, toast, cereal, coffee and milk! Another sings of seven arthritis specialists' new combined practice, apparently a gathering of the most brilliant medical talent on earth.

Such quasi-news articles don't even rehash the press releases from which they are plagiarized. If you're too lazy to get the real story for yourself—or if you can't write original material on deadline—take up some less strenuous trade.

4. Journalists acknowledge the newsman's ethic of protecting confidential sources of information.

This statement raises the question of who will be granted the privilege of confidentiality. Some sources should not be hidden—indeed, few merit secrecy. Rely on your editor's judgment any time a source asks for confidentiality. This is never something you should promise on your own.

When you make such a promise you must be prepared to go to prison for your principles. Some states have shield laws that protect journalists' confidential sources. In those that do not, a judge may send you to jail for refusing to reveal your sources.

Free-lance writers should never guarantee to protect a source. The reasons are two: (a) because free-lancers are independent contractors—not employees—publishers and editors feel little loyalty to them and so are unlikely to support or defend them; (b) a publication's insurance may not cover free-lance writers, should a lawsuit arise from any such agreement. If you incur legal costs, an employer may cover them; a publisher who has hired you as a free lance will not.

5. Plagiarism is dishonest and unacceptable.

A form of plagiarism common among journalists consists of lifting quotes. The theory goes that a spoken word cannot be copyrighted. Therefore, the parts of a story within quotation marks—i.e., the things a subject said aloud—are fair game.

Even if this rationalization is correct—which is questionable—the practice still smells.

- It's lazy journalism.
- It's stealing someone else's work.
- By placing the speaker's words in a new context, it may misrepresent what was said.
- It often repeats misquotations.

Under the fifth section, "Accuracy and Objectivity," the SPJ code tackles questions of truth and balance, in this order:

1. Truth is our ultimate goal.

Especially in magazine publishing, writers of feature articles are sometimes asked to subtly plug certain advertisers or potential advertisers, or to downplay negative aspects of a story for fear of offending powerful members of the community. These stories are presented to the public as objective journalism, but they are far from that.

If you refuse to go along, you may lose your job or find yourself unable to sell in a given market. You have to eat. But you also must look in the mirror and ask yourself if you're really *that* hungry.

The truth is what is real, not what some advertiser or power broker wants your readers to believe. As a journalist, your function is to transmit the truth. If your publisher will not permit you to do so, find another job.

In journalism, objective truth is not served by imaginative accounts that purport to transmit larger truths. This means we do not invent characters and circumstances to exemplify or illustrate our points. We do not write composite portraits of young children whom we claim are drug addicts and dope dealers. Nor does it help to qualify some tale with a remark like this: "Mary is not a real person, but her story is typical."

2. Objectivity . . . is a standard of performance toward which we strive.

Entirely true, in writing hard news. The feature writer, though, is permitted—indeed, expected—to take a stand on the issues. Whether you assume this stance explicitly or through artful presentation of the facts, you must present both sides of the story.

3. There is no excuse for inaccuracies or lack of thoroughness.

How to emphasize this enough? Check, check, and double-check your facts.

In the code's sixth section, "Fair Play," the operative tenets for feature writers are items one through three.

1. The news media should not communicate unofficial charges affecting reputation or moral character without giving the accused a chance to reply.

To report that a person was arrested for drunk driving is acceptable; to repeat a rumor that he drinks habitually is not. When you hear reports that reflect on an individual's character, talk to that person and tell him or her what others are saying. Do not fail to include the reply in your story.

The *Washington Post* and the *Richmond Times-Dispatch* reported that former Virginia Governor Charles S. Robb attended parties at which guests used cocaine. The rumors about the drug use were unsubstantiated; no one reported seeing the governor use cocaine; nor was there any evidence that the governor was aware any drug use might have been taking place. Ombudsmen for both papers agreed that questioning Robb's integrity on the basis of unconfirmed rumors was bad journalism.

2. The news media must guard against invading a person's right to privacy.

"Privacy" varies according to circumstances. The Associated Press Libel Manual notes that the right of privacy is "based on the idea that a person has the right to be let alone, to live a private life free from publicity." Then it adds, "When a person becomes involved in a news event, voluntarily or involuntarily, he forfeits the right to privacy. Similarly, a person somehow involved in a matter of legitimate public interest, even if not a bona fide spot news event, normally can be written about with safety."

A woman in Steele County, Minnesota, witnessed an assault near her isolated rural home. Later the victim was found dead of stab wounds. Before a suspect was arrested, the *Owatonna People's Press* reported the witness's name, despite her request for anonymity. She protested to the Minnesota News Council that her life could have been endangered when the newspaper identified her while the killer was at large.

The majority of the council agreed that the woman's fears were well-founded and that, given the circumstances, the newspaper should have respected her privacy. However, they added, reporters and editors are by no means bound to honor all witnesses' requests for anonymity.

In a more obvious breach of compassion and taste, *The Sacramento Bee* interviewed 18-year-old Peter Vanos after his brother, pro basketball player Nick Vanos, died in an airplane crash. The young man's college basketball coaches had asked that he be left alone while he was still in a state of grief and shock. But when Vanos was asked directly if he objected to an interview, he said no; so a reporter went ahead. During the exchange, the youth broke into tears. Family members and coaches complained that the newspaper had caused further anguish that affected the freshman student's ability to cope with his loss. An ombudsman agreed that the interview invaded Vanos' privacy.

3. The media should not pander to morbid curiosity about details of vice and crime.

Restrain yourself from reporting a detective's detailed comments on a murdered woman's life as a prostitute, for example. To illustrate a story on drug addicts who ignore the risk of acquiring AIDS through dirty needles, the *Philadelphia Inquirer* ran a page one photo of a man shooting up. Readers called the lurid picture unduly graphic.

Morbid curiosity extends beyond crime and immorality. Any unnecessarily detailed look at misfortune which does not add to the reader's understanding may be taken as bad taste. The *Ann Arbor News* once reported that firefighters found a dead man sitting on a toilet. Rescue workers at a building collapse in Bridgeport, Connecticut, had to hold up a blanket to shield a dead body from newspaper photographers; survivors complained that coverage of the story was ghoulish.

The American Society of Journalists and Authors Code of Ethics

The strictures and ideals cited in the SPJ code apply to all journalists. The ASJA Code of Ethics and Fair Practices, on the other hand, addresses free-lance writers and the publishers who hire them. ASJA's code is more a list of desiderata than an ethical standard.

It urges fair play between writers and editors, noting that the writer takes primary responsibility for the truthfulness of an article. Writers must be prepared to provide sources for all statements in a given story. Editors are not to alter the sense of a story without the writer's permission. When an assignment is not going according to plan, the writer is obliged to inform the editor before the deadline.

Some of the ASJA code's terms are idealistic. Although it is commendable to insist writers are "entitled to payment for an accepted article within ten days of delivery," even publications that pay on acceptance rarely deliver a check in ten days net. "Payment on acceptance" may actually mean "payment on scheduling," "payment during our next pay period," or "payment whenever the accounting department gets around to it."

Certainly, you should always try to negotiate for payment on acceptance and avoid entering pay-on-publication agreements— which often mean "pay never." Imagine what would happen if you walked into a supermarket, selected some lettuce, tomatoes, and cucumbers, and told the manager you would pay him after you had eaten your salad. This is what payment on publication means to writers.

Whether to insist on purchase solely of first North American rights depends on the market (Item 18. Copyright, Additional Rights). Often an article is salable only to a specific publication. When you recycle a story, you usually rewrite it to fit the new market—and that revision should obviate any "work for hire" or "all rights" agreement. However, if you have a story with broad appeal, something that might command the attention of *Reader's Digest* or lesser reprint markets, you should hang on to as many subsidiary rights as you can.

Article 9, on rewriting, is covered in most magazine contracts, which contain a clause stating that the editor may revise a writer's work as necessary. And though it is not nice to do so without telling the writer, as a practical matter editors commonly revise bad writing to make it acceptable for publication. You should protest rewrites that change your story's sense, introduce mistakes, or insert something you do not want published under your name. But an editor who cuts fat, switches paragraphs to form a more logical organization, and silently corrects inaccuracies is simply doing her job.

Article 22, concerning indemnity, is one about which every writer should take a hard-nosed stand. Never agree to indemnify a magazine or publisher against claims, actions, or proceedings arising from your work. Ours is a litigious society; imaginative plaintiffs sue for creative reasons that have nothing to do with accuracy, truth, good taste, or privacy—things that you do not foresee as you write. Publishers can afford libel insurance; writers by and large cannot.

LIBEL

Insured or no, writers and publishers rightly try to avoid accusations of libel.

The Associated Press Libel Manual defines libel as "injury to reputation." It says, "words, pictures, or cartoons that expose a person to public hatred, shame, disgrace, or ridicule, or induce an ill opinion of a person are libelous." As the same guide points out, this extends beyond the obvious: the *New York Times*, for example, was threatened with a lawsuit over its matrimonial column after practical jokers announced the engagement of two people who hated each other.

Omitting the name of a person you are defaming may not protect you. If a story's details identify, say, a rumored drug dealer who has not been arrested and charged, that person may have a case against the writer. Quoting someone else's defamatory remarks accurately is also not protected.

There are two main defenses against libel:

1. *Provable truth.* To succeed with this defense, you must show that the defamatory statement is substantially correct.
2. *Privilege.* This legal concept holds that some people, under some circumstances, may make false, malicious, or damaging statements without fear of prosecution.

There are two kinds of privilege:

A. *Absolute* privilege. It applies to legislative, legal, and official proceedings, and to the contents of most public records. A legislator, for example, may make a statement on the Congressional floor which outside those halls would be libelous. A criminal prosecutor may accuse a defendant of acts and motives in court, and may phrase the accusation in terms that would be actionable if they were uttered outside the courtroom. The theory behind absolute privilege holds that airing certain statements and accusations serves the public interest.
B. *Qualified* privilege. This covers the press. It means you can report a speaker's statements made under absolute privilege—*if* your report is fair and accurate, and *if* the statements really are privileged.

Remember, however, that public officials enjoy absolute privilege only when they are speaking in official proceedings. Statements made before a public gathering of a private group, such as the Rotary Club or Soroptimists, are not privileged. Also, legal briefs, complaints, or other papers are unprotected until they are filed in court.

You can lose qualified privilege by inaccurate reporting or by publishing statements with malice or reckless disregard of their truth or falsehood. Errors in reporting privileged statements may be taken as evidence of malice.

FAIR COMMENT

Commentary and criticism on matters of public interest, such as art exhibits, literary works, performances, architecture, athletic events, and the like, are protected by the defense of fair comment. Even severe criticism, as long as it is not written maliciously, is acceptable. Any facts cited must be accurate, and commentary must be pertinent. You may blast an actor's inept stage depiction of a philandering husband, for example, but you may not observe that his performance is disappointing compared to his fabled off-stage exploits.

THE WORD AS DEADLY WEAPON

Reporters have a power way out of proportion to their numbers and wealth. A writer who has the public's ear can ruin a person's reputation, business, or private life with a single remark—whether or not that remark is true. To compound the danger, it is easy for writers, particularly those who cover politics or crime, to grow self-righteous and arrogant.

Keep in mind that the subjects of your stories are not one-dimensional caricatures, not good guys and bad guys, not the great unwashed—but human beings. They have mothers and fathers, wives and husbands, children and grandparents. They must keep their jobs in order to live. When you prick them, they bleed.

−30−

FOR PROJECTS OR DISCUSSION

1. About that offer of a weekend at a Ritz-Carlton resort (above): would you accept it? Why or why not? In a cover letter, the hotel's public relations officer adds that you may take advantage of a special $75-a-night rate if your company does not permit you to accept free offers. Assuming you can afford it, would you go for that? Why or why not?

2. You are doing a story on teenage pregnancy. Two high-school students tell you they believe 95 percent of their classmates are sexually active, and a teacher remarks that students with free periods often leave the school for "a quick one" in a car or bedroom. Do you use these people's names in quoting them? Why or why not?

3. A photographer brings you a picture of the mayor touching up her lipstick while she sits at the head table at a luncheon. You're the editor. Do you run it? Why or why not?

4. A local priest has succumbed to AIDS. Before he died, he denied he was homosexual and said he often jabbed his fingers with dirty needles while cleaning out the pockets of drug addicts who stayed at his shelter. A doctor says this is plausible, although he adds that it is impossible to know how the priest became infected. Two members of the gay community claim the victim was homosexual. The archdiocese readily acknowledges the AIDS case; the archbishop says the priest wanted his parishioners to know. Do you report the cause of the man's death? If so, where in the story do you run a paragraph about the needles? Do you include any statistics about the number of clerics who have contracted AIDS? Do you run any comments on the priest's sexuality? Justify all these decisions.

SUGGESTED READING

The Associated Press Libel Manual. It is bound with the AP Stylebook. New York: The Associated Press, 1977. Available from the Associated Press, 50 Rockefeller Plaza, New York, N.Y. 10020.

Joel M. Gora. The Rights of Reporters: The Basic ACLU Guide to a Reporter's Rights. New York: E. P. Dutton, 1974.

John L. Hulteng. The Messenger's Motives: Ethical Problems of the News Media. Englewood Cliffs, N.J.: Prentice-Hall, 1976.

———. Playing It Straight: A Practical Discussion of the Ethical Principles of the American Society of Newspaper Editors. Chester, Conn.: The Globe Pequot Press, 1981.

William L. Rivers, Wilbur Schramm, and Clifford G. Christians. Responsibility in Mass Communication, 3rd ed. New York: Harper and Row, 1980.

The Society of Professional Journalists devotes much attention to ethical matters. The group's monthly publication, The Quill, regularly reviews ethical questions that arise in real situations and often runs full-length articles on ethical issues. For more information, write to SPJ, 53 W. Jackson Blvd., Suite 731, Chicago, Ill. 60604–3610.

12

Writers and Editors

Editors and writers view the world differently. To some extent, that's because their perspectives differ—although it's often a matter of temperament. The great muddy flow of bad copy that washes over an editor's desk tends to jade one's character. As I write this, I steal time from the following:

• An "author" plagiarized an article from a review copy of a forthcoming book; we discovered this after we had paid the writer and scheduled the story. I now must write a whole new story— against a ten-day deadline.

• A trusted writer dropped the ball on a fairly easy story. Little of the material she submitted on second rewrite is usable. To rescue it, I have toured a remote Indian reservation and interviewed tribal spokesmen. A massive revision awaits, pending the redo of the plagiarized piece.

• A recent journalism graduate submitted a story on assignment. Her inexperience showed in the copy. I had to revamp the piece, doing so in a way that made her feel involved in the revision. Before I submitted the final version to my editors, I asked her to check for accuracy, correctly spelled names, etc. She claimed to have done so. Much later—with the copy in second galley—she called to make some changes, revealing that she had not done this routine fact-checking. The corrections will now have to be made on boards, at unnecessary cost.

• An amateur writer sent us a glowing proposal. We made an assignment—only to discover that she was skilled at writing queries but hadn't the faintest idea how to handle a full-length article. Guess who gets to turn her effort into English!

THE EDITORIAL STAFF

Depending on the organization's size, a newspaper's staff usually consists of one or more copy editors who prepare for print stories sent to them from the wire service editor and other various sub-editors—the city desk, the state desk, the sports desk, etc. They supervise teams of reporters covering various beats. Large newspapers may also have photo editors, who supervise photographers and edit pictures. A managing editor oversees all these people; his boss is the publisher. This set-up is fairly constant, varying more in size than in operation. Most newspapers, even small weeklies, are now computerized, so that writing and editing take place on-screen.

In contrast, the magazine industry has few standard ways to organize editorial management. Typically, a magazine has a publisher who handles the business side and an editor in charge of filling the editorial (as opposed to advertising) space. On some publications, the editor is an administrator and the managing editor does the down-and-dirty work of putting out each issue. Sometimes the publisher, editor-in-chief, or editoral director is the senior executive and the editor does a managing editor's job. A magazine may also hire an assistant or associate editor and some junior editors or staff writers. The term "senior editor" often means "staff writer." Copy editing—the challenging job of reading a manuscript for accuracy, sense, grammatical correctness, and style—may be done by a single staffer or shared among editors. Some magazines have copy readers who proof manuscripts and galleys. A few have photo editors; only the most affluent can afford fact checkers. Magazines are also moving toward computerization, but because of the costs of magazine production this expensive process has been slower here than in newspapers.

WRITING FOR A MAGAZINE EDITOR

Most journalists who like to write features eventually work for magazines, either full time or on a free-lance basis while they hold down a newspaper job. Magazines represent the primary market for feature articles.

For that reason, let's look at a magazine staff and how it operates.

This hypothetical publication, a four-color regional, started as a

Chamber of Commerce organ but is now independently owned and supported by ad revenues. Its slant remains strongly probusiness. It has a circulation of about 50,000. The area it serves is largely urban, with a service- and tourism-based economy. The readers' median age is 50; their politics conservative; their average annual family income around $100,000.

"Editorial" has five staff members.

The *editor* supervises four subordinates, five columnists, and innumerable free-lance contributors. On publications with an executive editor or editorial director, this person might be called a *managing editor*. She handles her department's budget, speaks for the magazine at public gatherings, and writes television and radio spots advertising the magazine. Through the publisher, she acts as a liaison between her department and the circulation, advertising, and production departments. She supervises editorial and production during "deadline," the hectic last-minute preparation of each issue for the printer. She meets with the art director and publisher to dummy each issue—to prepare a cover-to-cover mock-up of its content and layout. At deadline, she reads boards (photo-ready copy, pasted up for the printer) and bluelines (printer's proofs). If the magazine's art department is computerized, she may review the laid-out copy on screen, instead of on boards.

She generates story ideas, and she organizes, assigns, and supervises six annual special sections: a high-season tourist guide, a low-season "things to do when the weather's bad" section, a round-up of commercial construction, a quasi-advertorial real-estate section, a purportedly humorous "Book of Lists," and an "update" of the past year's news on certain issues considered vital to the region.

She writes a monthly editorial column, a monthly restaurant review, and an occasional Q-&-A interview. She compiles the restaurant guide, which consists of one- or two-sentence distillations of her positive reviews. Before deadline, she writes titles and teasers for each article and column.

The editor does all content editing and some copy editing of every word in the magazine that is not openly billed as advertising. She edits the free-lance columns—personal finance, arts, travel, gossip, interior decor—and the in-house business, local travel, and gardening columns. She trains the assistant editor in content editing, whenever she can find the time.

The *assistant editor* writes one or two features a month, plus the fashion department and a monthly in-state travel column. Some publications would give this person part of our editor's responsibilities and call him the managing editor, second-in-command to the editor. He is in charge of obtaining photos and art for free-lance contributions—staff members arrange their own artwork. He works with the art director in controlling the quality of the photography, selecting a single picture from perhaps a dozen submitted by a photographer and checking the printer's color separations. He meets with the editor to help develop story ideas and determine the direction of future issues; he helps with content editing; and he contributes to four of the six annual special sections. With the editor, he stays at the office through deadlines, which usually entail many hours of unpaid overtime.

The *senior staff writer* edits a weekly business newsletter, which the magazine publishes as a sideline. She writes a monthly column based on the newsletter. To accomplish this, she reads every newspaper in the state, clipping material germane to her own and other staff members' projects. Because p.r. people are anxious to get their clients mentioned in the newsletter, her daily mail contains a mountain of press releases. She also writes two or three features a month, contributes items to the "front matter" department, and writes sidebars for free-lance articles. When necessary, she rewrites clumsy free-lance copy. She writes the annual commercial construction roundup and contributes to four of the other annual sections. She sometimes helps proof galleys, and at deadline she reads boards and bluelines.

A second *staff writer* does the garden column and compiles the time-consuming "Calendar," a monthly listing of local events. She supervises several stringers who contribute to this department. She writes the annual real estate section and contributes to four of the other six annual sections. Occasionally she writes a feature. She may help proof galleys or read copy, and she helps read boards and bluelines at deadline.

The *junior staff writer*, who doubles as *copy reader*, compiles the monthly public television schedule, which the magazine runs as a public service. He writes or edits the front matter, does all the copyreading, proofs galleys, and does some sporadic fact-checking. He contributes to four annual sections and sometimes writes a feature. At deadline, he helps read boards and bluelines. If there is any scut work to be done, this person, as low man on the totem pole, gets it.

At any given time, all these people are working on more than one issue. Stories are due by the copy deadline, two months before the printer's deadline. But each issue is planned about six months in advance. In other words, on June 16, our editors are thinking about the Christmas issue, beginning research on stories that will appear in October, writing stories for the September issue, and editing material for the August issue. Soon, they will face the printer's deadline for the July issue.

Suppose you offer our editor a query that intrigues her.

She presents your proposal at the weekly editorial staff meeting. The idea is well received. The editor, publisher, and assistant editor refine it and come up with a version slightly different from yours—shorter, but including an aspect you overlooked. They decide to accept your proposal with certain changes, and they pencil the story into the schedule. It will run in an issue three months hence; your copy will be due in one month.

After the meeting, she assigns a photographer and telephones you to say the story has been accepted. *Listen* to her instructions. Take notes, and read them back to confirm that you both know what you think you're supposed to do. If she writes you a memo, read it carefully. If you have questions, ask.

Before you start work on the assignment, be sure you have the answers to these important questions:

How long is the story to be?

When is it due?

What information will the editor be looking for? What questions does she want answered?

What slant does she want? Try to get her to specify the approach she expects: Breezy? Serious? Anecdotal? What?

If you are a free lance, how much will she pay, and when? Will she cover your expenses? And what rights is she buying?

Once you've landed the assignment and established its terms, your main tasks are to produce copy that does not require extensive rewriting, and to get it to the editor on time.

Set a deadline up front. If the editor is vague about this—I have had people ask for stories "ASAP"—target a completion date on your own calendar. Estimate how much time you need to do the research, interview people, and write the story. About three weeks is a reasonable period in which to complete a 2,000-word feature. Allow more for a long or complicated story, less for something short and simple. Mark this date on your calendar.

Then flag a date at least two days before the deadline. Try to finish a first draft by then—earlier, if possible. This will give you some time to let the copy cool before you begin to polish it. You should plan to spend at least a day revising and rewriting your story.

It's a good idea to keep your editor informed of your progress, especially if you have a long lead time. Discuss the story when both of you have a few minutes to speak casually, or be prepared to report on your work during editorial meetings. If you are a free-lance writer, call once or twice or send her an informal note to let her know whom you have interviewed, what problems or successes you're having, and how the story is shaping up.

Never miss a deadline. Although experienced editors will ask to receive free-lance copy a week or ten days before they absolutely must have it, some are more trusting. Violate this trust and she may not hire you again. Staff writers who are consistently late—costing the magazine hassle and dollars—may find themselves unemployed.

Adele Malott, editor of *Friendly Exchange*, has said that receiving a new manuscript is "like opening a Christmas present." Our editor feels a small rush of delight and curiosity when your story hits her desk. She reads the story quickly and decides that overall, it's adequate, although she estimates it's 300 to 500 words too long. One of the editors or a secretary types your copy into the computer network and prints out a hard copy for review.

The editor sets aside some time to read the copy carefully, paragraph by paragraph. She corrects a few grammatical and spelling errors, moves two paragraphs to a more logical place in the story's body, and prunes some verbose deadwood. Then she goes over the story again and cuts three marginally substantive paragraphs. This process removes about 200 words.

Now she gives the copy to the junior editor. He telephones the six people you quoted, reads their words back to them, and asks if you got them right. One thinks you've quoted him out of context, but further questioning reveals that what you wrote reflects his comments accurately. The junior editor goes to the magazine's reference library to verify four statistics and a question of geography. He corrects a spelling error the editor missed and flags a clumsy sentence, suggesting in a marginal note that it be recast. Then he routes the story back to the editor.

She gives it to the assistant editor with instructions to cut another 200 words as an on-the-job training exercise. This person, a young pup with more confidence than brains, takes a razor-sharp blue pencil to your manuscript. He combines sentences in ways that subtly change their sense, cuts a paragraph severely, and joins it to the next graf. He runs two quotes together, shortening the copy but making your source sound foolish. He amputates facts. Even though the editor reinstates some of your material, you will need the soul of a cucumber to stay calm when you see the published story.

Some editors send galleys to the author for final approval. Ours does not.

Meanwhile, the editor meets with the the art director. They decide whether your story's artwork will be illustration or photography, color or black-and-white, whether it will carry a boxed sidebar (to be written by the assistant editor), how many pull quotes will appear, and whether it will jump to the back of the book.

After this confab, the editor knows how much space she has for heads and teasers. She writes a title containing the number of characters required to fill the space, and she tries to make it snappy, attention-getting, and true to the story's contents. Once again, she goes over the copy, this time marking for the typesetter such details as dropped letters, bold face and italics, bullets, and subheads. (On some magazines, the art director or his assistant marks these specifications.) She selects three striking statements to be used as teasers, which will be set in bold face and worked into the page design. The story is now ready to go to the typesetter.

Meanwhile, two dozen color transparencies arrive in the mail from the photographer. The assistant editor meets with the art director to decide which three of these will run with the story, and then he writes the captions.

The typesetter returns the galleys, long strips of typeset copy, which now need to be proofread. The junior editor, who functions among other things as the proofreader, checks the galleys word-by-word against the edited manuscript, searching out and marking typographical errors. When he's done, he gives the galleys to the editor, who reads them again, belatedly noting a minor error in fact. She corrects this, plus a typo the copy reader missed.

Then she returns the corrected galleys to the typesetter, who resets the changes and runs out a clean set of galleys. The junior editor checks these again and declares them perfect.

Now the galleys go to the production department, where a paste-up artist cuts them to column length and glues them to a cardboard "flat" or "board" on which is printed a nonreproducing blue grid, a format guide that the printer's photographic equipment won't pick up. Following the art director's instructions, the paste-up person prepares a camera-ready version of each page, complete with "windows" where the printer will place photographs.

The story runs five lines too long. The art director asks the editor to "lose" those lines, so the copy will fit the space available. The editor reads the story again, cutting a few words here and a few there. This eliminates four lines. She agonizes; then ruthlessly kills another gem-like phrase.

All this will change in the near future, when the art department is computerized. The art director will design the layout on-screen; the copy as it appears in typeset form will be put in place and edited to fit before it is printed out. Editors will continue to read galley-like printouts, but the typesetter will be laid off and her duties redistributed among the editors and the art directors.

As each board is completed, it comes back to the assistant editor. He reads it carefully, checking for missed typos, dropped paragraphs, correct pagination and dates, correct pages in the "continued to . . ." flags, correct spelling of the author's by-line. He passes the boards along to the two staff writers and the junior editor, who each read and initial them.

Production has sent the photographs to a color separator, and they are now back in the office. Color printing processes require a procedure called "separation," in which the primary colors are photographically divided out of the picture. The assistant editor and the production manager study the separations; they accept two and send the third back to be redone.

When all the boards are finished to everyone's satisfaction, they arrive back on the editor's desk in a large stack. She now checks each page against the table of contents, to be sure the articles start on the pages listed. She reads over the magazine from beginning to end, verifying specific details against a checklist and watching for errors that might have been missed.

The boards now are ready to go to the printer, just in time to make the deadline. With them out of the office, the editor goes back to work on the upcoming issues. Having agreed to pay you on publication, she sends a pay requisition to accounting.

A few days later, the printer returns bluelines: proofs taken from the boards the magazine sent. Again, the editor checks each page carefully. Typography and facts had better be correct at this point; changes now will cost plenty. Nevertheless, she double-checks pagination and similar details. She looks for smudges, white spots, and other flaws in the reproduction. She makes sure the correct pictures are placed with the correct captions, and yes, even that they are printed right-side-up. When everything is as it should be, she signs her name to the blueline, indicating her approval. The production manager, art director, and sometimes one or more assistant editors do the same. At last the magazine goes to press.

By now, editorial and production staffers have read your story at least sixteen times. Keep this in mind if you ever detect an editor's impatience over some unduly tedious piece of copy you've concocted.

IN SEARCH OF A GOOD EDITOR

Editors are like all people: some you can work with, and some you can't. It's a matter of personal chemistry. But even the best editors have some characteristics you should know about.

If an editor thinks you can do the job for her, she may dish out some harsh-sounding criticism to prod you into what she regards as success. Editors rarely demand rewrites of people they think are incapable of doing the work.

The skill to set a writer straight in a few succinct phrases is a rare quality, as is the patience to spend time formulating those phrases. Good editors are the key to good writing. And they are as scarce as good writers: when you find one, treasure him as a pearl richer than all your tribe. The best editors have certain signal virtues:

- They doubt that you can do no wrong. If an editor publishes your copy virtually unchanged, he's probably not doing his job.
- They are unafraid to suggest improvements. But they possess a certain odd tact: they recognize that even the most arrogant writer's stainless-steel ego has micron-thin weak spots, and they deliver criticism so as not to cause permanent damage.
- They run major changes past you before printing them.
- They treat you fairly and defend you from elements in the publishing hierarchy who would short you on money and rights.
- They know the language. They know what is grammatically correct and they have an ear for what sounds right.
- They recognize that readers want substance, not hype, froth, or disguised advertising. They demand substance and accuracy from their writers, and they keep editorial copy free from advertisers' influence.
- If they believe you are in the right during a controversy, they defend you when you are criticized by management or by outsiders.

At times, writers and editors stumble over each other. You can avoid this, to some extent, by following a few principles of common sense and by keeping in mind some caveats about the publishing industry.

First, let's consider some typical writers' conundrums:

- You make a factual error, which you catch after you've filed the story.

You are in deep trouble if your editor catches an error in fact, and your goose is microwaved if she finds out after it's printed.

If you learn of an error after you've finished a story, call the editor instantly to report it.

To prevent this extreme misfortune, double-check *every* fact before you file the story. Ask every interviewee how to spell his name, even if it's something obvious like Smith or Blake. Double-check every figure—compare the numbers in the copy with the numbers in the source. In your copy, pencil a check-mark over every fact, spelling, and figure (including addresses and telephone numbers) that you have double-checked.

- You're running late.

If you see you're not going to make the deadline, let your editor know as soon as you realize it. This will spoil her day, but she will be even more annoyed if the deadline passes and she hears nothing from you.

- The *real* story turns out to be different from what you described in your proposal.

Never file a story that isn't quite what you promised. If you think you're going to have to change direction, phone the editor and explain what's happening.

- As you look into it, you discover there's no story there at all.

Better to sacrifice the work you've done than file unpublishable hot air. Don't try to hype up a story when you really have nothing. If you call the editor and explain that you don't think the piece will fly, she may be unhappy about it, but—provided you haven't dropped it on her a day before deadline—she will undoubtedly consider you for future assignments. She may even offer you a new story on the spot.

- Your phone bills are mounting up. It looks like you may bill the magazine more for your expenses than the agreed-upon fee.

If you have to make more long-distance calls than the editor might have expected, clue her in. But do it in a tactful way that precludes her telling you not to do the story right.

- Someone offers to pay you $500 to write a story about him and sell it to one of your editors.

Do not enter any such agreement. It is unethical to offer a story to an editor as disinterested journalism when you're really selling p.r. flackery.

If you have any conflict of interest—or anything that might smack of conflict—inform your editor. For example, my husband's former law partner is a prominent state legislative lobbyist. I have occasionally quoted him, because he knows a lot about local politics and regional and national issues. But before I did so, I told my editor about the business relationship. If you might benefit in any way by giving someone free publicity, consider that a potential conflict of interest.

CAVEAT SCRIBBLER

Lest anyone think writers are the only ones capable of blunders and outright mischief, let's look at a few difficulties you almost certainly will encounter if you spend much time working for magazine editors.

• Changes in editorial management.

This can work to your advantage or to your disadvantage. When a new editor arrives, she may not know the local writers well. Looking to breathe some fresh air into the publication, she'll give all comers a hearing. That means you may be able to break into a magazine as a new editor arrives.

However, a new editor often will bring her own stable of writers. If you're part of the former editor's stable, you may find yourself out in the back pasture. This is one reason free-lancers always get a written contract.

I wrote a story for an editor with whom I had worked many times. Just as I was winding it up, he informed me that he was out and a new editor and assistant editor were in. I didn't know the boss, but no love was lost between me and his assistant. I filed the story as assigned, realizing—from having perused the new guy's previous work—that he would never dream of running any such opus.

Sure enough, he called me into his office to harangue me about the piece. Fortunately, I had a very specific letter of assignment proving I had done exactly as I was asked. Without it, he would have rejected the story with no payment. I ended up doing a rewrite that pleased him and getting paid top dollar.

• Unclear directions from the editor.

Disaster. Make very sure both you and the editor understand what you are supposed to do. If you get instructions orally, read them back, so she knows what you think she wants.

• The editor rejects your free-lance proposal but assigns the same or a similar story in-house.

Too bad. Don't work with her again. Tell all your writer friends.

In fairness, someone else may have already thought of your idea, and the story could be under way. But it's bad form for the editor not to tell you so in rejecting your query. If she's that inconsiderate at the proposal stage, she'll be no fun to work with on a story.

- Without consulting you, the editors make changes that alter the story's sense, are poorly written, or add material you did not write.

Unless they send galleys for your approval, you may not learn about this until after the story is printed. Complain. Tell the editor as politely as you can that you want to know of major changes before your copy is published. The most tactful way to accomplish this is to say you want to "work with" the editors on "polishing" the copy. These buzz words make you sound eminently cooperative. If the editor declines to accept your "help" in the future, or if she proves unable to work comfortably with you, quit writing for her.

- You find she pays other writers with similar qualifications better than she pays you.

Time to move on. This is a common practice. Do ask for higher pay, but don't expect to get it.

- She promised to pay on acceptance. That was three months ago. The story just saw print, but you still haven't seen a check.

Call. Ask where the money is. Tell her baby needs shoes.

Sometimes the editor doesn't know accounting has delayed payment for its own arcane reasons. Sometimes she's been lazy about moving the pay requisition off her desk.

Don't threaten, but if you don't get paid within a few weeks, consider a suit in small claims court. These are easy and inexpensive to file, and if you get a judgment against the magazine, it damages their credit rating. One publisher tried to pay a street-wise writer half of what she had been promised, claiming the editor had no authority to offer her the agreed-upon fee. She went to small claims court, and the check went in the mail the instant the summons arrived at the publisher's office.

- The magazine goes bankrupt.

Tough. Chances that you'll get paid ten cents on the dollar are remote. If you have no contract, the chances are nil.

- The editor gives you an assignment over the phone or in person, but no contract arrives in the mail.

If you don't get a written contract within a few days, send her a letter outlining your agreement as you understand it. Be sure to discuss subject, approach, deadline, and pay, as described above. In addition, establish the amount of the kill fee (about 30 percent of the agreed-upon total fee) and pledge in writing to produce original work which, to the best of your knowledge, is accurate.

Send her the original and a copy, and ask her to confirm your mutual understanding by signing and returning the copy to you. Even if she doesn't do so, the copy in your files will serve as evidence of your agreement.

- The editor pays you for a story, but a year later it still hasn't been published.

Unless you have some understanding about when the piece is to be printed, you have a right to timely publication. If the story needs extensive updating, you should be paid for your added work. If they haven't published it after a year, the rights should revert to you. Call and ask them to return the manuscript. If they're not going to run the story, they should give it back to you without penalty or cost.

- The magazine rejects the piece.

Demand the manuscript back. I once had an editor re-assign a story that was not what the editorial director imagined she had asked for. I was naive enough to think she would throw my copy in the trash, as she said she would. The new writer lifted a third of my story, word for word, for which I was never paid.

Here are some things you should never put up with:

Inadequate instructions
Shifts in midstream
Demands that you produce a new article on a new subject without a pay increment
Assignments made without contracts
Unreasonable demands in the contract, or work that is not specified in a contract

I haven't covered all the bases here, because it's impossible to do so. Every time you think you've seen it all, someone comes up with something new.

$$-30-$$

FOR PROJECTS OR DISCUSSION

1. You sell an article to a national magazine and, before it hits print, win an assignment for a second piece. When pay for the second story is slow, you call to inquire after your fee. The editor tells you he hasn't time to rewrite your article and besides, another story on the same subject came in. So he will pay you a kill fee. He adds that he had to rewrite your first article so extensively that he decided to put his byline on it. How do you respond to this?

2. You regularly sell second rights to your stories to a news syndicate. Among the syndicate's buyers is a tacky tabloid, whose purchases result in fees to the writer as low as twenty dollars. One of your editors calls and complains that this tabloid picked up not only your article but its title, coverline, three teasers, the cutlines, and even the magazine's typestyle. Legally, the publisher can do nothing about this, but your editor is upset. What, other than refusing to deal with the syndicate, might you do about it?

3. An editor calls and gives you an assignment; the idea is his, something you never thought of. He asks you to do the piece on a "work for hire" basis, meaning all rights would belong to the magazine. Do you agree to this? Why?

4. Your editor calls and asks where you got information to the effect that Indians inhabited upstate New York in 12,000 B.C. You direct him to a specific chapter of a book you borrowed from his magazine's reference library. He accepts this cheerfully and hangs up. On reflection, you realize the date is absurd. You must have erred. A couple of days later, you ask him what he found out, and he says you knew so precisely where the date came from, he just let it go. You know the story is in blueline. What do you do?

SUGGESTED READING

Leonard Mogel. *The Magazine: Everything You Need to Make It in the Magazine Business.* Englewood Cliffs, N.J.: Prentice-Hall, 1979. See chapter 3, "The Role of the Editor."

Arthur Plotnik. *The Elements of Editing.* New York: Macmillan, 1982. A revealing discussion of what's involved in editing for publications.

13

The Business of Free-lancing

Someone once asked Don Dedera, author of seven books and innumerable magazine and newspaper articles, how he accounted for his success as a free-lance writer.

"I attribute it to two things," Dedera replied. "A working typewriter and a working wife."

Free-lance writing is a tough, unremunerative affair, not one for the frail ego or the free spender. Average incomes range from $4,000 to $10,000 a year, depending on the survey; an annual take of $25,000 can be considered exceptional. Editors rarely develop much loyalty toward free-lance contractors, and publishers try to extract as much work in return for as little pay and commitment as possible. Turnover in the publishing industry is breathtaking, as is the bankruptcy rate; when a magazine is in trouble, the first supplier it will short is the writer. If you have any ideas about free-lancing to support yourself while you stay home with the kids after school, live in a Rocky Mountain retreat, and work whatever hours you please, think again.

Given these grim facts, one might sensibly ask why on earth anyone would take up such a dismal occupation.

Three good reasons:

1. It's a way to eke out a few pennies and work a small tax break between jobs. Like many "business consultants," the writer who

calls himself a free lance often means he's unemployed. By free-lancing, you can keep your hand in while you look for regular work.

2. Because it lets newcomers display talents to many potential employers, free-lancing can open the back door to jobs in journalism. After selling several stories to an acceptable magazine, you let the editors know you need a job. Then you wait and keep writing for them. Sooner or later, someone leaves and you have the inside track for the position.

   This is the hard way to get hired, but for many a writer-turned-editor, it has worked.

3. For all its agony, frustration, and penury, free-lancing is just plain fun. It's one of the few jobs in which you never do the same thing twice and you truly learn something new every day. You meet people you would never encounter otherwise, and you get to ask all sorts of nosy questions. You go places and see things that a desk-bound editor can only dream of while he reads your copy. Established writers decide what they will write about and decline projects they dislike—a choice you don't have on staff. And yes, you get to pick your hours: any 18 hours a day you like.

BUILDING A PROFESSIONAL IMAGE

Let us assume, since office rentals are expensive, that you will work from your home. This alone tends to diminish your credibility.

If you are to sell magazine articles—or any other kind of writing —you must go about it in a businesslike way. Editors and other clients are not interested in dealing with amateurs. To persuade potential clients that you are a pro, you must act and appear professional.

Set aside some time *every day* for writing. Treat the time precisely as though you were in an office. Use it just for work.

Most people think of work as a place, not an activity. For this reason, friends and relatives will either disregard your new "office hours" or conclude that you are mentally sick. Your son's homeroom mother, who invariably calls while you are fighting a deadline, will evince annoyance when you decline to drive 12 children two hours into the country to visit a pumpkin patch for Halloween. A writer who spent most of her waking hours stringing for *Time* reports that her mother once asked her, with sincere concern, when she was going to get "a real job."

GOAL SETTING

Once you've staked out some time, you need to organize it by setting goals and arranging your time to meet them.

Assignments provide built-in goals. On your calendar, block out the time you'll need for backgrounding, interviews, and writing. Plan to finish a first draft several days before the real deadline; then schedule a day to let the copy cool and a day or two for revising and polishing.

Remember to build delivery time into your schedule. Figure four working days to send first-class mail coast-to-coast.

Meanwhile, you should aim to send out a certain number of queries in any given period. A reasonable goal is to launch four good, solid proposals a month. Not shoot-from-the-hip ideas, but well-researched, polished, carefully targeted queries. Even more than the number of proposals you float, quality counts.

When matters lapse, it can take about three months to land a new assignment. So the free-lance writer must always stay in circulation. While you're working on an assignment, search out new ideas, devise fresh angles, write up proposals, and keep them in the mail until they sell.

These, then, are your *short-term goals*:

- to meet your deadlines
- to develop a certain number of ideas each month
- to keep several proposals circulating at all times

Long-term goals address what you want to accomplish over, say, a year—or a lifetime. This is something you must decide for yourself and perhaps change as you mature.

Writers have various motives. The most common probably follow these lines:

- to get published, anywhere, at any price
- to make money
- to break into national publications
- to get a full-time job in journalism
- to quit worrying about money and produce high-quality writing on subjects that *matter* for people who care

The danger in writing for a living is that it often leads you to produce things about which you cannot feel proud. Writing a lot of second-rate stuff just to bring in money may dull what talent you have, so that after a while you can do no better than second-rate. I can tell you this from experience: it is an exercise in terror to turn down a highly paid assignment because you know the thing is schlock. But the best writing, in the long run, earns the best pay.

RUNNING A BUSINESS SINGLE-HANDED

The self-employed writer fills all the functions that several employees in a larger concern would perform. You are your own production line; marketing, filing, and accounting departments; secretary; and telephone operator.

Marketing

Successful free-lancers sell all the time. It takes nerve, persistence, and a stainless-steel hide. Selling article ideas is no different from selling cars or shoes. Watch good sales agents in action and read a couple of how-to-sell manuals. You can apply much of their technique to your own marketing efforts.

The key is to stay in motion. Never stop hustling. Never allow yourself to become discouraged, never waste time with people who aren't live prospects, and always make yourself keep trying to sell every day.

Records

You must maintain records of all your transactions for tax purposes. Keep every receipt, every canceled check, and every evidence of any financial exchange for at least five years. Large accordion-style folders are useful for this purpose.

Make records of your long-distance and toll telephone calls. Some magazines will pay these expenses; you can write the rest off your taxes, but only if you can prove you incurred them for business.

For the same reasons, maintain careful records of your automobile mileage.

Keep a copy of every manuscript you submit, as well as contracts and correspondence with editors. If you use a word processor, *always keep hard copy*. When an editor calls and wants to discuss page 8, paragraph 3, you'll not want to keep him waiting while you search through 15 computer disks, wondering where you stored the piece. Besides, computer disks crash.

A two-drawer file cabinet will suffice for this purpose. Use it to store ongoing projects, current marketing efforts, writers' guidelines, correspondence, and the like.

It's wise to keep old copy and research notes indefinitely. You can often recycle them, and occasionally a question comes up that can by answered by something you wrote five years before. Use inexpensive cardboard file boxes to store the stuff in a closet or garage. Those boxes are also convenient for collecting sample magazines.

Production

The production line generates the work you're doing for pay at any given time. Keep it moving. If your client doesn't give you a deadline, set one of your own. And *always* meet your deadlines, even if it means working all night to do so.

An odd phenomenon afflicts most writers. I call it "work-avoidance maneuvers." One starts the day with delaying tactics to keep from sitting down to work—brew another pot of coffee, write a personal letter, water the plants. Because I have never met a writer who doesn't do this regularly, I think it serves a psychological purpose. Some projects, for example, seem so huge you must back into them to keep from feeling overwhelmed. You can indulge the work-avoidance impulse in constructive ways. Try reading the newspaper, studying a potential target magazine, or reviewing and polishing yesterday's copy.

If your day's schedule requires you to telephone people you don't know—always a stressful task—start the morning with the toughest call. This makes the rest of the day feel like downhill sledding.

When you have a hard time beginning a story, skip the lead and start at the nut paragraph or some later point in the piece. You can work out the lead later. If that trick doesn't work, try writing a first-person narrative, like a letter to a friend or sympathetic editor, describing what you saw and heard as you interviewed people and did your legwork. If you still can't get a handle on the piece, set it aside and work on some other assignment; the momentum of accomplishing a small project will carry through to the more difficult one.

Secretary and Telephone Operator

The do-it-yourself secretary needs decent stationery on which to type correspondence. You can have letterhead typeset and printed, or you can visit a quick-print shop that rents time on a computer and laser printer, in effect typesetting originals and hiring the shop to print letterhead and envelopes. If you have a computer and a high-quality dot-matrix or laser printer, you can lay out and print your own letterhead. Whatever you choose, keep the design clean and simple. Avoid cute, frou-frou logos, like "Have Pen, Will Write." It is unnecessary and probably unwise to place the words "free-lance writer" or "published author" in your letterhead.

Consider the telephone a business instrument during business hours. If others use your household phone heavily, you may want to install a separate line in the room you use as your office. Refrain from telling the telephone company that you will be using the line for business, lest you be charged at a higher rate.

When you call people, they are always "in a meeting." This means you spend your day leaving word all over town—or all over the country. When someone returns your call, it is to your advantage to sound like a professional and not like a lady with a typewriter on the kitchen table waiting for her brownies to bake.

When I began free-lancing, I once left word with a top executive at Honeywell. He called back, and I answered the phone with my customary housewifely "hullo?"

A long, eloquent silence ensued. He clearly thought either he had the wrong number or something eccentric was going on.

Business people do not want to talk to eccentrics. Answer the phone during business hours as though you were in an office—with your name, with the last four digits of your telephone number, or with some phrase like "writer's office." This is an effective way to establish credibility.

You should use a telephone answering machine or an answering service while you are gone. Machines are cheaper and usually preferable to services, whose operators may be curt with your clients. Your outgoing message should make it sound as though callers are reaching a business number. Women may may want to imply that several people work at the establishment—"none of us can come to the phone right now." It is unwise to advertise that you are at an address alone or that no one is likely to be there for awhile.

Accounting

In this area, you must hire expert help. Have a tax professional—preferably a certified public accountant—prepare your tax return, at least the first time you fill one out as a self-employed writer. People who claim deductions for home offices make tax collectors itch. Because the tax laws are extremely complex and capricious, you should never try to deal with the Internal Revenue Service by yourself.

Deposit the money you earn from free-lancing in a separate checking account, and use it to pay your expenses. This makes it much easier to keep track of receipts and business expenses, and by not mixing free-lance income with other money, you can help a tax agent see how much you earn and how much you spend on business costs. Using a separate telephone line only for business calls also simplifies your accounting.

To deduct the costs of running a home office, you must prove you are truly in business—not playing at a hobby. You have to be earning money, and you must make a profit three years out of five.

The Internal Revenue Service requires self-employed workers to establish a permanent, *separate* place within the home to use exclusively as an office. The space must be demarcated from the rest of the dwelling with room dividers or portable walls—to be safe, however, you should reserve a separate room for this purpose. You must use the space on a regular basis, not on-and-off, and it must be your principal place of business. If you have an office somewhere else, you can't deduct a home office used for the same business.

Once you establish yourself as a for-profit enterprise, you may deduct "ordinary and necessary expenses." These include rent, utilities, supplies, research costs, travel, subscriptions to professional magazines, membership in trade groups, certain conventions and meetings, telephone and postage costs, and the like. Depreciate expensive assets that you will use for several years, such as a word processor or typewriter. IRS rules govern the period over which you must spread the deduction of depreciable items. You are permitted to take a one-time deduction for no more than $10,000 for such equipment, but the deduction may not exceed the income you earned in the year of the purchase.

The possibility of a tax audit is an important reason to establish a well-organized filing system. Copies of query letters, proposals, contracts, and manuscripts will serve as evidence that you are trying to make a profit. If you are audited, you will have to produce all your receipts and expense records for the years in which you are challenged. Keep careful, accurate records and store them for at least five years. Among these records you should include your appointment calendars.

AGENTS

Magazine writers do not need agents, and few agents will try to market magazine articles, because there's not enough money in it.

Agents are useful in marketing certain kinds of books. Most writers find agents by word-of-mouth, through recommendations from other writers. Agencies list themselves in *Writer's Market* and *Literary Market Place*; to choose one blind, pick out several names and start telephoning.

If you should seek an agent, bear this in mind: *legitimate literary agents do not charge reading fees.* Avoid those who offer to think about marketing your work for a price. A scam current as we go to press shapes up like this: the "agent" agrees to look at a writer's work. He sends back a qualified rave that assures the aspiring scribe that the subject matter is bound to sell, the writing shows signs of latent genius, and he knows a publisher who will certainly buy the book—if only it's polished a little more. For a fee, he adds, he will show the writer how to revise his stuff and then take it to this eager publisher. Nonsense. If you're that promising, you can polish your own material enough to catch an alert acquisition editor's eye.

Literary agents offer your work to prospective buyers and negotiate contracts and fees favorable to you. They retain 10 percent of the take as a commission and pass the other 90 percent along to the writer. Their services are worth this premium because they usually obtain higher rates than a writer can negotiate alone. If an agent agrees to represent you, he or she may provide advice and editorial guidance as a service—for free. Most effective agents live in or near New York City, because they depend on person-to-person contact with book editors and publishers, whose offices are concentrated on the East Coast.

WRITER'S CLUBS AND TRADE GROUPS

Unless you are desperate for moral support, clubs of amateur scribes have little to recommend them. A bunch of folks who are just starting out or who are hobbyists can offer nothing to a working free-lance journalist. They understand less about the business than you can learn by reading this book.

However, there are groups of professional writers. The National Writer's Union, 13 Astor Place, 7th Floor, New York, N.Y. 10003, accepts aspiring as well as established writers. The American Society of Journalists and Authors, 1501 Broadway, Suite 1907, New York, N.Y. 10036, limits its membership to professional, publishing free-lance writers of nonfiction; if you can meet their requirements, their newsletter is a marketing gold mine. The Authors Guild, Inc., 234 W. 44th St., New York, N.Y. 10036, also restricts its membership to published writers. Women in Communications, Box 9561, Austin, Texas 78766, tends to attract women in public relations and advertising; some chapters provide excellent word-of-mouth networks. The Society of Professional Journalists (53 West Jackson Blvd., Suite 731, Chicago, Ill. 60604-3610) caters to undergraduate journalism students with chapters on many campuses, and publishes a high-quality magazine, *The Quill*.

Beware writers' groups whose main purpose is to bleed money from you. They print useless newsletters—if they have any at all—and their meetings are basically lemonade socials. Usually local or regional operations, they frequently offer how-to-write "seminars" at rates several times higher than you would pay for more substantial courses at a community college. Often these outfits urge members to publish their work through vanity presses.

VANITY PRESSES AND SELF-PUBLISHING

A vanity press takes your camera-ready copy, runs it through a printing press, and delivers you a truckload of unedited, unsalable books, which you are free to try to market if you can. Slightly more reputable are publishing houses catering to authors who wish to self-publish their books; for a fee, they may help with marketing.

Yes, we all know of famous writers, among them Carl Sandburg, who started by publishing their own work. We don't hear about the ones who got taken for a ride.

If your writing is not good enough to persuade someone to pay for it, why should you waste your own time and money on it? Use your savings instead to support yourself while you try to turn out something salable.

OTHER JOBS FOR WRITERS

If you have the hustle, business has the money. Some people make good livings writing for businesses. They write annual reports; edit in-house newsletters; write press releases, reference and credit reports, company manuals, company histories, brochures, proposals —you name it.

Get this work by word-of-mouth, advertising, and chutzpah. One method is to print up a brochure describing your manifold skills and take it door-to-door, introducing yourself and offering your services. Another way is by advertising in business and trade journals. If you have any gift at translating technical language into plain English, advertise yourself in county and state medical, legal, dental, and veterinary journals.

Put out the word to your editors that you're interested in working for businesses. Magazines often receive calls from people seeking writers to free-lance brochures or press releases; if no one on staff wants the job, the editor may recommend you.

You can also take your brochure to printers, typesetters, graphic artists, and fast-print franchise owners. These entrepreneurs often have customers who need writers.

Public relations agencies are another source of free-lance jobs. When business is good, agencies often have more work than staff members can handle, and they will hire free-lancers to write press releases. Writers with magazine credits may be asked to hack out self-interested trade journal articles for clients, at much higher rates than the magazine would pay. Agency fees to free-lancers range from $20 to $40 an hour.

Associations and nonprofit organizations also need writers. They may not pay as well as businesses, although some do. They especially need people to write or edit newsletters.

You can write book reviews. They don't earn much, but you get free books. You can write resumés for job seekers. You can write genealogies. You can do public information for government agencies. You can handle public relations for schools and libraries.

Everybody needs a writer. All you have to do is see the need and fill it.

–30–

FOR PROJECTS OR DISCUSSION

1. How much per hour would you need to earn to live comfortably in your region? Assume you spend 30 hours a week on paying work and 10 hours soliciting business. Give yourself two weeks vacation. (One formula: desired annual income divided by 50 weeks divided by 30 hours equals the required hourly rate.)

2. Find out how much editors in your region pay for feature stories. Divide a typical fee by the hourly rate you arrived at in exercise 1. This will show you the number of hours you can afford to spend on the story. Do you think you could realistically expect to finish a full-length article in that time?

3. Keep track of the hours you spend on the next article assigned for this class. Would the fee your chosen market pays for such stories break down to a living wage? How many such pieces would you have to write in a month to earn a living?

4. Call a half-dozen public relations agencies near you. Ask how much they pay free-lance writers. How does the average hourly rate compare with the rate you would need to earn a living? With the rate you would have earned writing your most recent magazine or newspaper article?

SUGGESTED READING

Rosemary Guiley. *Career Opportunities for Writers.* New York: Facts on File Publications, 1980.

Kirk Polking, ed. *Jobs for Writers: A Complete Guide to Free-lance Writing Opportunities.* Cincinnati, Oh.: Writer's Digest Books, 1980.

14

Rights and Contracts

The question beginning writers most often ask is "how do I copyright my work?"

Just put it on paper. Under the Copyright Act of 1976, your rights in a work take effect the minute you write it. You do not have to publish it or register it with the Copyright Office to receive protection. A work written after 1978 is protected for its author's lifetime plus 50 years. A work written anonymously or under a pen name is protected for 100 years after the work's creation or 75 years after publication, whichever is shorter. Works done for hire (about which we will say more below) receive the same 100-year protection, except the publisher, not the writer, owns the copyright.

WHAT IS "COPYRIGHT"?

Copyright is a legal concept that gives you the right to reproduce your work; to prepare derivative works based on it; to sell, rent, lease, or lend the work; and to perform or display it publicly. Copyright permits you to recover damages from other people who do any of those things without your permission.

A writer owns many kinds of rights to a work and may choose to sell part of the ownership, to lease the right to use this work, or to sell all the rights to it. The law's purpose is to let you say how your work will be used and to guarantee that you will be paid for your efforts.

To be eligible for copyright, the work must be fixed in a tangible form—that is, copiable with a machine or other device. Literary works; musical, dramatic, pantomime, and choreographic works that have been notated or recorded; pictures, photographs, and sculptures; motion pictures, videotapes, or other audio-visual works; and sound recordings are protected.

Intangible works, such as improvised speeches, dances, or performances not written or recorded, are not covered by copyright. Nor are ideas, titles, names, short phrases, slogans, lists, and the like.

Note that copyright covers the creation, not its physical form. In other words, someone could buy a famous writer's manuscript for its value to collectors—but owning the paper and ink would not confer the right to reproduce the story.

Although you don't have to register your work to receive protection, registration does give you some advantages. Your work must be officially registered before you can sue someone for infringement, and if you registered the work after the offense took place, you can sue only for actual damages—that is, for the income or other benefits you lost as a result of the theft. Unless you had already registered your copyright, you would not be permitted to sue for statutory damages (a punitive award) or recover the costs of attorneys' fees. There is, however, a ninety-day grace period following the date of publication. If you register within this period, you can sue for statutory damages, actual damages, and attorneys' fees, even if the infringement took place before the registraton.

As a practical matter, it's not worth registering every magazine article you send out. Normally, you have a contract or letter of agreement that spells out the rights you are selling before you present a work to a publisher. But if you have some good reason to believe someone might steal your work, register it. Fill out a form obtained from the Register of Copyrights, Library of Congress, Washington, D.C. 20559. Return the form, a twenty-dollar registration fee, and one copy of an unpublished work or two of a published work.

If you wish to retain copyright on an article that is to be published in an uncopyrighted collective work, insist that your copyright notice be printed on the article's opening page. A copyright notice consists of the symbol ©, the word "copyright," or the abbreviation "copr.," followed by the year the work was written and the owner's name. This notice must appear on works that you send to the copyright office for registration, and anything that is printed or distributed in an unrestricted way should have a copyright notice on it.

Magazines and newspapers normally take the responsibility for registering all the work that appears in each issue. The copyright notice appears with each number, usually near the front.

The United States is a signatory to the Berne Copyright Convention, a multinational treaty that covers copyright questions. According to this international law, you don't have to put a notice on your published work for it to be protected in the countries that have signed the treaty. However, because under U.S. law you may not collect statutory damages and attorneys' fees unless the notice was on the work, you should be sure a copyright notice appears with all your published works.

As the owner of a copyright, you can sell certain parts of your rights to a work. Let's consider a few.

First Serial Rights. The word "serial" here refers to periodicals—works that come out "serially" or in a continuing manner. That is, the term means "magazines or newspapers," not "installments."

When you sell "first serial rights," you offer a magazine the right to be the first periodical to publish your article, poem, or story. The remaining rights belong to you. You retain the right to sell the same, unaltered work to another periodical after the story appears in the first publication, and to be paid should the original buyer reprint it.

Logically enough, then, you also may sell *second serial* or *reprint* rights. This allows a publisher to reprint a piece that has already appeared somewhere else.

Sale of *one-time rights* promises nothing about whether the buyer is the first to publish your work. It simply grants permission to publish the piece once.

First North American rights guarantee that the buyer is the first in North America to publish the work. *First U.S. rights* are restricted to the United States.

Foreign serial rights cover periodicals published in countries outside the United States. If you have sold only first U.S. rights, you are free to resell your story abroad.

Simultaneous rights allow two or more periodicals to publish something at once. The term is used by writers who self-syndicate articles by sending the same work to many different newspapers across the country at once. Make sure your editor understands this by typing "simultaneous submission" in an upper corner of your first manuscript page.

Syndication rights permit syndicators to sell works to several publications at once, taking a commission on sales and passing the rest to the author.

Subsidiary rights are additional rights, usually listed in book contracts. They include dramatic, motion picture, translation, foreign, and various serial rights.

WHAT IS "WORK FOR HIRE"?

Section 101 of the 1976 Copyright Act defines "work made for hire" as:

1. a work prepared by an employee within the scope of his or her employment; or
2. a work specially ordered or commissioned for use as a contribution to a collective work [i.e., a magazine or anthology] . . . if the parties expressly agree in a written instrument signed by them that the work shall be considered a work made for hire.

The employer and not the writer is considered the author of a work made for hire. In other words, when you take a job with a magazine or newspaper, everything you write belongs to your employer. And a free-lance writer who signs a contract with a work-for-hire clause signs away all rights to the article, just as if she were the publisher's employee.

Free-lance writers should resist signing such contracts. Often a protest to the editor will cause the magazine to change a work-for-hire clause to first serial rights. Sometimes you can quietly cross out such a clause without arousing any objection.

CONTRACTS

An experienced editor, free-lancing between jobs, hired on as a consulting editor to start up a regional magazine. Once the magazine was running, he hired a permanent editor and managing editor, and stepped into the background.

Shortly afterward, the new editor called and explained that a story had fallen through and he needed 2,000 words to fill the hole —fast.

Promised a healthy fee, the consultant raced around the city tracking down and interviewing people, spent a weekend cranking out the desired 2,000 words, and dropped the piece on the editor's desk Monday morning.

A week later, he had heard not so much as "thanks, we'll be in touch." So he called and asked after the story.

It was all right, said the young editor. But it was more copy than they needed, and so they had to cut it to fit their space. And by the way, since they couldn't use the 2,000 words they had asked for, they would pay him only for what they could use, at an arbitrary per-word rate.

"I should have had a contract," mourned the free lance, "but my god! I'm the consulting editor!"

There is no such thing as a gentleman's agreement in this business.

You should always have a contract before you write a story, because it protects you as well as the publisher. It spells out what is expected of you and what you can expect from the publisher, says how much you will be paid and when, and establishes your rights in the work. If a magazine folds before it pays you, a contract establishes you as one of its creditors.

A contract should cover these items:

- the title and length of the story
- a brief description of its content and approach
- the deadline
- the rights you are selling
- the fee you will receive
- the kill fee you will receive if the magazine cannot publish the article through no fault of yours (usually about one-third of the total fee)
- whether you will be paid on acceptance or on publication
- whether you will be reimbursed for routine expenses
- a guarantee that your work is original and, to the best of your ability, accurate

In addition to the work-for-hire clauses we discussed above, you should watch for these pitfalls:

INDEMNIFICATION

Some contracts include a sentence saying the author indemnifies the publisher against any claims for libel, invasion of privacy, defamation, or anything else for which someone might choose to sue or demand redress. Never sign a contract that contains such a clause.

Unless you are a lawyer, you have no way of second-guessing the reasons litigious individuals threaten to file suit. Nor is it your job to purge the story of all actionable material. It is the editor's responsibility to recognize passages that may be defamatory, libelous, or invasive. If any such statement makes its way into print, the magazine is as guilty as the writer. Nevertheless, publishers have been known to buy off people who claimed they were wronged and then to bill the writer for the cost.

If the clause is modified with words that say the article does not libel or defame *to the best of the writer's knowledge*, it is acceptable.

Payment on Publication

Agreements to pay a writer when an article is published too often mean "pay never." Magazine copy usually sees print months after it is accepted. Should the editors decide, for whatever reason, not to run your article, you get no pay. If the magazine folds before the story runs, a bankruptcy court will not number you among the magazine's creditors.

For full time free-lance writers, payment on publication makes it impossible to budget living expenses, because they never know how much they will be paid in a given period. One month $5,000 may come in; the next month, the take is $89. For this reason, established professionals hold out for *payment on acceptance* of the piece. If an editor will not agree to this, the writer declines the assignment.

A beginner may have to take payment on publication in order to establish some credits. Always ask to be paid on acceptance. As you gain experience, seek out publishers who will treat you fairly and avoid pay-on-publication markets.

–30–

FOR PROJECTS OR DISCUSSION

The first document printed below is a letter of assignment from *American Visions*, a publication of the Smithsonian Institution. The second is a master agreement that all writers who accept assignments from any Meredith Publishing Services magazine must sign. Meredith publishes *Ladies Home Journal, Better Homes and Gardens*, and some smaller consumer and custom publications.

As you read these contracts, consider the issues we have discussed. Most Meredith publications pay on acceptance. *American Visions* accepted a commissioned profile of college president Charles Green in July, 1987. In February, 1989—after having held the story without pay for almost two years—they decided not to use it. Whose contract would you prefer to sign?

From *American Visions*
March 31, 1987

Millicent V. Hay
000 East Erewhon Drive
Phoenix, Arizona 85000

Dear Ms. Hay:

Please consider this letter to be a contract between you, Millicent V. Hay, and American Visions magazine.

You agreed to submit eight neatly typed, doublespaced pages (250 words per page and 70 characters per line) by June 1, 1987 on the following subject:

Scottsdale sculptor Don Locke

You should provide attributions for all factual material, your social security number and a brief author's bio with the manuscript.

You agreed also to help locate appropriate illustrations and/or illustration sources by the manuscript deadline. Identifying captions and photo/illustration credits should accompany all illustrative material that you send. You should incur no photography or illustration costs without consulting American Visions magazine and receiving written confirmation.

You should discuss and negotiate all expenses with me before they are incurred. The expense limit shall be limited to a sum of $50 dollars unless other arrangements have been made in writing. You should submit your expense receipts at the same time the manuscript is submitted. Phone charge receipts may be submitted sixty days after the article deadline.

American Visions magazine shall purchase first North American serial rights for your article and shall reserve the right to reprint it. The sale of reprint rights to others will be negotiated separately.

In submitting the article, you guarantee that it is an original work and is solely owned by you; that you have no knowledge or reason to believe that the article will defame any person or will infringe upon copyrights, rights of privacy, or other property or personal rights of any person; that you are free to convey publication rights of the article to American Visions.

American Visions will pay you a writer's fee of $400 and reimburse you for all documented expenses within thirty days of the publication date. We will pay you a 1/3 kill fee, or $133, if we decide not to publish your manuscript.

If you have any questions, please call me at 202 000–0000, or write me at the following address:
American Visions
Frederick Douglass House, Capitol Hill
Smithsonian Institution
Washington, D.C. 20560

Sincerely,

Leigh Jackson,
Assistant Editor

From Meredith Publishing Services
MASTER AGREEMENT

WORK MADE FOR HIRE

This is an agreement under Iowa law and Federal law, between _____
(CREATOR) and Meredith Corporation (MEREDITH), Des Moines, Iowa, which shall remain effective until terminated in writing as provided in paragraph 6. CREATOR and MEREDITH therefore make the following promises:

1. CREATOR shall from time to time create separate works, such as contributions, articles, photos, etc., (hereinafter Works) for MEREDITH as requested by MEREDITH. During the time of this agreement all of the Works

created by CREATOR for MEREDITH are "work made for hire" unless specifically designated otherwise in writing by CREATOR and MEREDITH.

However, in the event any Work is not a "work made for hire" CREATOR hereby assigns and transfers all right, title and interest in the Work and any copyright in the Work to MEREDITH effective as of the date the Work was created. CREATOR further agrees to cooperate and execute any assignment or other document necessary to secure total ownership rights of all Works in MEREDITH since the intent of this agreement is to vest all copyright and ownership rights in the Works in MEREDITH including, but not limited to, all copyright, all extensions of copyright, all copyright renewal rights, all derivative rights, and all rights to reproduce, publish, perform, and display the Works.

PAYMENT

2. In return, MEREDITH shall pay CREATOR for the separate Works an amount to be determined by CREATOR and MEREDITH. This Master Agreement may be supplemented from time to time by separate writings (generally known as work acceptance letters, day rate photography forms, or manuscript billing forms) which specify Work to be created.

REVERSIONARY RIGHTS

3. In the event any assignment or transfer of a Work is subsequently terminated in the manner provided by the Copyright Act of 1976 (17 U.S.C. Sec. 203) and the owner of the termination interest in the Work shall offer to assign, license, or otherwise transfer the Work or any part of the Work to others, that owner shall first offer MEREDITH the right to secure the same interest upon the same terms and conditions as offered to others. MEREDITH shall accept or reject such an offer within thirty (30) days of receipt.

CREATOR'S WARRANTY

4. CREATOR warrants and represents that to the best of CREATOR's knowledge all Works submitted hereunder are original and have not been previously published or, if previously published, that written consent to use has been obtained on an unlimited basis; that to the best of CREATOR's knowledge, all Works or portions thereof obtained through CREATOR from third parties are original or, if previously published, that written consent to use has been obtained on an unlimited basis; that CREATOR has full power and authority to make this agreement; that to the best of CREATOR's knowledge the Work prepared by CREATOR does not contain any scandalous, libelous, or unlawful matter. CREATOR will hold MEREDITH harmless for any breach of this warranty. CREATOR does not warrant originality of any materials provided by MEREDITH to CREATOR.

NO OBLIGATION TO PUBLISH

5. MEREDITH is not obligated to publish the Work. MEREDITH has the right to edit the Work and use the Work in any manner desired and also has the right but not the obligation to identify the CREATOR

RIGHT TO TERMINATE

6. This agreement may be terminated by either party upon forty-five (45) days written notice to the other.

NOTICES

7. All notices and payments made with respect to this agreement shall be addressed as follows:

When to MEREDITH
Editorial Planning director
MEREDITH CORPORATION
1716 Locust Street
Des Moines, Iowa 50336

When to CREATOR

_____

NAME

_____

ADDRESS

_____

_____

NON-ASSIGNABILITY

8. This agreement is non-assignable by CREATOR.

BINDING EFFECT

9. This agreement is binding upon the heirs, executors, administrators, and successors to any of the CREATOR's rights.

INDEPENDENT CONTRACTORS

10. Both CREATOR and MEREDITH are and shall continue to be independent contractors and neither shall be or represent itself to be an agent, employee, partner, or joint venturer of the other.

MEREDITH and CREATOR accept and agree to all of the promises set forth.

MEREDITH CORPORATION

NAME _____

TITLE _____

DATE _____

CREATOR

NAME _____

TITLE _____ *Author* _____

DATE _____

_____

SOCIAL SECURITY NUMBER

Meredith person requesting Master _____

SUGGESTED READING

The American Society of Journalists and Authors. "On 'Work Made for Hire': A Statement of Position." *The Complete Guide to Writing Nonfiction.* Cincinnati, Oh.: Writer's Digest Books, 1983, pages 851–852. 2d edition. New York, Harper and Row, 1988.

Copyright Basics, Circular R-1, Copyright Office, Library of Congress, Washington, D.C. 20559. Washington, D.C., U.S. Government Printing Office, 1985.

The annual *Writer's Market* runs a section in the back of the book about the business of free-lancing. This department usually includes an overview of copyright.

15

Computers and Writers

Several years ago, an editor remarked to me—as I was handing in 2,000 computer-generated words—that if he ever caught one of his writers using a word processor, he would never hire that scribe again. I silently congratulated myself on the wisdom of having bought a daisy-wheel printer that mimicked the IBM Selectric typewriter.

That once-common attitude has pretty well disappeared. Indeed, the editor in question now owns a roomful of computer equipment and has become a disciple of the silicon chip.

But behind the discomfort with the electronic writer lay some reasonable concerns. Editors suspected that by making it too easy to draft an article, the computer would breed glib, shallow writing. Time has shown, however, that a thorough, painstaking writer will be just as careful on-screen as with a typewriter or pencil. A careless writer doesn't need a machine to make him sloppy.

The effect is more subtle.

Because the computer allows a writer to turn out more copy faster than before, you tend to overestimate the amount of work you can accomplish in a given period. It's easy to forget that the computer speeds only the story's writing—not the interviewing, library research, and travel. If you mistakenly accept too many assignments at once, your work will suffer.

In pre-silicon days, the old expression "run it through the typewriter again" had a literal meaning. Most writers think through their fingers. The physical act of retyping sentences and paragraphs can bring better phrasing and organization in a way that simply reading copy does not. Since the computer frees you from having to retype a passage to revise a few paragraphs, that aspect of rewriting is lost. Some writers, to make themselves concentrate on each word, line, and paragraph, will print out a story, read it and mark revisions, and then open a new file and retype all the copy, polishing further as they go.

Proofing and revising on-screen can be difficult, even for experienced editors. It's easy to miss typographical errors, possibly because of the way the eye perceives the glowing characters. Many writers and editors prefer to edit hard copy and then insert corrections on disk.

It's also easy to instill new mistakes as you edit. You may cut part of a phrase and forget to change the rest of the sentence to make it consistent. If you change a noun from plural to singular, be sure all the verbs in the sentence match; then confirm that the rest of the paragraph still makes sense. Because you don't see the whole page on your screen, you may alter a passage near the top of a printed page without realizing that you need to make changes 10 or 20 lines further on.

Sometimes, too, larger concerns of logic, organization, and clarity get lost inside the computer. What seems an obvious flaw on paper is invisible on the screen.

For all these reasons, it is wise to edit your writing on a print-out before making final revisions on disk.

COMPUTERIZING YOUR RESEARCH

We discussed on-line databases as a research tool in chapter 3. Most newspapers and many magazines now subscribe to large computer databases, such as Vu/Text, Dow-Jones News-Retrieval, or Dialog Information Services.

Databases come in two forms: as bibliographic services, which provide citations to articles, books, and other information sources; and as full-text services, which allow you to read entire articles online. If you can't find an item in your local library, some bibliographic services will mail you photocopies of whole texts. Interlibrary loan, though slower, is much cheaper.

Several databases are affordable for independent writers. CompuServe, originally a computer hobbyist's haven, now offers an electronic bibliography, news and stock quotes, and travel information. The Source has UPI and AP wires on-line. Dialog has an off-hours bibliographic service called Knowledge Index, which contains dozens of databases in every imaginable discipline. For a reasonable fee, you can call up Standard and Poor's Corporate and Biographical Registers, nine different medical indexes, Magazine Index, Books in Print, the full texts of stories carried on the UPI wires, indexes to government publications, and much more.

Many university research libraries offer computer database services to their patrons. If you have a large project that will require many hours of searching through indexes, you may find it worthwhile to pay for an on-line computer search, at least to give you a start.

To gain access to a computer database, you must attach a *modem* to your computer. This device allows your computer to "talk" to other computers over the telephone lines. The speed at which modems work is measured in *bauds*, or bits-per-second. They operate at 300, 1200, 2400 baud and up. Slower modems are cheaper, but because on-line database charges accrue by the second, a faster modem saves you money over the long run. Also, if you plan to use a modem to send copy to your editors, many newspaper and magazine computers cannot receive copy at rates slower than 1200 baud.

A WORD TO THE UNINITIATED

Some of this book's readers will be adult students in night or extension classes. Unlike younger undergraduates, many such students have little experience with computers. This section is addressed to them. If you are already familiar with computers and word processing, you may skip to the last section.

Computers make writing less like labor and more like fun. They don't remove the challenging work of research and creation, but they free you from the drudgery of retyping drafts.

Learning to use a word processor—that is, a computer, a printer, and a program that runs them as a glorified typewriter—is very simple. A determined person can master a fairly complex word-processing program, such as WordStar or XyWrite, in two or three days of concentrated attention. Many computer manuals, particularly Apple's, are more "user-friendly" than they once were; that is, they're close to intelligible and with some fiddling you can figure out how to work the machine without enrolling in a class. Enterprising authors have written easy-to-follow guides to word-processing programs whose manufacters' manuals are incomprehensible.

Most newspapers and magazines use video display terminals or personal computers. Basic operating principles transfer readily from home computers to in-house networks. If you hope to obtain a staff job in journalism, you should learn to use a computer now, not later.

Choosing a Computer

International Business Machines and Apple dominate the personal computer market. IBM has a lock on the commercial market, and Apple has insinuated itself into education and desktop publishing.

So-called IBM "clones"—machines that imitate IBM design well enough to run programs designed for its computers—are now relatively inexpensive. Because so many publishers use IBM-compatible systems, the beginning writer may find it wise to select an IBM or one of the clones, simply for the sake of familiarity with systems that future employers may use.

Many writers, however, prefer the "mouse-driven" programs of the Apple MacIntosh and its imitators. Instead of having to learn which key works what command, you use an external device to point at pictorial symbols of different commands. This is a matter of taste. The disadvantage to the mouse is that you have to take your hands off the keyboard to enter simple commands, which some writers find distracting.

Whichever you prefer, you should look for a computer with these characteristics:

- *Enough memory* to run a fairly powerful program—at least 640K; preferably more.
- *A keyboard whose design is large enough* to fit your hands comfortably. It should have a set of function keys (they are marked F1 through F10 or, on more powerful machines, F12) and a separate numeric keypad with cursor direction keys.
- *A high-resolution monitor* that displays crisp, easy-to-read text. If the computer will be used only for word-processing, you do not need a color monitor.
- *An 80-column monitor,* which allows you to see the width of an 8 1/2-by-11 page.
- *A built-in internal modem or RS-232C communications port,* which allows you to install an external modem.
- *A hard disk,* or, if you can't afford that, *two floppy disk drives.*
- *An MS-DOS operating system,* which is the standard for the major word processing programs.

A desktop personal computer is probably the best choice for most home offices. However, you can now buy laptop computers that weigh only about ten pounds, run on batteries, and can be carried into the field. These machines are as powerful as many desktop computers. Their only serious disadvantage is the small size of the screen and, in many cases, the monitor's poor legibility. A lap computer's monitor can show 80 vertical columns, but it will not display as many horizontal lines as a desktop monitor. Unless the screen is back-lit, the LCD characters are difficult to read in low light and at certain angles.

Choosing a Printer

Three types of computer printer are useful to writers:

Dot-matrix printers, which form letters and pictures with fine patterns of dots

Daisy-wheel or letter-quality printers, which work like typewriters, by impressing each character through a carbon ribbon

Laser printers, which through a sophisticated process can produce camera-ready copy

Dot-matrix printers are cheapest, and they can reproduce graphics. If dot-matrix is your choice, be sure to buy a "near letter-quality" (NLQ) printer, which produces sharp, clearly defined characters. If individual dots can be discerned, characters will be pale, fuzzy, and hard to read. Some publications will not accept dot-matrix copy for this reason.

Daisy-wheel printers produce copy that looks convincingly like an ordinary typewritten manuscript. Few editors, however, remain suspicious of writers who use computers, and so this is no longer the concern it was five or ten years ago. The main drawbacks to the daisy-wheel are cost and inflexibility; they will not reproduce graphics, nor can they easily change point size.

In shopping for daisy-wheel or dot-matrix printers, look for relatively quiet operation and for a built-in tractor feeder, which guides a continuous roll of sheets through the platen.

At this writing, laser printers are still beyond the average writer's budget. However, costs are coming down, and so you should keep an open mind to this possibility.

Choosing a Word Processing Program

Many fine programs exist, ranging from the wonderfully simple Bank Street Writer to powerful, complex systems such as XyWrite, WordPerfect, WordStar, and Microsoft Word. Recommending specific programs is outside this book's purview. However, some broad characteristics are useful to people who write for publication. Here are a few:

A comprehensible instruction manual. You should not have to devote the best years of your life to learning how to use a word processor. Before you buy, make sure the manual is written in clear, plain English.

Ease of learning. Commands should be logical and easy to re-member.

What you see on the screen should be what you get on the printer. Some word processors mark certain print commands with symbols on the screen. If you tell the computer you want to underscore a word, for example, WordStar shows you this: Sa wordS. The S symbol marks the beginning and end of the passage to be under-scored. A different word processor might show you this on-screen: a word.

Speed. The program should open and close files (individual doc-uments) quickly. In the computer world, this means almost instan-taneously, not over several seconds. You also should be able to move from the front to the back of long files (ten or more pages) very fast.

Page breaks and line spacing should be visible onscreen.

Boldface, italic, and underscoring should be available and easy to accomplish in a single keystroke.

Columns and tabulation should be easy to set up.

Word wrap, the function that frees you from having to hit a carriage return at the end of each line, is a "given" with word processors. But the program should also wrap words within columns.

Enough memory to hold at least fifty manuscript pages at once.

Split screen or windows, which allow you to see material in two or more files at once.

Ability to move words and blocks from place to place in a docu-ment.

Ability to restore material you accidentally delete.

Search and replace, a function that allows you to ask the com-puter to find a character or word and, if desired, replace it with something else.

Insert and overstrike functions, which allow you to insert words or type over undesired copy.

Word counting, preferably without having to leave the system and boot up another program.

Merge or mailmerge, which allows you to combine blocks of copy from different files.

Some word processing programs include *spelling* and *grammar checkers,* useful options for those who are weak at copy editing.

WHAT IT ALL MEANS

The computer has permanently changed the way writers, editors, and publishers do their jobs. If you intend to work on the staff of a magazine or newspaper, part of your preparation should include familiarity with word processing and on-line research. Free-lance writers need similar knowledge, simply to keep up with the publishing industry.

Nevertheless, the computer is a tool, not an end. You should avoid devoting large segments of your formal education to learning technology that may change before you get out of school. And you should never assume that the machine affects the basic way you think or create.

—30—

FOR PROJECTS OR DISCUSSION

1. Invite a veteran newspaper reporter to visit your class. Ask how his or her job is different from the way it was twenty years ago. Ask the person to bring and demonstrate a laptop computer. Find out how and when the reporter learned to use it, and ask if it has proven especially useful on any specific assignment.

2. Visit your library's computer research service. Ask the librarian to give you a quick overview of how to design a simple search project.

3. Many computer salespeople love to talk about their products. They'll answer your questions, demonstrate word processing programs, and even let you try programs in the store. Visit several retailers in your city; tell them you are interested in word processors and would like to know more. When you go, take a page or two of copy with you, and ask permission to try the store's pet program by typing and printing out your material. Report the results to your class.

SUGGESTED READING

Guide to Buying Word Processing Software. Madison, Wis.: P/K Associates, Inc. Address: P/K Associates, Inc., 4343 W. Beltline, Madison, Wisconsin 53711. A flyer by computer writers Judi K-Turkel and Franklynn Peterson; includes a brand-name comparison chart.

Bernhardt J. Hurwood. *Writing Becomes Electronic.* New York: Congdon and Weed, 1986. A compendium of writers' experiences with the computer.

William Zinsser. *Writing with a Word Processor.* New York: Harper and Row, 1983. Entertaining and instructive.

II

EXAMPLES OF FEATURE STORIES

Differences Between Magazine
and Newspaper Features

Writers and editors divide feature articles into various categories, according to subject matter and approach. Newspaper and magazine editors describe feature types in slightly different ways, because the newspaper is a different medium from the magazine.

TYPES OF NEWSPAPER STORIES

Newspapers usually carry a wider variety of writing. Most newspaper editors think of reporting—that is, *hard news*—as their publication's primary mission. Consequently, the thrust of the newspaper's content is news reporting. And yet, because readership is vastly more diverse than a magazine's, the paper contains much other material: lively editorials and editorial cartoons; op-ed columns; musings of local scribes such as Herb Caen or Mike Royko; agony columns like "Dear Abby"; restaurant reviews; arts criticism; how-to pieces on every subject from woodworking to health; recipes; automotive, sports, and outdoor stories; religious inspiration; the comic strips. All these are regarded as secondary to the news in importance.

Thus, on a newspaper the feature is subordinate to the news. Ask a city editor to list types of newspaper features, and he'll come up with something like this:

- The *news feature:* an article other than a news report whose subject is perishable, dependent on current events.
- The *sidebar:* a feature that focuses on one aspect of a related news story; for example, an article detailing the reactions of witnesses and bystanders following an airplane crash.
- The *human interest story:* a feature with no immediate news value, but which casts light on the motives and lives of ordinary people.
- The *personal profile:* an essay characterizing a person, usually someone in the news.
- The *aftermath piece:* a follow-up article that ties up loose ends or describes what is happening in the days after an important news event.
- The *color story:* a light, descriptive feature that captures the mood of a festive event, such as a state fair.
- The *seasonal story:* a feature highlighting a current holiday or season.
- The *enterprise story:* an analysis or elaboration of the meaning of current events.
- The *investigative article or series:* one or more hard-hitting stories, based on thoroughgoing research, exposing a problem or scandal in the community.
- The *bright,* sometimes cutely spelled "brite": a short, upbeat or humorous mini-feature, just a few paragraphs long.

TYPES OF MAGAZINE STORIES

By contrast, few magazines can run current, perishable news stories—a monthly publication schedule militates against that. With hard news dethroned as king of the editorial mix, the feature article takes a primary place. So, magazine editors see the feature as the most important part of their work.

On a magazine, the feature is independent of the news. Although it may have a news "hook," it stands on its own merits. So the magazine editor categorizes features not by how they relate to the news but by their subject matter and organization, like this:

- The *report:* an article whose main purpose is to tell the facts about some issue or event, current or otherwise.
- The *how-to-do-it piece:* a step-by-step guide to performing some activity or accomplishing a goal.
- The *service piece* or *round-up:* a consumer-oriented article that evaluates or presents several commodities, services, or places of the same kind, such as a *Consumer Reports* study of washing machines or a survey of day-care options for preschool children.

- The *personal experience story:* a feature relating one person's adventure or experience that is exciting, frightening, or inspiring enough to have general interest.
- The *inspirational piece:* a warm-fuzzy story designed to uplift the reader's spirits.
- The *profile:* fundamentally the same as the newspaper's "personal profile." A magazine profile is often longer and may offer more in-depth treatment. A subgenre, the *celebrity profile,* focuses on an entertainment star or similarly prominent person.
- The *travel piece:* an article describing a region, a resort, or some aspect of getting there.
- The *history story:* a report about a historical event, based on solid research.
- The *investigative article:* similar to the newspaper's investigative piece. It may treat a national subject rather than a local one; typically seen in magazines such as *The Atlantic* or *Mother Jones*; rarely appears as a series.
- The *opinion piece:* an article, based on expertise or research, whose avowed primary purpose is to present the writer's point of view on the subject.
- *Humor:* an article meant to be funny.
- *Filler:* similar to the newspaper's "bright."

To the magazine editor, the term *sidebar* means a short piece accompanying the main article and presenting ancillary or potentially boring information in brief.

It's important to learn these terms, because editors use them and assume that writers understand what is meant by "a round-up" or "a profile." But keep in mind that the distinctions tend to blur. A travel article, for example, might take the form of a how-to piece (how to deal with foreign customs officers), a round-up (weekend retreats within driving distance of New York), or a report (San Diego's famous Hotel del Coronado). Profiles, humorous pieces, and personal experience stories often slide into the inspirational category. Seasonal, aftermath, and human interest pieces could run as easily in a magazine as in a newspaper.

These ways of looking at the feature are anything but hard and fast. Your instructor may ask you to learn the basics of writing before you start molding stories for the tired cubbyholes of the marketplace, and that is probably a wise approach.

Anything is possible. Once you know your tools, don't be afraid to experiment.

16

Profiles

The profile is a story based almost entirely on interviews.

It is a fully developed feature, with a lead, body, and windup—not a Q-and-A interview. In a profile, you try to bring a personality to life for your readers. Your interpretation of the subject's character is the story's thesis.

In writing a profile, you create a character very much like the characters in a novel or a short story. Our lives, after all, are populated with fictional characters, impressions of the people around us formed through observation, gossip, and experience. Because no one can get inside another person's head, you can never really *know* someone else, no matter how much time you spend interviewing and following him around. The best you can do is empathize and approximate.

A nonfictional profile differs from a fictional characterization in that the journalist bases the portrait on a study of a single person and tries to represent objective fact. A fictional character may be a composite, based on several people the author knows. Too, an imaginary figure may possess attributes that exist solely to connect him to the story's plot. We discussed characterization in chapter 7. You should read or review that section before attempting to write a profile.

By the time you finish all your research and interviews, you will have reached some conclusion about the person. Your estimate of his character will govern your angle—the approach you take to the story.

Review all your notes to clarify your thoughts before you make up your mind. Then write a one- or two-sentence summary of what you want to say about your subject. Remember, you need never overtly state this conclusion in your article. A skilled writer lets readers make up their own minds; showing the subject in action gives them the evidence they need.

Esquire columnist Bob Greene is a master of this technique. In his essay, "Miss McNichol Will See You Now," Greene describes his passing acquaintance with starlet Kristy McNichol. He follows her on a shopping trip, accompanied by her chauffeur and grandfather. He shows her with a young admirer whose job is helping the blind, and later with her gigolo-like friend, Joey, to whom she has given a diamond earring. Not once does Greene make a judgmental comment or draw a conclusion. Yet by the end of the piece, the picture of Miss McNichol as a spoiled, self-centered brat is as crystalline as Joey's earring.

Greene's most overt summary remark surfaces about five lines from the story's end, concealed in a brief quote:

I asked her what she thought the greatest public misconception about her was.
"That I'm the all-American girl," she said. "Perfect and good and level-headed."

Choose descriptive details and quotes that characterize the person by showing how he thinks and acts. When you meet the subject, make yourself slow down and take conscious note of his workplace, home, tastes, gestures, clothes—everything that strikes your senses. Notice the color of his tie and the way she wears her hair. Are her shoes high-heeled? Are his oxfords or lizard-skin boots—and are they scuffed or polished? Does he cut his meat a bite at a time, or does he slice up the whole steak and set down his knife before he begins to eat? Does she drink bourbon or Scotch? Watch; listen; smell; feel—and take notes. Little things tell.

When you start writing, however, do more than just pile up random observations. The details you select should add up to a rational sum. Make them work together to support the impression you're trying to create.

In a short, jewel-like sketch, Charles Bowden portrays Keith Turley, chairman of Arizona Public Service Company and one of many industrialists insensitive to their firms' destruction of the Southwest's most fragile environments. Bowden draws the reader's eye to a collection of bald eagle figurines in Turley's office. Earlier in the passage, the writer has revealed his own stance in a single verb, by calling Turley's company "an empire that rips tens of tons of coal a day from the Indian lands of the Navajo and Hopi." Now Bowden asks Turley about the brass and porcelain figures.

> He offers that bewitching smile and says he doesn't know quite how it got started but it did and now everybody gives them to him. Yes, he likes eagles.
> He has never really seen one in the wild. Oh, once you know, someone said look up there, an eagle!, but he couldn't really tell. It was just a big bird. (*Blue Desert*, p. 149)

Don't belittle your subject by choosing details that detract from his dignity, unless that's what you intend. I was once asked to revamp another writer's profile of a Native American novelist. The author, a cultivated and distinguished gentleman, had dressed casually to meet the young journalist in an informal setting. After expressing awe that anyone growing up on a reservation could read and write English, much less win a Pulitzer Prize, our reporter focused on the man's loose shirttails hanging over his "bulging girth." The unintentional result, a hackneyed picture of a fat Indian, was tasteless, at best.

Use special caution when you profile members of races or genders other than your own. We all carry stereotypes with us, sometimes so unquestioned we don't recognize them as false generalizations. Treat your subject as a human being first, and then incidentally as black, white, brown, male, or female.

At the same time, don't feel you must believe everything your subject tells you—the reader won't, especially if you sound credulous or adoring. And don't turn the piece into an advertisement for your subject's business.

For any profile, you should interview several people in addition to your subject. Ask him for names of friends and associates who might talk to you. Explore sources outside his immediate circle. Talk to his competitors, to observers who know his business or trade, to people who have worked with him in civic activities. Your sources need not be friendly: sometimes an ex-wife or former business partner can provide all sorts of insights. *Wall Street Journal* reporter Joanne Lipman dwelt on premier publicist John Scanlon's endearing qualities for six paragraphs. Then she quoted a Yale ethicist describing Scanlon as "someone who doesn't know how to shut up," a lawyer who remarked that he had "all the tact of an ape at a Chinese tea party," and a colleague who disapproved of his high-profile tactics ("P.R. Man John Scanlon Can Wheel and Deal with the Best of Them," May 4, 1987).

For most magazines, a single interview with the subject will do—one to three hours. But if you can get the person to let you follow him around, to take you into his life for a few days, you will have a deeper, more insightful story. This is required for top-flight magazines such as *The New Yorker, Philadelphia, Esquire,* or *Reader's Digest.* Secondary-market editors can't pay you for your time, but they will bless you if you devote hours or days to getting to know your subject. Later, when editors with larger budgets see your clips, they will recognize your quality.

OLD JOKES NEVER DIE, JUST RETIRE

by Barry Bearak

The Los Angeles Times, Sept. 13, 1986

PEMBROKE PINES, Fla.—The piano player wants to know, does he have to stay for Sonny's act? The time before last, another old comic made him hang around 45 minutes just to play a little hut-tut-tut to close the show.

"No offense," the musician says. "I'll play for the girl singer, then give you your intro, then head out."

"Go, go," the comic answers, flipping his hand at the wrist. "Bob Hope, this isn't. I'm a hit with music. I'm a hit without."

Forty years in the business, Sonny Sands doesn't need a piano. He could use a few pounds since he had the surgery, and it would be nice if they paid him more than peanuts. But laughs he can still get without a piano, knock wood.

Audience Older

A half-hour later, slight as a pixie, he walks on stage. He is 69, and many in the audience have blown out more candles than that. He puts a cup of coffee by the piano for when his throat get dry. Then he opens his palms and shrugs his shoulders.

"I can see you didn't expect such a big, good-looking guy out here," he tells them—and off he goes, into his lifeblood, into his shtick.

This is the South Florida condominium circuit, and Sonny Sands is a condo comic, playing out the last laughs in the recreation halls of an American retirement capital . . . Sonny will tell you that at this stage of the game all he wants to do is to get on, get off, get the money and go home.

But that's a fib. Stay around a bit and he talks about what it is to be wanted, to be loved—to make people forget their aches and pains and to make him forget his own. The thing is to keep going.

"Life is like a composition," Sonny Sands says. "There's a beginning, a middle and an end. At first, everything is new and exciting. Then, in the middle, it all begins to look like Newark. Finally, life can become a little disappointing if you let it."

The condo crowd understands this. Like Sonny, they never made it big, never became a name or a millionaire. They had some ups, some downs,

---

The *lead* is a set piece. It opens by putting us on the scene—focuses on a person and place. It also establishes atmosphere up front.

Bearak has a feel for language; his narrative picks up the Yiddish cadence.

Simile

Where, who, what

Bridge summarizes what this story is about.

This is subtle stuff for newspaper writing: it suggests that the character of Sonny is a metaphor or icon for life in general. Bearak has used a telling quote to extraordinarily good effect.

Empathetic description.

A fine, original metaphor.

The patter is recognizably Yiddish, but not so much so that it becomes obscure. Most Los Angeles readers know what "kibitz" means.

Narrating part of Sonny's act allows Bearak to use some entertaining quotes.

Succinct description; nice simile.

some near-misses. Now the years have rocked their dreams to sleep, and there are more memories to remember than memories to be made.

Not that anyone should take up a collection. After all, these people have a place in Florida, a few bucks in the bank and white shoes to go with the new golf bag. Their hip may forecast the weather, but the weather is usually good. They like a good kibitz.

"I enjoy the condominiums," Sonny tells them, a blue pin stripe suit not quite camouflaging the skinniness of his 110 pounds. "I'm on by 8; the audience is asleep by 8:30. I'm home by 9:15."

"Recently, I worked a convention of doctors. I think they booked me because I looked like a patient."

The delivery is slow, with a rhythm that massages the room like ointment. What goes over are jokes about a visit from the grandchildren, the widows who want to dance with the widowers, a trip to the eye doctor.

"I told him my right eye is blurry. He said, I'm sorry, I'm only a left eye doctor. In the next building is a right eye doctor."

Dirty No Good

Mention a street in Brooklyn and applause fizzes up like seltzer. The birds and bees make good material, but never the pollinating. Dirty is no good here.

"She was wearing a V-neck dress. So I asked her, is that V for victory? No, it's V for virgin, she said. You're a virgin? I asked. No, she said, it's an old dress."

God bless, Sonny says, that there are still places to sell these jokes. After all, for a comic, live entertainment is not so alive these days.

The story reflects on Sonny's status. This passage leads into quotes and facts that must have come from interviews. It also establishes context.

Las Vegas and Atlantic City are for the big stars. Even in the Borscht Belt, the few remaining resorts in the Catskill Mountains—they mostly use names that at least ring a bell, a Red Button or a Henny Youngman or a Sid Caesar.

So, if not the Florida condominiums, where else could the old-timers go —guys like Sonny Sands and Lou Shor and Eddie Barton, guys who made a little noise but never so much it didn't die down?

"I Was Good"

This is a whisper on the purple side.

"I was never that big a talent," Sonny says, staring back across the spotlights of a thousand lounges, drinks on tables and hookers at the bar. "I was good. I was big. But I was never that big."

Fills out Sonny's background—essential to understanding the person.

Long time ago, when Sonny was a boy in Brooklyn, and the boy's name was Seymour Schneider, a comic could find all the work he wanted within a 5 cent subway ride. Then, in the summers, there was the Borscht Belt. Sonny started out in a tiny hotel. He was part bellboy, part chauffeur, part emcee.

After a while, he stole enough jokes to break in an act. He was lousy, but he didn't know it. That's a good thing. Being lousy is bad enough without getting hit in the eye with it.

Uses the language of the show circuit, at once tough and wistful.

In those days, every place needed some kind of show, and the comics worked doubles and triples, driving like madmen from job to job on the same night.

Success Story

Some of them eventually became big hits. Buddy Hackett, Jerry Lewis and the rest. Go believe in miracles. Jack Ray dropped out to sell paint for a living, then started over as Rodney Dangerfield and is now a superstar at 64. His new movie made $80 million.

But, looking back, only one in 100 climbed up to stay. "The rest just got a taste of it, enough to know what they were hungry for."

Sonny himself played Vegas. He did Jack Paar and Joey Bishop. He was on "The Jackie Gleason Show" six times in the three years up through 1968. Or was it '69?

"Who can remember," he says. "I must have had 83 comebacks."

He was always funnier than his material, a timing and delivery kind of comic with a knowing smile across a friendly puss.

Some years, the career seemed ready to take off. Other times, it was like a knock, knock joke. Who's there? Sonny Sands. Sonny Sands who?

Stalked off Stage

To be honest about it, he also liked to take a drink and sometimes two and sometimes kaplotz. One night, warming up for Paul Anka, he gave hell to a noisy audience at the Copacabana in New York, then stalked off.

This isn't done. The whispers start. When you're big, the agents and owners are working for you. But till then, you're working for them.

"You got to be a pro," Sonny says. "You got to show up and behave yourself. You can't be a drunk. And you have to have some business acumen.

"Bad habits, I had. Drinking and girls. And I was lazy. . . . But, what the hell, you can't buy back yesterday. There's no way."

Miami Beach Action

Sonny had fallen in love with Miami Beach in the '60s, and he made it his home base. The town was all action back then. Gambling was wide open. The bellhops made book, and the ladies wore mink. A $50 spot melted away faster than an ice cube on Collins Avenue.

Oh, was this a Miami Beach! The Art Deco hotels looked like wedding cakes and ice-cream cones. The ocean was waiting out the back door, where they served pastrami sandwiches on tables shaded by big umbrellas.

For miles up the shore, places had fancy names . . . the Fontainebleau and the Eden Roc and the Sherry Frontenac. The lobbies were decorated in something between brothel and chateau, one outdoing the next with circling staircases and velvet drapes and chandeliers that hung like sparkling wands.

Sinatra was always coming down back then. So were Sammy Davis Jr. and Jimmy Durante and every other name. The hotels had three shows a night, and Sonny's phone was ringing. Every two weeks, new tourists arrived to hear the jokes the old tourists had just finished laughing at.

"It was like a party," Sonny says. "There were girls, this and that. There were always people to talk to. The world was coming to you."

Miami Beach had a long run, but in time those glittering fixtures and golden moldings began to look old hat. Glamorous people found other places to plop down their tanned bodies and thick billfolds.

Margin notes:

History of stand-up comic routines: context.

Places Sonny in this context.

Sonny is no paragon. Serves to humanize him and to explain why a man presented as a charming professional hasn't made it big.

Background: biography.

Evocative scene-setting. Nice feel for language.

History; quote tells us what it has to do with Sonny.

In part, the town caved in from the weight of its own success. Many tourists decided they wanted to have their own piece of this paradise—why pay all that money on a room tab when you can buy a condo and build up equity? Even Sonny bought.

More Condos

History

By the late '60s, the hotels were crying the blues, and more and more condos were breaking ground. Much of the new money was cashed from Social Security checks, and the oceanfront strip turned into a hardening artery. Marquees began advertising early-bird specials instead of nightly entertainment.

Sonny in the Miami Beach context.

Much of the talent hit the road. Others, like Sonny, stayed put, making a last stand. Funny thing, the condominiums started becoming their own circuit, nothing to get rich with, but a thin living. Sonny Sands, and dozens like him, became condo comics.

The aging of Miami Beach seems to parallel Sonny's aging. Again, Sonny's life appears almost metaphorical.

"Show business, it's not, if you want to know the truth," he says now. "Some of the places, they don't even have a cup of coffee, they should drop dead. . . ."

Sonny enjoys the complaining. But he worries about giving the wrong idea. He's too old to hit the road now, anyway, he says. So what could be better than working these condos in his own backyard.

Laughter Is Reward

Sonny's acceptance of old age and death.

When he had an operation a few years ago the possibility of death made him realize something: You do the best you can with life, and you don't hurt nobody. That's what it's all about.

"The biggest reward is the laughter, the acceptance," he says. "I understand these people and they understand me. How much time you think you got in this world? I love this."

Description of the milieu.

There are hundreds of condos. Miami Beach to Palm Beach. Some of them are high-rises near the ocean, with the brawny look of refrigerators or of giant ice-cube trays that stand straight up.

Nice simile.

Others burst out of the swamps to the west, sprawling cities of 5,000 or 10,000 with names like Century Village and Ring's Point and Lauderdale Oaks.

Good verb.

The bigger ones have auditoriums, huge as university theaters, with cushy seats and professional lighting. They have dressing rooms in back, where Sonny combs his hair with the palm of his hands.

Admission Subsidized

Sonny's humor.

"Something is wrong with this mirror," he likes to say, "I've got wrinkles in this mirror."

Writer picks up the same wry, rueful humor.

The audience usually pays $1 each to get in, the entertainment subsidized by condo maintenance fees, same as cleaning the pool and spraying for bugs.

Catches the sad atmosphere of these ghettoes for the elderly.

Performing for this crowd can have its quirks. Frankie Man, the impressionist, was ready to go on when the emcee announced, "We're really sorry to report that Mr. Saperstein did pass away at 2 o'clock this afternoon, and we'd like a moment of silence before we bring on the comic."

But, mostly, it's easy work. This is a pushover audience—a lot of them Northeasterners, primarily Jewish, the same people who laughed at the jokes in Brooklyn and the Catskills. So they know a few of the punch lines already. They think it's a joy to hear them again.

"Don't Get Me Lost"

On a recent Wednesday night, Sonny drove west past the last street lights to where they've built yet another Century Village. He sometimes gets confused amid the clusters of white concrete slabs and moonlit artificial lakes.

"I'm the show," he tells the security guard at the perimeter gate. "Don't get me lost."

In through the stage door, he recognizes the lighting man. Then he pokes his head around, room to room. They have coffee.

"Thank God," he says.

There are plenty of mirrors to look at, and the comic has a joke for each one. "I'm going bald! How can this be?" he wants to know. "I'm 23 years old!"

He moves his bony face close to the glass. His eyes have settled deep into the sockets. His hair is thin and bleached.

The emcee sees him. A college student, he is just 25. He wants to be a court reporter. Emcee is his part-time job. To him, being with Sonny is like time-traveling and ending up in vaudeville.

> In three sentences, Bearak shows this character as a callow pup with no grasp of the humanity of the person he is addressing.

Talk with Your Emcee

"You can never retire, can you?" he says pleasantly, trying to start conversation.

> Naive. Is he trying to patronize?

"No, why should I?" the comic answers. "When people retire, what do they do, sit and play cards? I enjoy this more than they do."

The singer is already on. Her voice carries backstage, beyond the curtains. "She's not too bad," Sonny says. At least, she doesn't talk too much between numbers. Some of them, they make it sound like they were with Rodgers and Hammerstein when they wrote it.

> Sonny responds with grace and patience. Contrasts youth and age; also gives the character of Sonny depth.
>
> Description, context.

The comic looks at his watch and then pulls at the loose skin on his neck. It's almost time.

> A revealing gesture.

He asks the emcee, "How much you charging, $1 or $2?"

"One dollar tonight," the younger man answers. "We get $2 for some acts. One dollar tonight."

> Sad. Again, an unconscious insult from a man suffering from the insensitivity of youth.

Sonny sips coffee between tugs at a cigarette.

"How do I look compared to the last time you saw me?" he asks.

"You look thinner," the emcee reports.

"Really, it is bad?"

"Oh, no, no," the younger man lies.

> The obvious lie is less kind than a gently phrased truth would have been—were the young man capable of that.

It's Show Time

One more time, Sonny gets up to confront the mirror. He adjusts the lavender handkerchief in his coat pocket. Then he studies his face again, the lips and the eyes and the chin. It's both Sonny and what has become of Sonny.

"You'd think they'd fix these mirrors," he says.

Then, in a minute, the condo comic is on stage. He opens his palms and hunches up his shoulders.

Wrap brings us back to where we came in.

He tells them, "I can see you didn't expect such a big good-looking guy out here."

EDITORIAL OVERVIEW

Opening with a set piece was an effective approach to an article about a show-business pro. It makes us feel we are literally looking behind the scenes. First we see the act, and then we go backstage with Sonny. We learn a great deal about Sonny as a man, about live comedy, and about humanity in general. This effect is reinforced when the wrap directly repeats the lead.

Everything about this story—the tough-but-tender tone, the Yiddish cadences, the close and knowing observation—says that Bearak is the kind of reporter whose demeanor inspires his sources to trust. He shows a natural empathy indispensable to writers who rank among the best. For this kind of writing, you must go beyond observation and put yourself inside the people around you.

Note, though, that the portrait of Sonny, while gentle, is far from credulous. Bearak tells us the comic has had a drinking problem and repeatedly admits that as a performer Sonny is good enough, but not outstanding. While not unkind, the writer is honest.

This story was a finalist for the 1987 Pulitzer Prize in feature writing. It's wonderful stuff, of course—literary journalism, with all those similes and metaphors and, heaven help us, iconography. The picture is sensitively drawn. But one thing you must remember is that it *is* a picture, not the real thing. Sonny and the emcee are characters, exactly like people in a novel whose characters are drawn from real life. A man is not a symbol for a colorful period: no one is that complex, or that simple.

What Bearak has used here is probably the best approach we know to portraying a human being in the space of a few column inches. By focusing on one or two aspects of Sonny's personality, the writer produces something like an abstract painting. It's like Marcel Duchamp's *Nude Descending a Staircase*: the truth is in the suggestion.

—30—

17

Personal Experience Stories

Everyone has a story, and many of those stories are publishable. The personal experience piece relates someone's adventure—or misadventure—in the third person ("he" or "she") or the first person ("I"). Professional writers may tell another's story in the first person under an "as-told-to" by-line or under the subject's by-line. Whatever the wording, personal experience stories are always written from a protagonist's point of view (see chapter 7).

Reader's Digest senior editor Phil Osborne has said that his magazine likes simple adventure stories about ordinary people involved in life-threatening situations. The tale unfolds moment by moment. The writer should detail the victim's physical and emotional ordeal and end with "a ringing quote or message." Third person is best and suspense is critical.

Human-interest stories are so important to women's magazines that they make a relatively easy way to break in. Editors in this market will work with less-than perfect writers who present solid ideas. Diane Brown of *Good Housekeeping* says she wants personal experience stories that are newsworthy or issue-oriented. The issue-oriented piece focuses on the experience of a person involved in some national event or issue. *Good Housekeeping* ran a story about a woman who had been raped by her gynecologist, for example, at a time when assaults by doctors were in the news.

Also common in women's magazines is the "my problem and how I solved it" piece. Such stories usually deal with contemporary family relationships, and they confront a problem whose solution is preferably not a psychiatrist.

Medical personal-experience stories are popular, especially when they involve children. Typically, a person pulls through against great odds or is the subject of some new procedure.

Whatever the approach, the writer must always focus on the emotional and human angle. While these articles are "personal," they appeal to universal feelings; they are never so personal that they don't speak to every reader.

One student, for example, wrote a superb story about her struggle to get medical help for her deaf daughter in a tiny rural community where incompetent public-health practitioners refused to recognize that the child had a problem. She had to rework the story three times before she could transcend her own rage over the neglect the family suffered. By the time she finished, however, she had a moving article that appealed to any parent's sense of protectiveness, to the universal tendency to blame oneself for whatever harm comes to one's babies, and to the joy of seeing a child overcome a setback.

Personal experience stories follow a typical format. The first few paragraphs establish a conflict. As we saw in chapter 7, this conflict may occur between two or more people, between a person and an animal or Nature, or as an interior, psychological struggle. The conflict builds to a crisis. At this point, the protagonist—the person whose story you're telling—recognizes the problem. He takes some steps to help himself, and, as a dénouement, things start to get better.

Tales such as the ones that appear in Reader's Digest's "Drama in Real Life" department seem so startling that one might expect to encounter no more than one such story in a lifetime of writing. But they're commonplace. Watch local newspapers for reports of people who survive perilous misadventures. Over a few months in my region, for example, two women made a wrong turn and were stranded in snow for ten days—they escaped when snowmobilers ran across their buried car; a Boy Scout troop was rescued from bad weather in rugged terrain through the sensible and brave actions of their leaders; a hiker who fell from a remote trail was airlifted off the side of a cliff; a woman helped arrest a man given to raping real-estate agents; a man rescued a wheelchair-bound invalid from a trailer fire. These small dramas rarely make the wire services. National magazine editors rely on writers around the country to report them.

NIGHTMARE HUNT

by Marguerite Reiss

Reader's Digest, June 1986; condensed from *Outdoor Life* ("Bear Attack," November 1985)

Darrel Rosin and Rollin Braden pushed through the high brush along the path leading to the cabin and dinner. "Thought you told me I'd see some bears," Darrel chided his friend. "Seen plenty of moose in the last two weeks, but not a sign of a bear."

And just as well, Rollin thought. They were in bear country all right—the thick brush and tundra bogs of southern Alaska, 125 miles south of Anchorage and 50 miles south of Soldotna, where Darell, 32, and Rollin, 29, live. It was mid-September 1984, and Rollin knew that at this time of year Alaskan brown bears forage intensely before holing up for winter. Rollin didn't relish crossing tracks with one. But right now he had other things on his mind. It was the tag end of the hunting season, and Rollin, the owner of a small auto-parts company, still had not bagged a moose. Darrel had his. So did Rollin's brother, Wayne, and their father, Wes, who were at the cabin, a half-mile up the trail.

Suddenly Rollin sensed something. But the only sound he heard was a faint breeze riffling through the tall stands of spruce. Then there was a rustle in the brush 100 feet behind him.

"Hey," Darrel said quietly. "It's your moose."

"About time," Rollin answered. "I'm heading back to meet him."

"Okay," Darrell said. "Just shout 'yee ha' when you bag him."

Rollin picked his way toward the sound. Before long, he was 300 yards into the woods, then 400 yards. A chill rippled through his body. He knew that whatever animal he had heard probably was watching him right now.

A branch snapped off to his right, then another—louder and closer. As Rollin's grip tightened on his rifle, it happened. From 40 feet away, two huge Alaskan brown bears came hurtling toward him, growling, their dark faces full of anger. He guessed they were seven feet tall, maybe 400 pounds each.

"Y-e-e-o-o-w!" Rollin yelled, waving his arms to frighten them off. Their immense jaws opened wide, and he could see their massive fangs. Rollin fired his rifle from the waist, but the bullet pinged into a tree. Bear claws slashed through the air. With no time to run or reload, Rollin dropped his rifle and shielded his eyes with his hands.

Two heavy blows knocked him to the ground. A monstrous weight bore down on his back. Instinctively, Rollin thrashed his arms and legs to ward off the blows. He could hear guttural sounds and smell the heavy, foul breath of one of the bears. A searing pain shot through the side of his head. *Oh no!* he screamed inwardly. *My ear. The bear's chewing my ear!*

The best defense after a bear has attacked, he remembered, is to play dead. That way, the animal, no longer feeling its territory threatened, might lose interest. *Lie perfectly still,* Rollin ordered himself. *But dear God, how?* He could hear the tearing of flesh from the side of his head. He jammed his thumbs deep into the earth to keep from crying out. Needles of pain tore at his buttocks and up and down his spine. His body went limp. *Mustn't move. No matter what!*

Lead introduces the main character and sets the scene.

Throughout the story, Reiss traces what goes on in Rollin's mind.

Note the specific details. Also notice the high ratio of action verbs (pushed, chided, thought, knew, forage, relish) to verbs of being.

Foreshadowing.

Dialogue helps characterize the men.

Suspense builds rapidly as the story moves toward its dramatic conflict.

Minute-by-minute detailing of Rollin's physical and emotional state as the action moves forward.

"He guessed": the action seen through his eyes.

Not a single verb of being appears in these two grafs. The language *shows* what Rollin sees, hears, smells, feels.

This is one of the few places where many adjectives and adverbs appear. Note the care with which they are used.

Again, minute-by-minute narration of the action and what passes through Rollin's mind. Note that Rollin is doing something to

Rollin thought of his two children back in Soldotna with their mother. The divorce had become final a week before, and Rollin had planned this trip to get away from it all. *Now this,* he thought. *Please, God, let me see Max and Melinda again.* Seven-year-old Max, with those playful green eyes, and sweet Melinda, three. Rollin pictured them, here in these woods with him only two months before. The three had come to gather cranberries with Rollin's fiancée, Kathy, and her six-year-old son, Nathan, but the bushes had already been picked by bears.

Shooting pains jerked Rollin back to reality. As the bears tried to get a better grip on his neck, he bit deep into the cold, damp earth. Now one bear was clawing at his back while the other gnawed at his skull. A brief pause. Then Rollin heard the creatures shuffling around. *Dear heaven,* he realized. *They've changed places!* Rollin could not feel the pain anymore. *So this is what death is like. Please end it fast.*

Abruptly the pummeling and chewing stopped. Rollin could hear the bears nearby, panting heavily, resting from their labors. His head, back and leg throbbed. He fought against gagging on the blood, grass and moss that filled his throat. If he blacked out, Rollin knew his muscles might go into spasm. That could bring another attack.

As the seconds ticked by, he waited, motionless. Bears have been known to begin eating a moose immediately after the kill. But they are more likely to cover their prey with leaves and twigs and wait until later. *My only hope,* Rollin thought.

The heavy panting subsided. *Are they gone?* Slowly he turned his head and squinted into the pale twilight. The bears were there, not six yards away, their small, piglike eyes glaring at him, their jaws dripping and bloored. Seeing him move, they bellowed and lunged furiously, ripping at the loose flesh along the back of his skull. *Oh no! Not again!*

Rollin struggled against the white-hot pain. *Keep still as death. . . . Still as death.* He repeated the phrase over and over. The bears were now tearing at the soft skin along the side of his stomach. Rollin felt himself slipping away. *Can't hold on . . . much longer.*

The silence seeped into Rollin's awareness. No more slurping, grunting, crunching. Only dead quiet. His blood-soaked body seemed glued to the earth. A kind of inner peace took hold, giving him courage to lift his head.

The bears were gone. But were they lurking nearby, preparing to charge again? Rollin knew he couldn't survive another mauling. Somehow he had to find the strength to get away before they returned. He struggled to his feet. *Thank God! At least my legs still work.* As he lifted a hand to his head, his fingers slid under his warm, soggy scalp as if it were a hat. Holding the scalp in place with one hand, he used the other to unbutton and pull off his wool shirt. Then he wrapped the shirt around his head to hold the scalp in place.

He knew the cabin was only a half-mile away. But which direction? "Help," he called weakly. Then, taking a deep breath, louder: "D-a-r-r-e-l! H-e-l-p!" Slowly at first, then faster, he started loping toward the spot where he had last seen Darrel. Rollin heard something. *The bears?* He froze, afraid to yell again. Then he heard a voice: "I'm coming!"

Darrel broke through the trees. At the sight of Rollin, he went white. "Just hold on," Darrel urged, throwing an arm around his friend. For Rollin, every step took enormous effort. It was almost dark when they finally made it to the cabin.

Working swiftly, Darrel wrapped a towel around Rollin's forehead to keep the oozing blood out of his eyes. Wes cleaned his son's face and body. He couldn't believe what he saw. The entire back of Rollin's head, ear to ear, had been opened and lifted. The scalp was falling to the front like a slipped wig. Large pieces of skull showed through the openings. His back and legs were covered with deep gashes. The bears' teeth had chewed more than three inches into his buttocks.

"You can make it, boy," his father told him. "But you gotta fight. We have a long way to go." It was six bumpy miles in an all-terrain vehicle to their pickup truck, then back to Soldotna, where they would charter a plane to Providence Hospital in Anchorage.

But nothing went right. The pickup had a flat tire. After changing it, they raced to Soldotna, only to find they would have to order a charter plane out of Anchorage. It wasn't until 3 a.m. that Rollin finally arrived at the hospital, nearly eight hours after the attack.

Rollin was in the operating room for five hours. He had lost three quarts of blood, roughly half the body's normal supply. It took more than 200 stitches to close all his injuries. Dr. James Scully, Rollin's surgeon, was surprised anyone could have survived such wounds.

Rollin spent eight days in the hospital, including two in intensive care. Today he is fully recovered—and a different man, he feels, from the one who went hunting that fateful day in 1984.

He realized this last fall when he went after moose again with Darrel, Wayne and Wes in the same area where the attack had taken place. But this time, for protection from bears, each hunter built a platform in trees overlooking a large clearing.

Rollin was on his platform when he heard a bear grunting nearby. "Right then," he says, "the memory of the attack came rushing back, and I started shaking uncontrollably." The shaking subsided only when Rollin realized he was safe and had the upper hand.

"On that other hunt I got myself into a situation I shouldn't have," he says now. "And that's the key thing I learned from all this: no matter what, keep in control. This goes not only for hunting. It goes for everything else in your life."

In a few minutes, the still-unseen bear wandered by. By then, Rollin was no longer afraid.

Side notes:

From this point on, we are in the dénouement—what happens after the main dramatic action. The moment-by-moment narrative stops, replaced by a summary style.

Personal experience stories typically show how an event changed an individual's life.

Cliché.

The story ends with a ringing quote *and* a message. The final quote is chronologically out of synch. To here, the narrative relates an anecdote that took place some time before; then it jumps to "now;" then back to an earlier time. Possibly more effective to reverse the two final grafs.

EDITORIAL OVERVIEW

"Nightmare Hunt" exemplifies most of what we discussed in the first few chapters of this book. The spare, tight writing uses literary devices that serve both nonfiction and fiction, and its structure, a conflict rising toward a climax and then falling off in a dénouement, mirrors the classic fictional plot.

The narrative is dense with specific facts: each sentence carries its weight in information. All those details represent the payoff of careful, intense interviewing, close observation, and accurate research. Typical of stories edited for *Reader's Digest*, the piece is melodramatic but clear of fat and froth—it contains no unnecessary words.

–30–

18

How-to Stories

The cover lines on a single issue of *Redbook* trumpet six stories:

Easy to Mix & Match Clothes with Workday Class
Keep Your Weight Down, Energy Up: The Best Diet for Busy Bodies
Cut Clutter: Closet Makeovers to Make Space Fast
Saucey! 30-Minute Skillet-Pasta Dinners
Sex and the Worried Man: How His Secret Fears Can Come between You
"Because I Said So" . . . The 9 Worst Discipline Mistakes Even the Best Parents Make

Of these, five are how-to-do-it stories and one is a fashion spread with a how-to twist. "Sex and the Worried Man" is a report.

How-to pieces are the stuff of women's and lifestyle magazines ("15 Make-Ahead Gifts!" "Problem-Solving Furniture Arrangements"; "Step-by-Step Microwave Main Dishes"; "Build a Playhouse Bunk Bed for Kids"; "Strengthen Your Immune System"; "Talking to Kids about Drugs"). But business, technical, and men's magazines are also full of them ("Your Money: The Art of Speculation"; "Tips for Late-Season Whitetail and Mule Deer"; "Great Ways to Recycle Your First Computer"). City and regional magazines, with their gardening columns and home improvement stories, often use them, too.

The market for this dreary reading matter is vast. Such stories appear most frequently in magazines whose audience reads more for short doses of pragmatic information than for pleasure, a group that may very well include most of the American public.

One sub-species is the recipe or simple crafts guide. Usually such stories, if they can even be called that, first list the ingredients or materials and tools needed, and then explain step by step how to combine these items. A series of recipes may be linked to form a larger story, with a frothy lead and sometimes a one- or two-sentence windup (*Sunset* often runs such pieces; a recent one is titled "Having Fun with Peanut Butter, for Lunch or Breakfast").

This type of article, which boils down to a step-by-step guide to some project, is invariably organized in chronological order: first *a*, then *b*, then *c*. For the beginning writer, a serious stumbling block in how-to stories is the deceptive simplicity of this structure. What seems obvious to someone who has already done a project may confuse the reader if a step is overlooked or a term undefined.

Keep in mind that many cooking or crafts terms are unfamiliar to readers new to the subject. Suppose, for example, you are explaining how to lay a brick-on-sand patio. You write, "Prepare a smooth sand surface."

Your reader, who was five years old when she last played with sand, wonders *how*. You must explain how to level the grade beneath the sand, how deep the sand should be, how to mark out a work area with stakes and twine, how to use a level—and you will have to define terms such as *screed* and *header*.

Even everyday terms, when used in an unusually precise way, may puzzle readers. What does *braise* mean? Most publications avoid such words, instead briefly describing the process: "Cook the meat in oil over high heat until browned. Add vegetables, broth, and wine and simmer over low heat for 45 minutes."

How-to stories must be meticulously organized; it's easy to forget a step that seems too obvious to mention. When you have finished a draft, read the story carefully to be sure each step follows logically and in the correct order, and that no details have been omitted.

A popular variation on the how-to is what I call the "Ten Tips for Success" piece. The number need not be ten: it can range from five to twenty. The idea is to come up with staccato bursts of helpful information on the same subject: "Nine Ways to Enhance Inexpensive Fabric for Interior Decorating"; "Six Tips for Achieving a Better Complexion"; "Seven Ways to Turn a TV Kid on to Reading"; "Ten Fashion Do's and Don'ts."

Such stories are organized in a series of self-contained paragraphs, each with a short, bold-face lead sentence summarizing the "tip" in a nutshell. In the TV-kid story, for example, *McCall's* department editor Maureen Smith Williams elaborated on these helpful hints:

Read aloud
Set a good example
Don't turn leisure reading into a chore
Limit your child's TV time, and use TV as a point of departure for reading
Make reading a special privilege
Create a reading nook
Join your local public library

She devoted no more than two paragraphs to each precept. The copy for these stories must be kept short, bright, and clear; when appropriate, the "tips" should appear in chronological order.

How-to stories, however, can take a much more sophisticated form. They may appear as serious discussions of challenging problems likely to affect the reader. *Savvy*, for example, has a department called "Tools of the Trade," which offers detailed, thoughtful approaches to situations female middle-managers encounter at the office.

These pieces are organized in the classic manner of the feature article: an arresting lead, a logically ordered body based on interviews and solid research, and a satisfying wrap-up. When possible, the facts are presented in chronological order, because a how-to story consists of a series of steps that build on each other.

The following selection from *Money* opened a special section that won the 1988 National Magazine Award for personal service stories. It amounts to a how-to piece. We include a *sidebar*, which also plainly exemplifies the subgenre.

AFTER THE CRASH: ANSWERS TO ALL YOUR QUESTIONS

by Diane Harris

Money, December 1987

Lead: a rather dry reprise of the market crash, no doubt a subject of riveting interest to *Money's* readers.

In the long run, October's unprecedented stock market collapse could prove to be a perverse blessing. A number of respected economists, including former Federal Reserve Board chief Paul Volcker, argue that the stunning loss of some $500 billion in equity values in a single day may expunge speculative excess from the overblown markets, thereby paving the way for more realistic gains next year. Interest and inflation rates, which had been rising, suddenly reversed course to provide another long-term plus for the financial markets. And politicians, shocked by the looming threat of recession, are finally talking seriously about extraordinary efforts to cut the massive budget and trade deficits—the two problems that had long threatened to topple the prosperous-looking house of cards that Reaganomics built. "This is no time to be morose," says Henry de Vismes, a director of Kleinwort Benson International, a London investment firm. "In retrospect, the crash may be the best thing that could have happened to the U.S. economy."

Perhaps. But the cloud cast by that blackest of Mondays is still awfully dark. Some six weeks after the fact, only one conclusion can be drawn with certainty: the historic 26% two-day drop in stock prices in mid-October and the wild market gyrations that followed raise profound questions about your personal finances that this special report endeavors to answer. Among them: Will you have to revamp investment strategies and re-allocate assets? Should you alter your plans for retirement? Will the crash affect your spending and saving?

Bridge: What does it mean to *you*? This article will present some economic forecasts and advise readers how to handle their investments in the aftermath of the crash.

The magnitude of the market crash makes accurate predictions about its repercussions nearly impossible. Of past declines, only the 23% two-day fall in October 1929 came close in size. And everybody knows what followed that one. Not that most forecasters are saying there will be a repeat of the Great Depression—slower economic growth certainly, as anxious consumers cut their spending; recession possibly, but not outright financial catastrophe. Yet with economists confessing lack of faith in their own forecasts, the consensus view is not terribly reassuring. Atlanta resident Yvette Greune, a caterer whose mutual funds have lost 20% of their value since early October, spoke for many when she said: "What scares me most is that nobody seems to know what's coming next."

Uncertainty about crash effects. Quotes a person typical of *Money*'s readers.

A few lonely bulls still insist that the primary trend in stock prices is up and that the October massacre was nothing more than a dramatic correction in the most powerful advance in postwar history. But by the widely accepted definition of a bear market—a drop of more than 20%—this one growled like a genuine grizzly. Despite the partial comeback in prices since mid-October, the Dow Jones industrial average remains 28% below its August peak of 2722. Moreover, the momentum of the market, a broad measure of the direction of stock prices, still shows declining issues outpacing advancing ones by nearly 2 to 1.

Describes post-crash conditions.

Just how long it will be before equities can mount a lasting recovery depends, of course, on the economy. In agreement with most other forecasters, Allen Sinai, chief economist at Shearson Lehman Bros., estimates that the gross national product will grow by a sluggish 1.5% to 2% in 1988, 1.5 percentage points less than had been expected before the crash. He also expects inflation to run 3.5% to 4% next year, down one percentage point from pre-crash forecasts. Interest rates, which were expected to rise modestly next year, are now more likely to fall by one percentage point, as consumer spending and borrowing moderate. With U.S. officials no longer trying to prop up the dollar through higher interest rates, the trade deficit may begin to shrink as the weakening greenback increases demand for American goods abroad by lowering their cost.

Cites a believable source making a modestly positive prediction.

But economists cannot rule out the possibility that the downturn could deepen into a recession—two or more consecutive quarters of negative economic growth. The odds on Wall Street of recession next year are as high as 3 to 1. After all, the stock market is a reasonably reliable leading economic indicator. Of the 13 substantive declines in stock prices in the

Brings up the specter of recession.

postwar period, eight have been followed by a recession. Moreover, market declines as large as the one from August through October have *always* resulted in recession. Yet many economists aren't convinced that a recession looms in 1988. "It's not a done deal yet," says Robert Brusca, chief economist of Nikko Securities International, a brokerage firm. "The policy-makers still have it in their power to change the economic outcome."

For investors, the difference between sluggish growth and recession adds up to a lot of money. If the economy keeps expanding, even slightly, the worst of this market turn may already be behind us. Although most securities analysts believe that stock prices will remain well below their August peaks for the foreseeable future, the steady if smaller increases in corporate profits anticipated under a slow-growth scenario would probably stop prices from falling much below their October lows. But severe ongoing bear markets always accompany the first stages of recession. During the 1973–74 economic slump, for example, the Dow dropped 45% over a period of 23 months. If the current market follows that pattern, within the next 18 months or so the Dow would hit bottom around 1500—13.7% below Black Monday levels and some 25% off recent prices. The average record of postwar bear markets: a 31% decline over a 15–month period. Even after the bear retreats, the suffering is not over. According to a study by Yale professor of finance Roger Ibbotson, investors who held on to their stocks in bear markets since World War II have had to wait from 14 to 42 months just to break even.

Forecasters' lack of faith in their current economic predictions—about the direction of interest rates, inflation, and especially about the likelihood of recession—suggests that you may want to do your own sleuthing in coming months to determine the direction of the economy and the financial markets. Among the indicators to watch for in the press:

Retail sales. Consumer spending is crucial to economic growth. Reports on retail sales, released in the middle of every month by the U.S. Commerce Department, will flash early warnings of consumer retrenchment. A decline of about 1% for at least two to three months running would indicate a significant slowdown on consumer purchasing; repeated drops of 2% or more over the same period could signal recession.

Orders for business plant and equipment. Corporate planners anxious about a downturn tend to cut back on capital spending to shore up the bottom line. In fact, business investment has already fallen by one-half of one percentage point in the third quarter, according to the Commerce Department's quarterly reports on orders for plant and equipment. The next report is due out in mid-December. Progressively larger declines could be a clue that corporate executives smell recession in the air. If so, you should too.

The federal funds and discount rates. The federal funds rate (the interest rate charged by Federal Reserve banks to banks borrowing funds overnight) is the most sensitive indicator of the future direction of interest rates because it is set daily according to market conditions. The federal funds rate has been falling since Black Monday, indicating less fear of inflation. Announcement of a cut in the discount rate (the rate the Fed charges member banks for longer-term loans) would confirm a downward rate trend.

The financial markets. Lower interest rates and reduced risk of inflation are good news for stock and bond prices. While percentage changes in major market indexes such as the Dow reflect the general direction of stock prices,

Quotes another expert.

Immediate implications for small investors: at least two divergent possibilities.

Transition to how to read economic indicators in coming months.

Four things to watch.

they can sometimes be misleading because of the limited number of companies represented. For the big picture, turn to two measures of market breadth—the number of advancing stocks vs. declining issues and the number of shares hitting new highs vs. those dropping to new lows. Successive weeks of contraction in the number of issues rising in price and reaching new highs relative to the number that are declining or falling to new lows is a sign of basic market weakness.

Be prepared for a blurry picture. Harbingers of recession or resurgence, while useful tools, nearly always flash confusing signals at first. Some forecasters believe, for example, that a few months may pass before consumers respond fully to the stock market's decline. Retail sales during the 1929 Christmas season, they point out, were robust—hardly a prescient warning of the tight money, failed banks and 25% unemployment that followed.

Disclaimer: these indicators may prove nothing.

You needn't—indeed, shouldn't—wait until you are sure where the evidence is pointing before making some cautious, reasoned adjustments to your portfolio. Whether the economy tumbles into recession or rebounds smartly, one underlying investment theme is clear, the very uncertainty of the outlook combined with the recent violent market moves dictates a shift from aggressive strategies that strive for maximum gains to defensive maneuvers that protect your capital. "What happened in October is the financial equivalent of an earthquake, and we still don't know what the aftershocks may be," warns investment adviser Richard Young, author of *Financial Armadillo Strategy* (William Morrow, $17.95). "This is no time to compromise on safety."

Transition to advice on active steps the reader may take.

Leading investment strategists recommend several specific moves:

1. Regard market rallies as opportunities to dump your riskiest stock. Even analysts who were superbullish before the crash now say that the prospects are slim for a sustained surge. For example, Prudential-Bache analyst Joseph Feshbach, who predicted that "it's clear sailing to a 3500 Dow" next year in *MONEY's* October issue, now agrees with consensus forecasts suggesting that the index will trade between the low 1700s and 2200 over the next six months. The prime candidates for sale are volatile stocks that typically rise or fall more than the market average and issues with lofty price-to-earnings ratios of 20 or higher, vs. a recent P/E of 14 for the market overall. From October 1 through 19, when the market P/E averaged 18, the 20% of stocks with the highest multiple—27 and above—fell 15% more than the average issue.

Five helpful hints. Explains in clear language what to do and why. Here and there, the editors sprinkle in a comment from an expert.

2. Park 50% to 75% of the cash you get from selling stock. If there's a recession, cash investments, such as CDs or money-market accounts, may give you the safest and greatest return on your money. And if both the economy and stock prices confound the experts by recovering quickly, you will have the cash on hand to move swiftly back into the market.

3. Invest the rest of the cash from stock sales in high-quality bonds. If interest rates continue to fall, as experts expect, your bonds will increase in value. And if rates reverse course, the interest from top-grade issues will provide you with a safe income. You might also consider putting 5% to 10% of your money into gold as a hedge against inflation, though that investment is becoming increasingly risky.

4. Don't sell stocks that are fundamentally sound unless you really need to do it. It's only human to panic when all those around you are stampeding for the exits. But fight the urge. The time to sell shares is when prices are rising; selling into a decline only turns your paper losses into real ones. "View your high-quality stocks as long-term holdings," advises William Melton, chief economist of IDS Financial Services in Minneapolis. "Don't be panicked into selling good companies at bad prices."

5. Reassess the way your retirement funds are invested. Start with the money that you and your employer contribute to company-sponsored retirement accounts, such as a profit-sharing, thrift or 401(k) plan. Typically these plans allow you to choose the mix of investments in your account periodically from among a stock fund, fixed-income fund, money-market fund or shares in your company's stock. How much you may already have been hurt by falling stock prices depends on the choice you made. Overall, these plans fell about 15% in value from the August market peak to early November, according to the nonprofit Employee Benefit Research Institute in Washington, D.C. The losses in accounts that were fully invested in stocks, however, averaged 26%.

What to do or not to do with retirement funds, and why.

If you have sustained losses of that magnitude, your first instinct may be to run for cover by shifting all your money to fixed-income investments as soon as you can. But don't rush to that decision. While diversifying into nonequity investments will enhance the safety of your account, the best balance of risk and reward requires more thought. If you are at least a decade away from retirement, you are better off sticking mainly with stocks, advises Paul Westbrook, a financial planner in Watchung, N.J. Over a 10-year period, equities will usually outperform fixed-income funds by an average of 6% to 7% a year, and thus allow you to recoup your current losses. If you are less than 10 years away from retiring, focus on preserving your capital by shifting 40% to 80% of your money into your plan's fixed-income or money-market fund. And if you are within two to four years of retirement, put the entire amount into cash as soon as you can. Short term, Westbrook says, "the chances of making back what you have already lost in stocks in a bear market is about zero."

Other aftereffects of the crash.

The problems that investors are grappling with in the aftermath of the market crash are not limited to financial losses alone. If you tried to trade stock or get professional advice during the hellish week that began on October 19, you may also be struggling with a loss of confidence in brokerages and mutual fund companies. Although most people who sought help got it, complaints against brokerages and mutual fund firms doubled during the frantic trading days that followed Black Monday, according to Bonnie Westbrook, director of the Securities and Exchange Commission's Office of Consumer Affairs. The most common grievances: an inability to reach brokers, especially discounters, by telephone to place orders; delays in mutual fund redemptions; and difficulty in learning whether trades ordered had been executed and at what prices.

To be fair, no one could reasonably have expected brokers and mutual fund companies to handle the stupefying volume of trades that week without a glitch. But it is hard to accept big glitches that cost you big bucks. Some investors may conclude that the low fees charged by discounters and no-load fund companies—the two sectors of the industry that provoked the most ire—are no longer a compelling reason to do business with them. "Over the past five years, investors were conditioned to a long-term bull market and thought they could do it all themselves," says James Stack, editor of the newsletter *Investech Market Analyst* (2472 Birch Glen, Whitefish, Mont. 59937; 18 times annually, $150 a year), who believes that full-service brokers will be the principal beneficiaries of the market chaos.

"Now that they've learned differently, investors are not likely to shun the need for investment advice anymore."

Beyond all, the lasting lesson of the worst week in financial history could well be a renewed appreciation of the risks inherent in investing—and a greater respect for the strategies that help to reduce them: Thinking long term. Diversifying your portfolio. Dollar-cost averaging. Taking capital gains after major price advances instead of getting greedy and going for that last elusive buck. Says Robert Edwards, director of education services for the American Association of Individual Investors: "If the crash teaches people to concentrate on the risks as well as the potential rewards of their investments, maybe it wasn't a complete disaster."

Wrap: reprise of lessons to be learned.

WHAT TO DO ABOUT YOUR FINANCES NOW.

Sidebar

The stock market crash calls for a reassessment of all your personal finances, not merely your investments. For example, now that an economic downturn appears more imminent than before, you need a more cautious attitude toward debt. If the crash caused you to sell stock or mutual fund shares, you must take a fresh look at your 1987 tax bill and plot appropriate strategies. Crash-induced drops in mortgage rates and weaker real estate markets have created opportunities for some home buyers. You may also need to change the way you save for retirement and for your child's college education. Here's what to do now:

The *lead* puffs a little to introduce four more helpful hints.

Your Debt

Refrain from unnecessary borrowing. Graydon Calder, a San Diego financial planner, says that with tougher times ahead, you may need a larger cash reserve, especially if you lose your job or must take a pay cut. Try to pay down your credit-card balances too. Rather than sending Visa or MasterCard a monthly check of say, $300 on your balance, pay $400.

The 1986 income tax law provides added incentive to reduce your debt load in 1988. Only 40% of interest on consumer loans and credit cards will be tax deductible next year, down from 65% this year. In 1989, a scant 20% will be.

Solid facts

Your House

"The next few months may well provide a welcome opportunity for first-time home buyers and homeowners interested in trading up," says John Tuccillo, chief economist at the National Association of Realtors. That is because the October crash led to lower mortgage rates. A pre-crash 11.5% 30–year fixed-rate loan is now only around 10.75%, and adjustable rates dropped from roughly 9% to 8.5%. Take a fresh look at your ability to come up with a down payment, however. If you had planned to use stock or mutual fund proceeds, you now have less cash to tap.

More facts and what they mean to the reader.

On the other hand, homeowners may suffer. Assuming the market crash slows the economy enough to lower the inflation rate, chances are the value of your home will level off. Economists at the National Association of Home Builders now expect resale house prices to rise about 7% in 1988, roughly one percentage point less than they had forecast before stocks plunged.

Believable source prognosticates.

Houses in financial centers may be hit the most as area brokerages and banks cut back. Some prices in New York City and Chicago have already plateaued.

Your Retirement

Many people, such as Mary Boulay, 57, the Eden Prairie, Minn., widow shown on the cover, are worried about whether the stock market collapse will reduce their retirement funds. Their concern seems overdone. In all likelihood, you may not need to change your retirement strategies as much as you think. If you are either retired or still working and are covered by a traditional pension plan, there is little to worry about. According to the Employee Benefit Research Institute, such defined-benefit plans—ones that pay a preset amount at retirement—had built up a surplus of more than

$450 billion in late August 1987. The plans lost about $200 billion during September and October, leaving most still well funded. In addition, about 90% of defined-benefit pension benefits are guaranteed up to $22,295 this year by the Pension Benefit Guaranty Corporation, a federal agency.

You may need to save more than before the crash, however, if you expect to retire on proceeds from a company savings or profit-sharing plan that accepts employee contributions, Keoghs or Individual Retirement Accounts invested in stocks. None of these plans that invested in stocks are federally guaranteed, and many lost 20% to 30% of their value this fall. Conventional pension plans of professional service employers, such as doctors and lawyers, with fewer than 25 employees, are also not guaranteed.

You can safeguard your retirement by diversifying the investments you earmarked for it. Most businesses with company savings plans let an employee choose once a quarter whether his funds will invest in stocks, money-market securities or bonds.

If your only savings plan invests solely in the company's stock, you must diversify your investments for retirement on your own. One idea is to force yourself to save by opening an IRA, even if you are not eligible for a tax deduction.

Your Child's Education

As the crash demonstrated, if you are a parent with a college-bound teenager, it is unwise to plan to pay tuition bills solely with stock proceeds. History shows that since World War II the chances of encountering a bull market in any five-year period have been very good, but not so for shorter periods.

If your child will enroll in college within five years, buy Treasury bonds or corporate or municipal bonds (rated at least an A in quality by Standard & Poor's) whose maturity dates will coincide with his high school graduation. This way, you will know in advance exactly how much income and appreciation the bonds will provide between now and college. Zero-coupon corporate and Treasury bonds do not pay interest until the bonds mature. But their accrued interest is taxable each year.

Parents who have children about 13 years old or younger should still buy stock or stock mutual funds to help pay for college. You and your younger children can wait out a poor market. Growth stocks and funds will be lightly taxed too, because they probably will not pay out much in taxable dividend income.

—*Jersey Gilbert and Lisa Shea*

EDITORIAL OVERVIEW

Even though this article and sidebar helped *Money* win a major editorial award, I find the prose about as exciting as a dust mouse. The dull leads, terms like "ongoing" and "house of cards," and the overall effect of uncertain hedging mark the copy as the product of a committee—it probably was edited into the ground.

Nevertheless, the two stories have a single sterling quality: solid research. Harris, Gilbert, and Shea cite nine experts in the rather short article and four in the sidebar; they also manage to quote a couple of worried persons-on-the-street.

Armed with evident expertise and plenty of information, *Money* dares to tackle as complex a problem as human society has yet invented: the vagaries of the stock market. Boiling the difficult questions posed by the 1987 crash down to a few thousand words— easily understood words, if dry—is quite an achievement.

The main story follows a typical feature format: lead, bridge, body with strong transitions, wrap-up. How-to stories often provide considerable background, as this one does, before they get to the list of helpful hints. Here, we have two sets of steps the reader can take: the first amounts to advice on how to interpret certain economic indicators; and the second offers specific advice on what to do next. The article helps readers make sense of the crisis by explaining not only what to do but why.

This story and the section it introduces provide useful information, clearly presented. It undoubtedly performs a public service. And it shows you don't have to write like John McPhee to win journalism awards.

–30–

19

Travel Stories

Travel writing looks easier than it is. Students often think they can whip up a "how-I-spent-my-summer-vacation" essay and sell it to *Connoisseur* for a quick $500.

Not so. Travel articles make the same demands of writers as any other kind of feature: strong lead; crisp, tight writing; careful organization; and a decent wrap-up.

In addition, good travel writing is extremely detailed. It is not enough to say a scene is "beautiful" or a hotel is "gracious." You must tell what specific attributes make for beauty or grace, in a convincing way free of purple prose. With effective description must come a strong grasp of the practicalities: directions, distances, costs, transportation, accommodations, and even the weather.

Travel stories occur in two varieties. There are *destination pieces*, in which you describe a specific place to stay, be it a five-star resort or a homey bed-and-breakfast. These commonly appear in such magazines as *Travel and Leisure* and *European Travel and Life* and on newspaper travel pages. Less narrowly focused is the type we will call *regional stories*, overviews of an an entire vacation setting. You often see these stories in *National Geographic Traveler*, *Travel-Holiday*, and airline magazines.

As important as description and reporting are, the best travel articles go beyond setting to mention local history and bring an individual perspective into the picture. You will notice, for example, that almost every story in *National Geographic Traveler* is written in the first person. Travel articles in the *New York Times*, often done by prominent writers, narrate the details from the observer's point of view.

Travel writing, particularly the destination piece, often raises ethical questions. Hotel and restaurant proprietors, business groups, and others interested in good press regularly offer writers free trips, accommodations, and meals—just trying to be polite; never meaning to influence your judgment.

It would be hypocritical to tell you to refuse these opportunities, because they are commonplace. I once worked on a magazine whose management expected the monthly travel columnist to take every perk that came along. Indeed, the choice of destinations for that department often depended on which resort would put up the writer and her husband for a weekend.

However, if you *must* accept blandishments, do refrain from calling yourself a journalist. What you are writing in such cases is not journalism but extremely low-paid public relations.

Better publications ask writers either not to reveal their purpose until they have a chance to observe the scene, or to identify themselves as reporters but firmly decline gifts.

Rarely will you see a story that pans a resort or hotel. What if you cannot in good conscience recommend a place? First, try to avoid writing about it: tell your editor that a puff piece surely will elicit complaints from disappointed readers. If, as a staff writer, you are assigned to cover an unsatisfactory hotel, resort, or restaurant, be frank without doing a hatchet job. If service or accommodations are poor, say so and say why. Balance these reports with whatever saving graces you can find.

THE ARIZONA STRIP OF CLARENCE DUTTON

by Page Stegner

Arizona Highways, September 1988

How many times have we driven this road? How many river trips over the last 10 years have washed us out somewhere in the vicinity of Four Corners, only to be confronted once again with the realization that the quickest way west and home starts out southward? South out of Utah to Page, Arizona, and on toward the Arizona Strip through a slot in the Echo Cliffs; across Navajo Bridge at Marble Canyon and along the foot of the Vermilion Cliffs, then over the Kaibab Plateau to the little town of Fredonia; over the northern extension of the Kanab and Uinkaret plateaus toward the valley of the Virgin River. Off the Arizona Strip to accelerate madly on to St. George, Utah, Littlefield, Arizona, and Mesquite, Nevada. On to Las

— Leads with several rhetorical questions.

Specific detail: not just "across the Arizona Strip," but where and what specifically. Catalog of place names gives a poetic ring —Quivira, Cibola, and El

Dorado have historic and mythic significance; others are evocative.

Summary statement or "nut graf": the reader will join Page and Lynn Stegner on a sightseeing journey across some exotic terrain.

Geographic description of wide-open spaces; again, very specific. This story weaves a great deal of fact into a narrative about an automobile trip.

Specifics.

Mentions an environmental controversy.

Literary allusion. Draws our attention to a rarely read writer.

Quotes Dutton.

Description and narrative.

Vegas and a different sort of strip. Out across the great Mojave Desert to Quivira, Cibola, El Dorado.

What, we always wonder afterward, was the hurry?

This time it's going to be different, my wife, Lynn, insists. We are going to stop. We are going to wander. We are going to peer into the "great arroyo" (as the first Spanish explorers called the Grand Canyon) from vantage points heretofore unvisited. Or at least less visited.

Except for the highway route described above, and a spur road across the Kaibab Plateau from Jacob Lake to the Grand Canyon's North Rim, there isn't much pavement on the Arizona Strip—that part of the state lying north of the Colorado River. Bounded on the east by the Echo Cliffs and on the west by the Virgin Mountains, the area is in great part roadless, or traversed by dirt tracks that often resemble goat trails and are only sporadically marked. You guess where you want to go by the direction in which tracks disappear through the scrub and by a general understanding that the sun travels east to west. If you turn north, you regain the highway. If you go south, you eventually fall into that "horrid abyss."

Some of the Strip is officially designated wilderness, which by definition is *supposed* to be roadless: 19,600 acres in the Beaver Dam Mountains, 36,300 acres of the Grand Wash Cliffs, 84,700 acres in the Paiute Wilderness, 7,900 acres around Mount Trumbull, 14,600 acres around Mount Logan, 110,000 acres of the Paria Canyon and Vermilion Cliffs, 6,500 acres in the Cottonwood Point section, 77,100 acres of Kanab Creek, 40,600 acres around Saddle Mountain. Included in the National Wilderness Preservation System by the Arizona Wilderness Act of 1984, the total comprises about 397,300 acres. That's a drop in the bucket, actually; but fortunately—or perhaps unfortunately—it is hard to tell where the protected lands end and the unprotected begin. You can fool yourself into ignoring the threat to more than 600,000 acres of this roadless region by proposed uranium mining. And there's nobody out there directing traffic.

That is one of the reasons I'm amenable to a leisurely crossing. Another is that I have been browsing in Clarence Dutton's *Tertiary History of the Grand Cañon District*, and for the first time since John McPhee's *Basin and Range* I have actually enjoyed reading something about geomorphology. Published in 1882, Dutton's study—despite its austere title and the fact that it is a U.S. Geological Survey report—is an extraordinarily entertaining book. Dutton takes his reader along. As he examines the Canyon district, he entertains; he gives his science lessons without forgetting that most of us are poor students and easily distracted; he commands our attention with a power of descriptive narration that so exceeds our own meager scribblings we forget all this is about drainage and erosion, faulting and flexing, rainfall and declivity rate.

"I have taken the liberty," Dutton writes, ". . . of attacking the reader through his imagination, and while trying to amuse his fancy with pictures of travel, have sought to thrust upon him unawares certain facts which I regard of importance. . . ." He has made me want to go look at it all again, now that I have viewed it through his eyes and better learned how to see.

The five elongated plateaus that lie between the Virgin Mountains along the Nevada border and the Echo Cliffs near the western boundary of the Navajo Indian Reservation make up much of the territory Dutton's survey concentrated on during the summers of 1879 and 1880—territory through which we now travel as we turn off U.S. Route 89 onto 89A and head across the Marble Canyon platform. The road winds down toward the river over a sloping desert of sage, rabbit brush, and Indian rice grass, and crosses the gorge a few miles below the confluence of the Paria and Colorado rivers at Lees Ferry. The parking lot just across Navajo Bridge is empty, except for a motor home and a pickup with a "cramper" on the back. The proprietor of the latter is having his picture taken in front of a monument to the fugitive and ferryboat operator John D. Lee—"frontiersman, trailblazer, builder, a man of great faith, sound judgment, and indomitable courage." I have to wonder about the "sound judgment," since John D. was the only Mormon ever tried and executed for his part in the Mountain Meadows massacre near Cedar City, Utah. His judgment might have proved sounder had he blazed a trail somewhat south of the crossing where he was eventually caught and which bears his name. (See *Arizona Highways*, January 1988.)

Foreshadows what they encounter at the North Rim of the Grand Canyon.

We stop to tie down a flapping tarp near the Hatch River Expeditions warehouse at Cliff Dwellers Lodge. Behind us to the south, in the direction of Flagstaff and the San Francisco Peaks, House Rock Valley spreads out in a vast, undifferentiated plain of rocky washes and low, barren hillocks. Bracketed by the blue rim of the Kaibab Plateau on the west and the sheer wall of the Echo Cliffs monocline on the east, it appears less than inviting —though it seems to have served well enough as winter range for cooperative livestock companies during the late 19th century, and still is home for one of Arizona's two buffalo herds. One pioneer spoke eloquently of its hospitality when, on a rock at the spring near the head of the valley, he carved his name, "Joseph Adams," and the inscription, "To Arizona and Busted on June 6 A.D. 1873."

History, woven into narrative.

Word pictures of what they see as they proceed.

Again, works in historical fact.

In front of us, the Paria Plateau terminates in the farthest extension of the Vermilion Cliffs, a 1,000- to 2,000-foot escarpment that stretches more than 100 miles from the southwestern end of the Markagunt Plateau in Utah to the Paria Valley. Powell named these walls for the color they turn at sunset, but in the cloudless heat of this midday they seem washed out, the folds of their vertical surfaces flattened, and the distinctions between horizontal strata blurred to a uniform hue of pale rose. Dutton observed the phenomenon more than a century ago. Without the middle tones of light and shade, "the cliffs seem to wilt and drop as if retracting their grandeur to hide it from the merciless radiance of the sun whose very effulgence flouts them."

Exotic landmark described; again, with historic allusions.

I join them in retraction when we pull over for lunch at a former campsite of the Dominguez-Escalante party, now a historical marker near the foot of the monoclinal flexure comprising the eastern front of the Kaibab Plateau. Lynn does what she can with limp lettuce, peanut butter, and a loaf of bread that resembles in color and texture the carboniferous rock on which we are parked. I sit muttering in the shade of the truck, pouring sweat, idly wondering what the good friars had for their lunch when, returning to Santa Fe after a five-month counterclockwise circumnavigation of Utah's high plateaus, they stopped at this place in October of 1776 to open their picnic basket. Escalante remarked in his journal that the party had been rather discommoded by its recent diet of seeds and cactus fruit; Father Dominguez, indeed, had been flattened for several days by a terrible "pain in the rectum." Grumblers. I acknowledge that it was not all skittles and beer for the Franciscan explorers, but they fared better than many and, except for aspects of the cuisine, were treated well by the Utes and Paiutes they encountered along the way. While the route to the Pacific for which they

Narrative gives a sense of history and of place.

had been searching did not materialize, they were the first Europeans to see the valley of the Virgin, the first to climb the Hurricane Cliffs and cross the Arizona Strip, the first to ford the Colorado above the Grand Canyon, the first to map this country in detail and with remarkable accuracy.

The sage, rabbit brush, and cactus of the Marble platform give way to juniper and piñon, mountain mahogany, and finally ponderosa pine, Engelmann spruce, and aspen as our map leads us 4,000 feet up into the green forest of the Kaibab. Then we make our first grave mistake (for it is Memorial Day weekend) when we turn south from the junction at Jacob Lake toward the North Rim of the Grand Canyon. In a few miles, we begin to flank a long series of grassy meadows where wildflowers spot the terrace with color, and afternoon thunderheads are reflected in shallow mirrors of standing water. In less than an hour, we have been transported from slickrock desert to alpine retreat. Indeed, by the time we reach the national park boundary a few miles below Deer Lake, we are caught in a freak spring snowstorm that forces us to the side of the road. Two hours ago, I was hyperthermic; now I'm hypothermic.

Four out of the 12 chapters in the *Tertiary History of the Grand Cañon* are written about the Kaibab and its unceremonious southern termination in what Major Powell alternately referred to as the "black depths" or "the most sublime spectacle on earth." Some of Dutton's most elegant prose is reserved for that particular moment on the densely forested plateau when, as he rides sedately across a meadow and through the pines, leaning from his saddle to pluck a wildflower from a shaded bank beside a stream, "the earth suddenly sinks at our feet to illimitable depths. In an instant, in the twinkling of an eye, the awful scene is before us."

There are two awful scenes, actually. The first (as in *awe* plus *full*) derives from the incomprehensible chasm itself, from the power of one's emotional reverence for the majestic, from wonderment inspired by the ensemble of terraces, buttes, walls, amphitheaters, pilasters, gorges within gorges, that constitute the vision before one's eyes. One's ecstasy, it has often been noted, is tinged with a little fear. A little dread. There is nothing to say about all this, no way to articulate it, except to echo Dutton's own disclaimer: "Surely no imagination can construct out of its own material any picture having the remotest resemblance to the Grand Cañon." It is, as J. B. Priestley once remarked, a kind of landscape Judgment Day, "not a show place, a beauty spot, but a revelation."

The second "awful" derives from a spectacle unavailable to Messrs. Powell, Dutton, Priestley, et al.—to wit, what appear to be 10,000 tourists at Grand Canyon Lodge (presumably one per vehicle) staring at the void with cocktails in hand, gawking from the terrace, the dining room, the bar, the cafeteria; some hobbling down the Transept Trail, the Bright Angel Trail, the North Kaibab Trail, neoprene coolers in one hand, cameras in the other. It is humanity in such appalling, achromatic, featureless number that the moment we are reminded of our membership in this assembly, we flee the scene, screaming out the truck window our paraphrase of Captain Dutton's words: "Surely no imagination can construct out of its own material any picture having the remotest resemblance to Grand Canyon Lodge on Memorial Day weekend." It is not the fault of the National Park Service (except for allowing these accommodations in the first place). We cast two votes for a national program of euthanasia.

It is long after sunset when we reach Pipe Spring at the northern end of

Not just "chaparral," but specific names of changing flora.

A literary, intellectual response to the chasm—in character with the story's narrative voice.

A powerfully negative reaction, again in character. Stegner brings up an issue and lets his opinion show without worrying whether we agree with him.

the Kanab Plateau. Once the headquarters for various pioneer cattle cooperatives (whose wards had overgrazed most of the Arizona Strip even by Dutton's time), later established (in 1924) as a national monument, the site lies within the Kaibab Indian Reservation. On this holiday, the parking area is stuffed with motor homes, all running generators to keep air-conditioners humming.

No matter. We are on our way, headed down a dirt road that leads southwest across Antelope Valley and eventually into the Toroweap Valley, the lower end of which drops in several abrupt descents nearly 5,000 feet into the inner gorge of the Grand Canyon.

I assure Lynn that we are not missing anything by crossing this part of the Kanab Plateau at night. She can take Dutton's word for it when he describes the Kanab as "a simple monotonous expanse, without a salient point to fix the attention, save one [Kanab Creek]." The Toroweap Valley, however, is a different box of rocks. I have seen the valley's canyonside edge from the top and from the bottom—in fact, from the bottom of a capsized raft at Lava Falls—and I would like to take this opportunity to stand on Vulcan's Throne, the volcanic cinder cone so representative of the basaltic nature of this region, and hurl a few selected insults at that treacherous rapid down below.

But somewhere in the dark, ignoring the carping voice in the adjacent seat reminding me that this is a leisure trip, that we could stop, that *we don't have to do this marathon thing again*, I make a wrong turn. "Just around the next bend," I continue to insist. "We're almost there." But it isn't; and we aren't.

Eventually I relinquish the helm, and we throw down in a sandy area strewn with prickly pear and agave. When we waken at 6:00 A.M. after a brief and sullen sleep, it appears that we have somehow tacked quite far to the windward of the Toroweap Valley. In fact, judging from the position of the volcanic heights of Mount Trumbull and Mount Logan, the entire Uinkaret Plateau seems to have drifted to the east of us, and we are lying in our sleeping bags looking back at the Hurricane Cliffs. To the best of my knowledge, which is admittedly negligible and utterly unassisted by any of the maps in my possession (no topographic maps included, of course; it's too easy to find one's way with topo maps), we are somewhere in the middle of a 2,500-square-mile section of the northwestern corner of Arizona and about 20 miles from Wolf Hole. Maybe.

Wolf Hole is an address occasionally used by writer Edward Abbey (quite possibly as a joke); otherwise it is indistinguishable from the rest of the Shivwits Plateau, a broad, gullied plain of desert scrub rimmed by flattopped hills, a nursery of great silence.

Even the literature specializing in the Arizona Strip and the Grand Canyon district is quiet on the subject of the Shivwits. Dutton sidesteps a description of its geophysical features on the grounds that it resembles the Uinkaret, the facts about which he feels are more "compact, intelligible, and, on the whole, more complete." Other observers offer a line or two about its geological history ("the Shivwits Plateau is crowned by scattered volcanic cones") or about its one bit of human history that has captured attention: the killing of three members of the Powell expedition who had left the party at Separation Rapid, climbed out of the Canyon, and presumably were discovered by a hostile band of Indians a few miles north of Mount Dellenbaugh. Powell's narrative itself devotes only about 10 pages to that part of the river canyon that cuts through the Shivwits, and on the subject of the plateau above he has nothing to say other than to note evidence of its volcanic origins and to remark, "I know enough of the country to be certain that it is a desert of rock and sand. . . ."

There is, to be sure, a lot of rock and sand. But there is more. There is unequaled solitude. We have not encountered a single soul since we turned off the pavement at Pipe Spring. There is magnificent early light on the eastern face of the Virgin Mountains, in stark contrast to the dark and illegible slope across the valley from our camp. There is a pungent smell of sage and piñon and damp dust that triggers the memory of other wakings in other deserts. There is a walk I take down in the wash (while Lynn works her magic on instant coffee, rye crackers, and a wizened apple) discovering the astonishing colors and multiplicity of wildflowers—yellow ragleaf, purple phlox, orange globemallow, red verbena, and prickly poppy with its white petals and egg-yolk center. And there is the strong, sweet perfume of the lavender snapdragons called Palmer penstemon that I pick in a groveling gesture of atonement for last night's forced march. But the *bella doña*, I find, has already provided her own bouquet of white trumpet flowers of the sacred datura, or nightshade, nicely displayed in an empty mayonnaise jar.

At a crossroad somewhere in Wolf Hole Valley, we turn west into the afternoon sun and bump along toward Jacob Well. The route descends a long gulch spotted with cholla and grizzly bear cactus, both in flower, then begins to climb through Lime Kiln Canyon toward the crest of the Virgin Mountains along the Nevada border. This is clearly not a habitat to visit in one's BMW. Rocks that have fallen from the palisades above threaten to block the narrow, precipitous passage, and the old truck bed, burdened with its load of rafts and oar frames, bangs on the axle at every pothole and ledge.

We pull over for a moment near the top of our ascent to look back across the canyon in the direction of the Grand Wash Cliffs. A congregation of turkey vultures drifts in a clockwise eddy below us. The meridian sun shimmers off chocolate rocks, bleaches cross-bedded sandstones to the palest pink, washes the entire plateau in bluish haze. Distant buttes dance on mercurial vapors. Again the text is Dutton's: "There are no concrete notions founded in experience upon which a conception of these color effects and optical delusions can be constructed and made intelligible. A perpetual glamour envelops the landscape." Again it is a scene that inspires awe—and a little dread.

Onward. At a turn just over the summit I encounter a cow, who stares at me in stupefaction before commencing a suicidal dash down the trail and out of sight around the next hairpin turn. Following, I encounter two cows. Then three. Soon I have collected a small herd, all of them bawling, stiff-tailed, befouling the road in a beef-witted dash for sanctuary.

Can't get distracted here. Must press on. Hope the rancher who owns this stampede doesn't see the dust cloud down there in Mesquite. Where again the quickest way west is southward, through that other strip and out across the great Mojave to Quivira, Cibola, and El Dorado. I am now less sure than ever there is any cause for hurry.

Sights, scents, solitude.

Very specific: names the individual flowers.

A sophisticated pun: datura, like belladonna (in Spanish, *bella doña*— "pretty lady"), is lethal. A variety of nightshade is called belladonna.

Specific description, again with a literary twist.

Real places whose mythic connotations seem more tangible after this essay.

EDITORIAL OVERVIEW

This story pleases because on the other side of the print is a genial, intelligent mind. We feel Page Stegner's presence in every sentence. That, more than forced charm or "objectivity," gives the article real quality.

Literary presence, in this case, comes from the story's narrative voice. The writer's habit of describing what he sees as much through bookish sources as through his own eyes; his curmudgeonly love of solitude; his familiarity with the country and with the dreams and adventures of those who came before; his amiably grudging admission that he was wrong and his wife was right: all these things draw a picture of the person who is speaking.

The story's sophistication could be a drawback; the refined, subtle wit may go past many readers.

Although the action is low-key, a little plot unwinds, narrated in the first person from the author's point of view. Page and Lynn Stegner decide to see the sights as they drive from Utah to their home in California. They cross a rugged, chromatic landscape and are reminded of the area's history and geology. Arriving at the North Rim of the Grand Canyon, they are dismayed by hordes of tourists and flee. A wrong turn gets them hopelessly lost and causes a quarrel. They reconcile and push on. From this narrative hangs much solid fact, vivid description, erudite commentary (the piece draws on five literary sources), and subjective opinion.

Point of view, plot line, voice, character, setting: they make the piece a *story*. These are the stuff of the feature article.

−30−

20

Roundups or Service Pieces

A roundup gathers a lot of information under one heading. Unlike a report, which may draw some implicit or explicit conclusion, the roundup presents only what amounts to consumer information. For this reason, roundups are sometimes called "service pieces."

You can "round up" many categories in single stories. You might cover a service: where do you go to get good fake fingernails? How do you find the best day-care centers, the best housecleaning services, the best lawyers? It might be places: resorts, fishing holes, ice cream parlors. You could cover goods: telephone gadgets, Christmas presents, scale-model trains. Or businesses: what are your city's best private schools? What stores retail antiques, Persian rugs, ceramic tiles? Or activities: things for kids to do during summer vacation. Or even people: which young men and women are most likely to be influential leaders in your state by the end of the decade?

Roundups present several advantages to beginners and to free-lance writers:

- They're popular with readers.
- They're popular with advertisers.
- Sometimes they're well paid.
- You can do a roundup on almost any subject.
- Staffers hate to write them.

- They consume so much time, many editors farm them out and use experienced staff writers' time more effectively.

Before you head for your word processor, though, consider the drawbacks:

- They're not strictly journalism. They often verge on puffery or advertorial. Frequently, the advertising department has something to say about what will go into them.
- They're harder to do than they look.

The reason they can be difficult is that you must cover the field. You can't include *every* fern bar or resort or whatever, but you'd better not forget any of the big boys. You also must be alert enough to catch the latest development—and since that usually means The Competition, you can't rely on your sources to clue you in.

As usual, you must get the facts exactly right. This always involves triple-checking many telephone numbers and addresses—fussy, tedious work.

The best roundups come from writers who go in person to investigate the place, product, or service in question. You usually have to interview a phenomenal number of sources, and that means plenty of driving. If you're doing the job on a free-lance basis, be sure the magazine will cover your mileage.

It is often possible, nevertheless, to do the research by phone. Since staff writers rarely are reimbursed for mileage, one is strongly motivated to take this route. As we have seen, it often takes two or three calls to reach a source. So, if you have to talk to 20 people, you could end up making 60 telephone calls!

And finally, the material that goes into roundup pieces tends to bore. That's one reason veteran writers dislike them, and it explains why such stories are so often full of froth. It takes special skill to sustain interest when you're repeating essentially the same thing 15 different ways.

Michael Robbins writes sparkling, informative roundups for *New York* magazine. As the following example shows, the stories succeed when the writer personally knows whereof he speaks.

DREAM WEEKENDS

by Michael W. Robbins

New York, April 28, 1986

New York is, arguably, the most stimulating city in the world. What a New Yorker needs, therefore, is an occasional break from all that input. To gaze at the sea from a breezy bluff. To cycle through patches of sun and

Frothy leads are typical of roundups. Some editors seem to think this ap-

shade on a hilly country road. To fish a fine trout stream, amble through a beautiful, somnolent village, reflect on life from a rope hammock under the shade of tall oaks. These eleven destinations provide that kind of escape — dream weekends.

Shelter Island
New York

The Ram's Head Inn is just the spot for a spring getaway. It's on the water: The back lawn falls away in a shady slope to a tennis court just above Coecles Harbor, which is part of Gardiners Bay, at the eastern end of Long Island. Set on a bit of a bluff, the inn catches the breeze. But, most important, it's on an island — Big Ram — that's as remote as you can get and still be within 100 miles of Wall Street. So remote, in fact, that you can stroll around and watch the ospreys (they nest on poles, and they'll watch you too).

Big Ram is connected to Shelter Island by a narrow causeway flanked by pebble-and-shell beaches. The inn is a long, simple, three-story frame building shingled in the weathered grays of far-eastern Long Island. It claims some fame as the house where in 1947 a stellar band of scientists, including J. Robert Oppenheimer and Linus Pauling, met to consider quantum mechanics.

There's a sunny, open feeling about the Ram's Head: Even when you're inside, it seems as if you're outdoors. The long lawn below the flagstone terrace is canopied by enormous oaks: in the dappled green shade, the scattered white Adirondack chairs seem irresistible, and so do the *ménage*-size rope hammocks. The yard has great appeal for children. Rope swings are hung from those sturdy oaks; there's a swing-and-slide set; a wood rowboat is grounded on the wavy grass.

Adults who insist on some kind of activity will find enough to do at the Ram's Head. There's that tennis court. At the inn's dock, two small day sailers are tied up for guest use. Just off the dock, there's a wood float for swimming and sunning.

Shelter Island is ideal for knockabout bicycling. There are some hills, but they won't require bikers to expend too much energy. Most of the roads — which are lanes, really — carry only light automobile traffic. You will roll past fields, houses, and flowery yards, through patches of sun and shade, catching flashes of the small bays and inlets. And this island is so free of crime that the bicycle-rental agencies don't even issue locks with their rental bikes.

Cycle to the beach. The one nearest Ram's Head — a mile away — is on a typical Upper Beach, a long crescent of sand that eases into the shallow and calm waters. The firm beaches that surround Shelter Island are good for walking, and even when it's still too cold for swimming, beach-rambling is a pleasant pastime on a bright afternoon. More-organized activity is possible — there are several marinas, a nine-hole golf course, fishing stations — but this is a lazy kind of place. If you can't stand indolence, the North Ferry will convey you to the comparative hustle of Greenport, or the South Ferry will deliver you in the direction of Sag Harbor, the old whaling port that seems bent on becoming a Hampton.

Try to move around enough to work up an appetite, because the Ram's Head has an impressive kitchen. When we stayed at the inn last summer, the chef was Ray Bradley, who has worked at the Polo and Le Cirque. This season the chef will be Stefan Larsen, who is an executive chef for the Norwegian Caribbean Lines. We dined on the candlelit terrace on a warm evening. The scene had a sort of Caribbean feeling: whiffs of salt water, light breezes, and glimpses of silver waters against the dark shore, on which a few points of light sparkled.

We had salads of endive, romaine, watercress, and warmed Montrachet, followed by braised flounder and a sautéed breast of chicken in cream with a green-mustard sauce. All was excellent. (Entrées—baked salmon, sautéed veal, flounder, roast duckling—range from $12 to $15.) There's a decent wine list, mainly French. You ought to make an evening of it, watching the light and the wine go down.

The owners are serious about relaxation; they provide no telephones or televisions in the rather austere, vaguely Colonial, maple-furnished rooms. The only trouble is, there's nowhere to relax in the bedrooms, except on the bed, and there's no real living-room area downstairs, only the large bar (which *does* provide a couch by the fireplace). The Ram's Head is a very open place, with people drifting in and out, and evidently you're supposed to spend your time out of doors. Try the hammocks.

Rates: In low season (May 2 through June 19), shared-bath rooms are $55 a night, double occupancy; private-bath rooms are $72; a private-bath suite (sleeping four) is $115. Rates are higher in high season. Add 7.5 percent tax. A Continental breakfast is included. M.C., V., personal checks. The inn will be closed from October 27, 1986, through May 1, 1987.

Directions: The Ram's Head Inn, Shelter Island, New York 11965 (516–749–0811), is about 100 miles—a two-hour drive—from New York City. Take the Long Island Expressway East until it forks; bear to the left on Route 58, which eventually turns into Route 25 to Greenport. Follow signs in Greenport to the North Ferry Dock, and take the ferry across to Shelter Island. Follow Route 114 South to Winthrop Road, and turn left. Once you've gone around Dering Harbor, veer right onto Cobbets Lane and follow it past the firehouse to Ram Island Road. Turn left, then turn right onto Ram Island Drive, and proceed past Little Ram Island to the first right turn, on Big Ram Island; the inn's on your right.

The Eastern Shore
Maryland

Chestertown, Maryland, is not a resort town, and unless you keep a boat nearby or need to visit Washington College, you might never go there. That would be a serious error of omission. If the point of travel is to be somewhere that's unlike where you are, you ought to try Chestertown: Try to remember the last time anyone said to you, "Your car is perfectly safe on the street." I can tell you, from actual observation, that some sane people do not lock their cars in Chestertown.

Try to remember the last time you parked your car, walked across the street to a movie house, did not stand in line, and paid $3 to see a current film.

Try to remember the last time you were in a drugstore that had a soda fountain—the kind with those stainless-steel hand pumps that deliver squirts of fizz. These details suggest that things don't change rapidly in Chestertown; indeed, the town doesn't appear to have changed appreciably in the

cause later Robbins uses a first-person singular, "I." First-hand description gives the story immediacy and authenticity.

Tells how it looked and smelled. Good stories let the reader know how it feels to be in a place or action.

In a service piece, one often is expected to state prices.

Better publications allow writers to give honest appraisals, rather than purely gushing.

This kind of information is often requested by the editor, and the format is usually specified. Dates, prices, acceptable methods of payment, etc., must be double- and triple-checked before publication.

The same is true of route numbers, distances, and directions. All these details must be checked against a map.

Characteristics bound to appeal to city-weary New Yorkers.

Quasi-nostalgia, again sure to tempt urbanites.

last lifetime or two. But these details are not what's most striking about the place: Chestertown is a stunningly beautiful little town, with the ordered, mellow quality of a place that has been good for generations, a place where things have worked out. Like much of the Eastern Shore, this quiet town has kept the flavors of the eighteenth and nineteenth centuries: All along the banks of the Chester River stand houses that date clear back to the 1720s. Most are of warm brick, some with a faded haze of worn-away whitewashing; all have white trim. They stand tall, three stories or more, with the era's characteristic multi-pane windows, double-end chimneys, and formal entrances. The brick sidewalks are set in a herringbone pattern. Toward the river, there are gardens, and the smell of boxwood sharpens the air.

In a place this suffused with its own past, family counts. Lineage counts. Roots count. When I stopped at a shop to ask directions to another store, I got not only directions but a genealogy of the owner and a description of his family seat. That's characteristic of a small town—Chestertown has fewer than 4,000 souls.

Staying in the White Swan Tavern is like being left alone for the night in a museum of decorative arts. The effect is especially marked if you choose the tavern's "John Lovegrove Kitchen" room—a semi-attached structure large enough to be a tavern in its own right. Built about 1725, it has a brick floor and a smoke-darkened, rough beam-and-plank ceiling. You could not find a more authentic, atmospheric sleeping room in Colonial Williamsburg.

In fact, the White Swan is a rare combination of period-room museum and public bed-and-breakfast inn. It was thoroughly investigated by a team of historical archaeologists in 1978 and 1979; near the innkeeper's desk there's a tasteful, museum-quality display of some of the objects they recovered—pottery, clay pipes, fragments of wineglasses and bottles, iron tongs. In 1981, after the inn had been professionally restored, it was opened to the public.

There are four upstairs rooms, each with a (nonworking) fireplace and a four-poster, canopy, or elaborately carved bed, each meticulously furnished with antiques of the eighteenth or nineteenth century. Downstairs is the Lovegrove Kitchen, which we were lucky enough to draw. It was the tavern's kitchen for the first half of the nineteenth century; it makes a splendid bedroom now. Despite the coolness of the brick pavement, the room has a real warmth, a glow contributed to by the patina of the wood chests and stands, the well-used tavern table, the light from the half-dozen lamps and the tin chandelier. Two sturdy wood bedsteads, one double and one single, face the cavernous fireplace. Fitted with period-design spreads (and contemporary electric blankets), they are comfortable indeed. Other nice touches, old and new: a high-backed settee, copper and tin pieces around the fireplace (which, alas, cannot be used); bunches of dried flowers; a small refrigerator complete with a chilled bottle of decent white Bordeaux; a contemporary bath and shower.

Our snug refuge was so quiet that flights of migrating geese were heard from indoors; we heard no sound from inside the building. This room was big enough to live in, big enough for an evening of wine and talk with a gathering of friends. Still, we wanted to get outside: Spring is truly rewarding in Chesapeake country, with early warm sun and flowers blooming before they do in New York.

So we took our ease outdoors, on the large patio—the old tavern yard—where we found benches and tables for early sunning and coffee. Those who wish to lounge about indoors can use the dayroom, furnished with an abundance of comfortable wingbacks and Windsors, a working fireplace, even a concealed color television. Or they may use the two front rooms, which look out across sycamore-lined High Street to the red-brick, 1720 County Courthouse, around which much of the life of the town revolves. Afternoon tea and morning breakfast are served in one dayroom; the other, the Joseph Nicholson Room, is furnished with antiques and reproductions in exact accord with Mr. Nicholson's final inventory. (Nicholson, a Revolutionary War notable, was the tavern's owner from 1733 to 1793).

Clearly, the past is heeded in Chestertown. One thing this means, evidently, is concern for *order*. Both the White Swan Tavern and the Imperial Hotel, across High Street, are extraordinarily orderly, clean, neat places; in both it's clear that the task of restoring an old place to better-than-new condition has been taken seriously and done right, apparently with scant consideration of the cost.

Neither place is inexpensive, but considering the quality, both seem like bargains. It is disheartening to recall how many places charge as much or more without returning a fraction of the warmth and character of these places.

Wherever you stay in this part of the Eastern Shore, the Imperial Hotel is the place to dine. Not because the country-French menu is so extensive or so daring, but because the ingredients and the cooking are of such high quality.

The choices are a combination of American standards and French treatments, with some regional influence: duck, of course (no Eastern Shore restaurant dare ignore it), but boned duck, roasted in dark amaretto sauce and dusted with crushed almonds. Seafood, of course, but grilled tuna in béarnaise sauce, or grouper Rebecca with sautéed mushrooms and shrimp.

Dinners, served in the two relentlessly Victorian dining rooms—one rose and one very dark green—begin with one or two soups. A favorite is the oyster stew, flavored with bits of Smithfield ham. The half-dozen "appetizers/salads" include Scottish smoked salmon, mussels Cassino, and a "salad composé"—a bright, crisp pinwheel of limestone lettuce, endive, tomato, mushrooms, and peppers. Among the eight or nine entrées are veal piccata, sirloin or filet, lamb—boneless medallions with a garlic sauce and fresh mint—smoked chops, and fish dishes.

Our roast duck was very tender and richly flavored, without the strong game taste of inferior fowl, and moist throughout. It arrived quite hot— served, like all the dishes at the Imperial, at the appropriate temperature. The details were excellent, too: warm, just-baked rolls and a side dish of tender asparagus with hollandaise.

Desserts are worth serious consideration. Each is a special creation. The mille-feuille approaches the monumental: layers of fresh sliced strawberries alternate with layers of sliced kiwi fruits and layers of puff pastry, the whole running over with strawberry liqueur and whipped cream and topped with mint cuttings. As for the wine list, it has depth—there are over 100 champagnes, reds, whites, and dessert wines—and sophistication.

On our visit last summer, chef Bruce Campbell was in residence, and what his kitchen turned out was first-rate. But Campbell was only filling in for a time; the inn has long been negotiating for the services of Ernest Belmore, who starts work this month. He expects to keep the inn's commendable menu essentially the same.

The Imperial was built as a hotel in 1903. The current owners, George

Again describes the amenities.

Describes the setting.

Works some history into the piece.

The residents' pride in their town must have struck Robbins; he doesn't fail to note it.

Transition to a new place.

A decidedly sophisticated repertoire for a quaint small town that hasn't changed in a generation.

Language suggests he tires of the antique decor.

Note the wealth of detail here. He probably kept the menu.

Beware the infelicitous rhyme!

Here, too, note that the description goes beyond "the food was good" to explain *why* it was good.

Plenty of descriptive detail.

Evidently interviewed the proprietors and employees.

From those interviews, he obtained enough to focus briefly on the people involved.

"Not in demeanor; more elaborate; dominate; took up much of our room": the language suggests Robbins found this style oppressive.

Wordy construction.

Also verbose. How would you tighten this sentence?

Again, bringing people into the narrative adds warmth and interest.

Specifics. Always be specific!

Each section of this story winds up with these practicalities.

Translating miles into time spent on the road is useful.

and Jane Dean, are responsible for the elaborate (and evidently painstaking) renovation, which was completed only sixteen months ago.

Most rooms, except for the third-floor suite and the Early American carriage-house apartment, are modest in size but not in demeanor: Furnishings—both original and reproduction—in the more elaborate Victorian styles dominate the rooms. A new queen-size brass bed took up much of our room. There were a couple of upholstered Victorian side chairs, but for sitting and reading in comfort it was necessary to step across the hall to the dayroom, where there were plush couches and chairs. At the foot of our bed, a very tall armoire, an antique, contained and concealed a color television with a wireless remote-control device. Light was furnished by brass-and-glass-globe fixtures flanking the bed, as well as by a brass extravaganza of a four-globe floor lamp.

The Deans are new to the hotel-inn trade (he's a trial lawyer), but they have paid attention to details, and they have introduced some of those touches that distinguish a fine hotel from routine lodgings. Every closet has a white terry robe and a large green-and-white umbrella for guest use; very thick white towels wait on a chrome pipe rack that's filled with hot water, so the towels are always pleasantly warm. All very thoughtful.

Rates: Year-round, the three smaller rooms at the White Swan, all with private bath, are $75 a night, double occupancy; the John Lovegrove Kitchen is $90, double occupancy; the Victorian Suite is $90 for two guests, plus $25 for each additional occupant. Add 5 percent tax. A Continental breakfast is included. No pets, no credit cards; personal checks. The inn is closed for three months in wintertime.

Year-round, rooms at the Imperial Hotel, all with private bath, are $95 a night, double-occupancy; both the Carriage House Suite (sleeping four) and the Hotel Suite (sleeping two) are $200 a night, and the Double Suite (sleeping four, with two bathroom) is $300 a night. Add 5 percent tax. No meals are included. For pets, there is a heated kennel. No credit cards; personal checks.

Directions: The White Swan Tavern, 231 High Street, Chestertown, Maryland 21620 (301–778–2300), is about 200 miles—a four-and-a-half-hour drive—from New York. Follow I-95 South to the Delaware Memorial Bridge. Cross the bridge, follow Route 13 South to Odessa, Delaware, and turn right (west) onto Route 299. Follow 299 to Route 301 South, then go right onto Route 213 and take it into Chestertown. In Chestertown, Route 213 becomes Washington Avenue. Drive about a mile on Washington Avenue, then turn right and go one block on Queen Street. Turn right onto High Street; the White Swan's on the west side of the street.

The Imperial Hotel, 208 High Street, Chestertown, Maryland 21620 (301–778–5000), is just down the block from the White Swan, on the east side of High Street. Follow the above directions.

EDITORIAL OVERVIEW

The story goes on for five more sections but sustains the same level of interest. Robbins can hold the reader's attention because he has so plainly been to these places; he makes that clear with specific, detailed description. He adds interest by mentioning the people he met, by telling us his personal reactions to what he experienced, and by *showing*, not telling, wherever possible. Even in a consumer roundup, it is possible to give the reader a feeling for places and events.

The narrative might have been improved if Robbins had identified his companion, so that the reader could have a clearer sense of being with a traveling couple. The more human interest you can build into a service piece, the more engaging the story is likely to be.

Robbins' article goes beyond the unreserved gushing one sees too often in this kind of journalism. When something strikes him as a shortcoming, he says so, albeit it in a low-key way. We learn, for example, that he likes the Ram's Head but wishes it had an indoor lounge or space in the rooms for relaxing; we suspect that elaborate Victorian antiques give him the creeps. Good: this is what puts the "service" into service pieces.

–30–

21

Reports

A feature "report" is different from a straight news report. It's usually longer. It opens with a feature lead, not the standard who/what/when/where/why lead of the news article. And of course, it's organized like any feature, with a lead, transitional nut graf, in-depth discussion of the issues, and a lively ending—as opposed to the news article's inverted pyramid.

Like a news story, however, it presents the facts on a single subject, usually one of topical interest. It does not tell the reader how to do something or relate someone's gut-wrenching personal experience. Although the writer may take a stance on the issues in question, it is not a review nor should it necessarily proselytize the writer's opinions.

If you could take the most interesting term paper you have ever written, augment it with some interviews, and present it in journalistic form, you would have something like a feature report. The writer undertakes a great deal of research and presents it in a congenial, readable style.

This characterization will seem, to many experienced writers, an oversimplification. Let's make it clear that the journalistic report is *not* just a glorified term paper: the best are complex, lengthy articles that synthesize difficult, hard-to-find information under a single thematic heading. The report calls on an author to bring all of his or her research and writing skill together in one place. The lazy reporter and the clumsy writer will not do well.

As a nonfiction form, the report is the cornerstone of the feature writer's genre. And yet it is here that we face the greatest challenge: how to offer potentially tedious data without boring the reader.

One way: focus on human beings rather than on dry facts. Introduce a person in the lead and show how the issue at hand affects him or her. Use anecdote and other fictional techniques to keep emphasizing what the facts mean to the reader or to people like him.

Another method is to bring your reader's attention to some surprising fact first, and then show how your other information explains the oddity. There's a danger in the "gee-whiz" approach: it can seem patronizing, like a grade-school textbook ("you will be surprised to learn that . . ."). Be sure an amazing fact really *is* amazing when you present it as such.

It's important to translate large, incomprehensible figures into meaningful terms. In the United States, for example, about 30,400,000 people are older than 65. A browse through *Statistical Abstracts* gives a clue to how to bring this home: the population of Canada is only 25,858,000. Hence, "The number of Americans over 65 exceeds the entire population of Canada." Use metaphor and simile to compare the unfamiliar with the familiar. And, to cite another example, in an article describing the earth's hot, molten interior, physicist James Trefil says the layer of rock immediately beneath the planet's outer skin "boils," and then compares this action with a pot of water on the stove.

The report is the nonfiction publisher's meat. Even magazines heavy on personal experience, how-to, and inspirational stories are full of reports—think of all those medical reports in the women's magazines, and *Good Housekeeping*'s monthly department, "The Better Way." Many newspaper features fall into this category, too. Information that is ancillary to breaking news may be presented in feature form, as will relatively nonperishable hard news.

The report takes many forms. Some are updates: "whatever happened to . . . ?" Others treat topical subjects in the manner of the weekly newsmagazines.

Some science, medical, and technical writing requires the writer to possess both expertise in a subject and skill to translate abstruse concepts and language into everyday English. Medical reports commonly appear in women's magazines. Technical stories—articles and columns about computers, for example—are ubiquitous, particularly in newspapers and trade magazines. Science reporting, too, is not restricted to magazines like *Discover* and *Omni*; most urban dailies hire science writers, and reports on science or nature appear almost everywhere. Many such writers, by the way, have undergraduate and even graduate degrees in science, with journalism or liberal arts minors.

With the story below, Steve Twomey won the 1987 Pulitzer Prize for feature writing.

HOW SUPER ARE OUR SUPERCARRIERS?

by Steve Twomey

The Philadelphia Inquirer, October 5, 1986

Extended narrative *lead* is long for a newspaper piece. But the short sentences, plain words mark it as newspaper rather than magazine writing style. "Bird Farm," Air Boss," "cat stroke"—sparing use of jargon gives flavor and color. This entire passage is packed with specifics: names of planes, weights, speeds, lengths, etc.

Air Boss looked aft. Through the haze of a June morning off Sicily, an F-14A Tomcat fighter was already banking in low over *America's* wake, a couple of miles out and coming home to the Bird Farm. Air Boss looked down. Damn. Still no place to put the thing.

On the flight deck below, opposite Air Boss's perch in the control tower, an A-7E Corsair II bomber sat astride the No. 4 stream catapult amidships. By now, the A-7 should have been flying with the rest of the day's second mission. Nobody would be landing while it straddled *America's* only available runway.

"What's taking 'em so long down there?" Air Boss growled. He had left his leather armchair in his glass booth in *America's* superstructure. He was standing up for a better look, which he always does when the flight deck crunch is on.

Dialogue, focus on *people* up front humanizes a complex, potentially impersonal subject. Helps communicate sense of urgency and tension.

The ship's 79,724 tons suddenly shuddered. Steam billowed from No. 4. The A-7 had vanished, rudely flung out over the Mediterranean by the "cat stroke," like a rock from a slingshot. Finally.

"Launch complete, sir!" said Mini Boss, his assistant.

"Clear decks!" Air Boss boomed into the radio to his launch crews. It would be close, maybe too close. "Secure the waist cat! Prepare to recover aircraft! Hubba, hubba!"

Simile.

The F-14 was closing at 150 miles per hour. A mile out now. On the deck, crews were frantically stowing launch gear. They had to seal the long slit down which the catapult arm—the "shuttle"—races as it yanks a plane along the deck and flips it heavenward. They had to shut hatches and make them flush with the deck. *America* had to become seamless for its bird.

Communicates the scene's tension and speed.

"Commmme on, commmme on," said Air Boss. His eyes flitted from the looming F-14 to his crews working below. The plane's variable wings were swept wide for landing, 64 feet tip to tip. Its wheels were down, its twin tail jets were spewing heat waves. It was a pterodactyl about to prey on the carrier.

Metaphor.

"We're not going to make it!" said Air Boss.

"We'll make it!" said Mini Boss.

Facts and explanation woven into the narrative.

Unless they made it, the F-14 would have to be waved off, sent around for another approach. In peacetime, that is not fatal. It costs fuel—266 gallons a minute for an F-14, $1,100 an hour—but no more. In war, a carrier's ability to cycle its jets in seconds—to launch them, land them, rearm them, refuel them, launch them again—could mean victory or defeat. *America* is not at war now. But *America* trains as if it is.

Effective use of repetition as a literary device. This technique recurs twice in

"We're not going to make it!" Air Boss said again.

"We'll make it!" said Mini.

Catapult crews had almost finished. The F-14 was just off the stern and plunging, a long hook dangling from its belly that would, it was hoped, catch one of four cables laid across the rear flight deck to stop the plane cold. It was time to decide: Wave it off or land it. The last of the crew was scampering out of the landing area.

"They made it!" said Mini.

Over the stern, down, down.

Bam.

Fifty-six thousand pounds of F-14 slammed home. Simultaneously, the pilot pushed to full throttle. Heat blasted down the aft flight deck. If the hook missed all the cables, the pilot would simply keep going, over the now-dormant site of the No. 4 catapult, flying off and coming around again. But he was no "bolter." He snagged a wire for a clean trap. Time from the last launch to the first land: 45 seconds.

Air Boss grinned.

Mini Boss grinned.

Hubba, hubba.

It is hard not to love the dance of the carrier deck—the skill, beauty, and sheer guts of men launching and landing warplanes on a 1,000-foot slab on the sea.

Seventy-five times on an average day, up to 400 times during crises such as Libya, *America*'s crew members dodge sucking jet intakes and whirring props to hitch aircraft to the catapults and send them flying. That many times, they help them home and snare them and park them. They can launch planes a minute apart. They can launch and land at the same time. They can do it in the dark or in the rain. Their average age is 19 1/2.

Engines whine, then race—and a plane disappears from the deck in 2.5 seconds. Its exhaust heat bathes launch crews. The air reeks of jet fuel. Steam seeps from the catapult track. The next plane is already moving forward to take the "cat stroke," and there's another behind it. Noise overwhelms the deck. All the while, the carrier slices through the blue.

"There's no way to describe it," said an A-7 pilot aboard *America*. "There's no way to see it in a movie. You've got to come out here and smell it and see it. It's too dynamic. The whole thing's like a ballet."

In all, the United States' carriers number 14; no other nation has more than four. They are the largest engines of war; no one else's are half as big. They bear the names of battles won. *Coral Sea*, *Midway*, and *Saratoga*; of leaders gone, *Eisenhower*, *Forrestal*, *Kennedy*, *Nimitz* and *Vinson*; and of Revolutionary War vessels, *Constellation*, *Enterprise*, *Independence* and *Ranger*. One evokes the place where man first flew, *Kitty Hawk*. And one is called *America*.

With their pride of escorts the 14 carriers and 878 carrier-based fighters and bombers are the most tangible sign of U.S. power that most people around the world ever see. They are the heart of the nation's maritime defense, its glamour boys. They are the costliest items in the military budget, the price of one carrier and its escorts equaling the bill for 250 MX ballistic missiles.

Yet, for all their impressiveness and for all the importance the Pentagon attaches to the vessels, many congressmen and defense analysts argue that the supercarriers' day is history. The critics fear they are now unnecessary,

the remainder of the lead. Note that the repetition is neither redundant nor monotonous: it serves a specific purpose.

Clear, crisp description.

Of the lead's 93 verbs and verbals, only 10 are verbs of being. Just two are in the passive voice.

This *bridge* is also very long for newspaper copy. It summarizes the gist of the story: an aircraft carrier and its planes make a dramatic, glamorous, expensive whole—one that may be a white elephant. In vivid language, Twomey describes the carrier's appeal and impressiveness; yet he wraps up the bridge with a summary of critics' arguments.

Interesting detail; again, humanizes.

Sights, sounds, smells.

Use of quotes has ironic effect: Twomey has just tried to "describe it."

A covey of facts. Note short sentences and variety of sentence structure. Yet one long, complex sentence— with semicolons!—surfaces.

Summarizes criticism of the carrier.

too expensive, and, worse, easy marks. Some of the doubters are even Navy men: Stansfield Turner, a retired admiral and the former director of the Central Intelligence Agency; Elmo Zumwalt, the retired Chief of Naval Operations, and Eugene J. Carroll Jr., a retired admiral who once commanded *Nimitz.*

"Like the battleship the carrier replaced, its magnificence cannot nullify basic changes in the nature of war at sea," Sen. Gary Hart, the Colorado Democrat, writes in a new book on U. S. defense, *America Can Win.* "The day of the large aircraft carrier . . . has passed."

As Twomey moves into the story's body, he focuses on the criticism. This four-sentence paragraph martials 12 solid facts to support critics' assertion.

Today, all surface ships are highly vulnerable to two things—missiles and submarines. A British frigate was sunk in the 1982 Falklands War by a single Exocet missile fired from an Argentine jet it never saw. The Soviet Union has 304 attack submarines, enough to dispatch 21 to hunt each U.S. aircraft carrier. By opting for 14 big carriers—a 15th, the 91,487-ton *Theodore Roosevelt*, will join the fleet soon—the United States could lose, perhaps fatally, a very large portion of naval power in a very short time from a very few Soviet missiles and torpedo hits.

Quotes a source with strong credentials.

In short, it might have the wrong navy for the late 20th century. "When you concentrate your total offensive capability into 15 platforms, the targeting system of the adversary becomes very focused," said Carroll, the ex-carrier captain, who is now deputy director of the Center for Defense Information, a private Washington research group.

No one doubts that the United States ought to have carriers. They have uses. The answer to vulnerability, critics say, is to have more of them, to spread the risk. The big ones, however, cost big bucks. *Roosevelt* and two other new, huge, nuclear-powered carriers authorized by Congress, the *Abraham Lincoln* and the *George Washington*, will cost $3.5 billion apiece. Without planes. Add those and add the cruisers and frigates that must

Effective way to make sense of incomprehensibly huge figures. Brings the cost home to local readers.

escort any carrier—the Navy concedes they need protection—and it costs $17 billion to put a carrier group to sea. That is 10 times the 1986 Philadelphia city budget. The cost of the three carrier groups combined would be enough to pay for all city services—police, fire, sanitation, everything—for 30 years without any resident paying any taxes.

Again, explains *what it means.* Quotes a believable source.

That is money that cannot be spent on other military items. And most of that money goes for "the purpose of protecting this goddamn carrier," said Robert Komer, who was an undersecretary of Defense for policy during the Carter administration. Even most of the carrier's planes are there to protect it.

Presents critics' alternative.

Instead, many critics say, it's time to think small. Overhauling the big carriers at the Philadelphia Naval Shipyard—*Independence* is there now, under the Service Life Extension Program—is merely fixing up the past. The nation should have smaller, cheaper carriers. They can do the job. And the nation could then afford more carriers, and more would cut the impact of losing any given one if war comes.

Discussion of the issues.

Of course, to speak of cutting losses in any war seems surreal. Only the Soviet Union could really challenge the U.S. Navy. But any sea battle with the Soviets would trigger nuclear war, many analysts say. In that case, it wouldn't much matter if the United States had 15 supercarriers or 30 medium ones. The game would be over. Still, the Pentagon plans for old-fashioned conflict. Its theory is that because nuclear war is final, no nation would start one. But the Soviets might be willing to start a regular war, so it's vital to have good conventional armed forces. In that context, debating what kind of navy to have does make sense.

And the U.S. Navy has no doubt that it wants big carriers. It would even like seven or eight more, up to 22 or 23. In fact, the Reagan administration, under Navy Secretary John F. Lehman Jr., has made big carriers the key to a strategy that would take them right into the teeth of Soviet defenses in wartime. That is how much confidence it has in carriers' ability to survive today. Critics, said Adm. Henry H. Mauz, commander of America's battle group, "are well-meaning people, I'm sure. But they're wrong."

Navy's response to critics.

Lehman even said in testimony before Congress last fall that to build small is communistic, to build big is American. "Should carriers be bigger or smaller? There is no absolute answer to that question," he said. ". . . [But] our tremendous edge in technology is a permanent edge built into the nature of our culture and economic system, compared to the Soviets. It is to that advantage we must always build, not to go to cheaper, smaller, less capable ships in large numbers. That is an area in which a totalitarian, centralized, planned economy excels."

Big is beautiful.

America's crew sometimes gets lost. There are so many decks and passageways that sailors don't know where they are. "I get fouled up all the time," said an officer who was consulting a deck plan on a bulkhead.

Nifty transition into a "how big *is* it" passage.

Crew members can ask someone for help, though it'll often be a stranger. With 4,950 men—there is not one woman—who work different hours on different decks, most don't know each other, even after spending six months at sea on the same ship. Usually they learn about a fellow crew member by reading about him in the ship's daily newspaper or seeing him on one of two television stations that beam live news and old movies and TV shows. (The most popular fare is a raunchy movie about a riot in a women's prison, one aired repeatedly and so bad that the crew says it's great.)

America is a floating small town—all male.

Many days, there is no sensation of being at sea. Unless they stand on the flight deck or work in the "island"—the starboard-side command structure that rises above the flight deck—crew members can't see the ocean. There are no portholes. And *America* is so massive, it is often unaffected by the water's roll. Being belowdecks can feel like being in a building.

Physical sensation: how it *feels* to be there.

When it left Norfolk, Va., on March 10 for a Mediterranean patrol, *America* took $9 million in cash because at sea it becomes its own economy. The crew gets paid. The crew buys things at the ship's stores. The proceeds are then used to pay the crew. Eighteen thousand meals are fixed a day, 280,000 gallons of sea water is distilled. The Navy loves to boast that there is a barber shop, a bakery, a photo lab, a post office, a printing plant, a tailor, and a public relations staff. In other words, much of the crew has nothing to do with weapons or war. They are service-sector Navy.

Specifics.

A lengthy passage of pure exposition.

The bigness does have an objective, of course: to fly a lot of planes and carry fuel and bombs for them. A U.S. carrier has 80 to 90 planes, more than all four Soviet mini-carriers combined. *America* has eight types of planes, more types than either the three British or two French carriers can hold. Besides 24 F-14s and 34 A-6 and A-7 bombers, *America* has four planes to refuel its planes in the air, four to detect enemy planes, four to jam enemy electronic equipment, 10 to hunt for submarines, and six helicopters to find downed pilots and to hunt for submarines. All told, there are 86 aircraft, which together can deliver 480,000 pounds of bombs, as much as 10 World War II-era aircraft carriers. When they're not flying, the planes can be stored and repaired on the hangar deck, which runs almost from bow to stern below the flight deck.

Comparisons of more specific details.

Another image designed
for Philadelphia readers.

Again, what the figures
mean in a reader's everyday terms.

The aircraft fly off a deck that is 1,047.5 feet long, not the biggest in the Navy, an honor that belongs to *Enterprise* at about 1,100 feet. But if stood on end, *America's* flight deck would be almost twice as high as William Penn's hat on City Hall. It is 252 feet wide. All told, the deck covers 4.6 acres, an expanse coated with black, coarse, nonskid paint. The crew has plenty of straightaway to jog in the hot sun when the planes aren't flying. Five lengths is a mile.

The flight deck is so big, *America* can launch four planes almost at once, two from box catapults and two from catapults amidships, on an extension of the flight deck that angles left. The angle enables the ship to launch and land simultaneously in some cases. While a plane is launched forward, another lands on the angle. If it misses all the arresting cables, it keeps going left, thereby avoiding the bow catapults.

Despite its weight, *America*, which is 22 years old, can glide through the water at 30 knots. The power is not nuclear but conventional boilers that drive four 22-foot-high propellers. In fuel for the ship and planes, in crew pay and in food and supplies, each hour of patrol costs taxpayers $22,917. That is $550,000 a day. That is $99 million for the normal six-month cruise —not counting the bills that its escorts run up.

Introduces and character-
izes the captain. His quote
defends the carrier against
the criticism we've heard
above.

Overall, *America* exudes seductive and expensive power, a sense magnified by the stateroom of Capt. Richard C. Allen. There, in the bowels of a ship designed for war, is an elegant living room with coffee table, sofa and wing chairs. The carpeting is bulkhead-to-bulkhead. The dining table can seat at least 10. Several lamps lend a soft light to the room.

Its occupant is a serious man who was born 46 years ago in Wisconsin and flew carrier jets until his eyes went bad. He wears wire-rims now; they give his soft and narrow face the look of a teacher. Allen, who has commanded *America* since July 1985, seemed perplexed by a suggestion that his ship might be at risk or should be anything but the size it is.

Two carriers half as big, for example, would mean two of everything. Allen said, two engine rooms, two sets of catapults, two bridges. Thus, two small carriers would be more than the cost of one big one. But neither would be as stable in rough seas, hampering flight operations, and neither would have so many planes able to do so many things. Even with the advances in missile and submarine warfare, he would much rather command a carrier now than during World War II. Besides, because *America* is big, it can take many bomb hits. And it is much harder to find than an airfield ashore.

"It's mobile, it's moving, it's never in the same place," the captain said. "Like right now. You're on it. Do you know exactly where we are? I'll share with you: We're southwest of Sicily. Tonight, we'll go north of Malta. This morning, we were east of Sardinia. The carrier moves. As a result, the targeting problem against a carrier is very complex . . .

Anecdote, related from
Capt. Allen's point of
view. Twomey must have
learned what was going
through Allen's mind from
the captain. Don't write
"he thought" without
confirming that the sub-
ject really thought it.

"It's extremely remote a carrier would ever be totally put out of—I mean, *sunk*. I think it's just something beyond imagination as I see it, by any threat that we see today or in the near future. This is a very capable piece of machinery."

Libya. They were actually going to hit Libya. Night had fallen. It was April 14, 1986. Allen looked down from the bridge at a dimly lighted flight deck jammed with aircraft, bombs and bullets bound for Benghazi. It was no drill. "I don't believe we're really doing this," he thought. "It's just unbelievable."

The crew had manned battle stations in record time. "All you have to do is tell somebody, 'We're going to go kill something,' and the level of interest goes up logarithmically. I mean, people become—they're *motivated*."

Thirty-eight planes from *America* would go. Somewhere in the darkness of the Mediterranean, the scene was being repeated on the *Coral Sea*. One by one, planes roared away. The most beautiful were the F-14s because, in order to get extra lift, they always flipped on their afterburners just before the "cat stroke," sending twin cones of flame 20 feet down the flight deck and lighting up the dark sea.

He was proud, Allen said, "to watch the complexity of the carrier pull together and to watch the thing take shape, until *boom*, there you are at night, and the cats start firing, and things happen just as they were planned."

And in the early hours of April 15, as the planes began coming back, crew members belowdecks watched the closed-circuit television shot of the flight deck to see whether the bombers had bombs under their wings. They didn't. And all 38 planes returned. The crew cheered wildly. (Fearing terrorist reprisals against the crew's families in the United States because of the carrier's role in the raid, the Navy requested that no crew member's name be used in this article, except Allen's, and it told crew members not to discuss Libya.)

"I just never thought the national decision would be to engage," Allen said. "I'm extremely proud of the President for having had the guts to do what he did."

Whatever its merit or morality, the U.S. raid on Libya to counter terrorism showed what carriers do best. They can sail to remote places and deal with Third World crises. They can, as the Navy puts it, "project power." Virtually every day of 1985, four U.S. carriers were somewhere at sea on patrol. Not the same four, of course, but a rotation that enables crews to avoid prolonged periods away from home. No other nation can deliver so much airpower wherever it wants. It is this ability to pop up anywhere swiftly that even critics of big carriers say makes carriers worth having.

It was carrier planes that forced down the civilian jet bearing the four hijackers of the cruise ship *Achille Lauro*. Carriers stood off Grenada and Lebanon during land operations in 1983. It is carriers that would be called on to reopen the Strait of Hormuz should Iran ever carry out its threat to cut oil lanes in its war with Iraq. Often, the mere arrival of the carrier is enough; none of its jets has to fire a shot.

"The carrier is an enormous politico-military capability," said Rear Adm. Jeremy J. Black, assistant chief of the Royal Navy Staff. "It is evident power. As you approach the thing, it emanates power. And wherever it will be, it will be a symbol of *American* power. That in itself is so significant."

"The aircraft carrier," said Norman Polmar, a noted U.S. defense analyst, "has demonstrated that it can move to the troubled area. It can remain offshore, in international waters, for days or weeks or months. . . . You're going to see many more low-level conflicts and confrontations, and aircraft will be necessary for us to observe, deter and, if necessary, fight."

Used this way, carriers are not at much risk. Grenada or Libya do not have the military skill to mount a serious threat. Or so the Navy thinks. Carriers stood off North Vietnam for years, launching air strikes but never taking one in return. The Navy has plans for big carriers, however, that would put them at risk.

Imagine: On May 30, 1987, Soviet tanks and infantry swarm across

This graf opens with a phrase that in effect says, "We will not discuss the well-publicized maiming of Khadafy's children." It forces the reader back to the story's point, which is the carrier, not the raid on Libya.

Good quote. Summarizes the gist of this passage.

Transitional quote moves the narrative to the next topic.

Subtle. With no loaded language, Twomey suggests an image of a bully picking on little guys. He does it by juxtaposing facts against quotes.

central Europe. For the moment, the conflict is conventional. The European Allies are barely holding on, and they need troops from the United States. Convoys are pieced together, civilian 747s commandeered. And carriers flood the Atlantic to baby these sea and air fleets across to Europe. They are to sink submarines and shoot planes. They are to sweep Soviet surface ships out of the sea lanes linking Old World and New.

Background: how the Navy is pushing for more carriers, larger fleets.

That has been part of U.S. strategy for years. Navy Secretary Lehman has added a twist, however. After carriers make the oceans safe for passage, he wants to send them on aggressive forays close to the Soviet Union to finish off the Soviet navy and then bomb land targets. Carriers would sail near the Kola Peninsula, off the Soviet Union's far north coast. They would sweep into the Baltic Sea. They would cruise off the Soviet's Pacific coast. By crushing the Soviets on their flanks with carrier power, Lehman argues, the United States would take pressure off the war in central Europe.

This "forward strategy" fuels a push by Lehman for a 600-ship Navy. The number of warships had slipped to 479 after Vietnam, and the Carter administration had decided not to build carriers to succeed the aging *Coral Sea* and *Midway*, which were both due to be retired. It thought big ships were too vulnerable and expensive. The number of carriers was set at 12.

But Lehman sought—and got—congressional approval during the first Reagan term for three giant nuclear-powered carriers and all their escorts, which together will consume 41 percent of Navy construction costs from now to the year 2000—$60 billion. Two of the carriers will replace *Midway* and *Coral Sea*, and the third will represent a net gain. So, the number of big carriers will actually rise to 15.

Lehman says the fleet expansion centered on big carriers is crucial to the "forward strategy." The United States must get the enemy in his lair, and only big carriers can do it. But it's not the same enemy as it used to be.

Interesting anecdote leads into a discussion of Soviet naval power. These scenes move the article forward, much as do scenes in a fictional story.

"Captain said to tell you we got a Udaloy coming in."

Churning on an opposite course in the twilight, the sleek visitor whipped past on *America*'s port side, swerved across its wake and pulled up off the starboard side about 1,000 yards away. Its speed and course now matched the carrier's. From the flight deck, a few crew members gave a look, but they had seen one before.

The Udaloy is a new class of Soviet destroyer. Each has 64 surface-to-air missiles, eight torpedo tubes, eight antisubmarine missiles and two helicopters. The ships steam at 32 knots. *America*'s crew calls them "tattletales."

Soviet destroyers and frigates routinely weave in and out among U.S. battle groups. The high seas belong to no one; the Soviets have every right to sail wherever they want. The encounters are always courteous. Both sides follow the rules of the road. What the Soviets are doing is taking notes. They watch the pattern of flight operations and the types of exercises. They see how the task force moves. They watch how different planes perform.

"The Soviets? Oh yeah, they'll come right off the quarter, 1,000 yards, 500 yards, follow us around, back and forth," Allen said the next day as the Udaloy hovered. "Whatever we do, they do. If we turn, they turn. . . . They take pictures. They pick up garbage. They do weird things. Usually they just follow you around."

Such open-ocean presence reflects the new Soviet Navy. Russia had never been a sea power, under the czars or under communism. Just 20 years ago, Soviet ships spent a fleet total of 5,700 days at sea, according to U.S. estimates. Last year, they spent 57,000. The Soviets now have the world's largest navy, with 283 major surface ships and 381 submarines, split between 77 ballistic missile-launching submarines (for delivering nuclear warheads to the United States) and 304 attack submarines (for sinking ships, such as U.S. ballistic missile-firing submarines or the carriers). That is 664 warships, compared to the 541 the United States has at the moment. That is three times the total of U.S. attack submarines, the kind needed to find Soviet attack submarines before they find U.S. carriers.

More exposition. Comparisons help make sense of figures.

Assigned to the Soviet navy are 1,625 aircraft, mainly operating from land. Their job, too, is to sink U.S. ships. Most formidable, perhaps, is the new Backfire bomber, which can fly at 1,100 knots for 3,400 miles without refueling, bearing big air-to-surface missiles. At the end of 1985, there were 120 Backfires, with more being added each year.

Some Soviet planes are even at sea. Four modest aircraft carriers have been built, and each has 13 planes and 19 helicopters. Like British "jump jets," the planes take off and land by moving vertically. Last year, the Soviet Union launched an American-size carrier of at least 65,000 tons and designed for 60 planes and helicopters. It will not be operational for several years, however, because the Soviets must first master the dance of launching and landing so many aircraft.

Though the Soviet navy is large, there is disagreement about how much of a threat it is, at least away from its coastal waters. In a study last year, the Center for Defense Information said that 145 of the Soviets' surface ships were too small, less then 2,000 tons, to venture into the open sea for long. It said the Soviets have a limited ability to resupply ships at sea, which America does very well. (It has to: A battle group gulps 10,000 barrels of fuel a day.) Nor do the Soviets have as many anchorages in other countries as the United States has. And while the Soviets now have carriers, no one argues that the vessels are any match for U.S. carriers.

Another passage explaining what the facts mean.

Nonetheless, Lehman and other Navy officials tout the Soviets as a huge, aggressive force, plying waters they never did before with power they never had before. They point to the Gulf of Mexico, where major Soviet naval forces sailed twice last year. "In many areas of the world, the Hammer and Sickle now overshadows the Stars and Stripes," the unabashedly pro-Navy magazine Sea Power intoned last fall.

Much of this gloom-and-doom, of course, is to justify the need for 600 very expensive ships: The Pentagon must face a worthy foe. And even the Center for Defense Information, in its study, said the Soviets would be very tough adversaries close to home if Lehman's "forward strategy" were ever tried. And farther out to sea, Soviet attack submarines and Backfire bombers could, indeed, threaten convoys and their carrier escorts.

Yet even while highlighting Soviet power, the Navy says, in effect, no problem. It's got a system.

Transition to the next passage. Effectively links the two segments.

Much of the time, America seems alone in the Mediterranean, free of Soviet tattletales and steaming toward an empty horizon. Not even fishermen chug by. But the Small Boys are never far away.

There are 10 sprinkled in a circle around America, two cruisers, four destroyers and four frigates, sometimes moving in close, sometimes sailing out of sight. One or two U.S. attack submarines are often there as well, but because they are underwater, it's hard to be sure; Allen said only that they are not there all the time.

America never leaves home without the Small Boys, whose crews say that they are the true sailors and that the carrier is just the Bird Farm. Battle groups are the key to what the Navy calls defense-in-depth. The idea is to keep the $3.5 billion airfield at the center from being sunk.

The first sentry is not a ship, however. It is a plane, one that does not carry any weapons and cannot fly fast. The E-2C Hawkeye looks like a small AWACs plane, the Air Force's Airborne Warning and Control aircraft that seem to have a giant mushroom on their backs. The mushroom has radar.

Often the first plane to leave the carrier during launches, the E-2's job is to park in the sky and see what else is up there. Its radar can scan 100,000 feet up and in an arc 250 miles around *America*. If it identified enemy planes, the E-2 would call in what deck crews call the Super Hot Fighter Pilots, only they use a more descriptive word than *super*.

The men who fly the $38.7 million F-14 fighters are just about as smug and smooth as *Top Gun* portrays them. *America*'s pilots haven't seen the movie because they have been at sea. But they've seen the Kenny Loggins video clip, featuring shots of twisting, blasting F-14s. It was flown out to the ship. They love it.

"Yeah, that's us," said a 28-year-old pilot from Drexel Hill. "We're *cool*. We're *fighter pilots*."

Most are in their late 20s or early 30s. Handsomeness seems to be a job requirement. Catapulting off a carrier, which subjects them to a jolt seven or eight times the force of gravity, "is a lifetime E-ticket at Disneyland," said the Drexel Hill pilot.

"To be sitting in that machine and to know that 300 feet later you'll be going 200 miles per hour and the whole thing takes 2 1/2 seconds—well, the level of concentration in sports or whatever has never reached *that* adrenaline high," said a 42-year-old pilot from Philadelphia, who has done it 1,250 times.

Their job is to hunt down enemy planes and destroy them before they can launch missiles at America. Or, as Adm. Mauz, the battle group commander, put it, "We want to shoot the archer rather than the arrow."

F-14s, which can fly at more that twice the speed of sound, have Phoenix missiles with a range of 120 miles, as well as shorter-range Sidewinder and Sparrow missiles. The F-14s would be helped by four EA-6B Prowlers from the carrier, planes whose task is to scramble the radar of attacking enemy planes and baffle their missile guidance systems. Needless to say, the fighter pilots don't think anyone will get past them. What a silly suggestion; without the carrier, they would get wet.

"This is home," said the air wing commander, 40, who is in charge of all the pilots of all the various types of planes. "This is where dinner is. This is where the stereo is."

If attacking planes did skirt the F-14s and fire missiles, the next line would take over, the Small Boys. They would rely on Aegis, a defensive system just entering service aboard a new line of cruisers and destroyers; America's battle group has one of the new ships, the cruiser *Ticonderoga*. The Aegis is designed to find and track dozens of hostile missiles. Judging by a test one day on *America*, the gun's noise alone might destroy them.

Soviet submarines would be found by *America*'s 10 S-3A Viking planes. Their electronics can look down through the water and spot a submarine. The plane then drops a depth charge or torpedo. The battle group also scours with sonar and can fire an array of weapons at submarines.

Actually, Navy officials hate to talk about all this defense. They say outsiders spend too much time worrying about how vulnerable carriers are. The ships are for offense, first. "It's sort of like your house," said the air wing commander. "You take steps to protect it, but you don't go around protecting it all the time. I'm not worried every day my stereo's going to be stolen. I'd rather go bomb something."

Reveals personnel's mentality; final remark—presented without editorial comment—is chilling.

It came out of the west just after launch, skimming 10 feet above the South Atlantic at 680 miles per hour. On the bridge of *Sheffield*, a British frigate, Lts. Peter Walpole and Brian Leyshon had seen a puff of smoke on the horizon but didn't know what it meant and hadn't seen the Argentine Super Etendard fighter. One mile out, they both recognized what was coming their way.

Abrupt shift to anecdote about *Sheffield*. Seems to support critics and . . .

"My God," they said simultaneously, "it's a missile."

Four seconds later, the Exocet hit starboard amidships, above the water line, and veered down into the engine room, where its 363 pounds of high explosive detonated. In an instant, *Sheffield* lost electrical power and communications. Fires broke out. The edge of the hole in the ship's side glowed red from the blazes, but there was no water pressure to put them out. As flames crept toward the magazine, where ammunition is stored, the crew abandoned *Sheffield*.

A new, $50 million ship had been destroyed—and 20 of its crew killed —by a single, small computer-guided missile costing one one-hundredth as much.

What happened that Tuesday, May 4, 1982, during the Falklands War was the most stunning example in history of the power of the anti-ship missile. These weapons can strike from much greater distances than naval guns and, unlike shells, can be guided to their targets. Photos of *Sheffield*, listing and burning, depict the critics' nightmare of what will happen to carriers.

There is little chance, certainly, that one, two or even three Exocets could sink a U.S. carrier. It is just too big. And the Navy accurately says that the British had less ability to detect, track and destroy enemy planes than a U.S. battle group has. Britain's two Falkland carriers had no planes like Hawkeyes to spot the Super Etendards. They had far fewer fighters to attack them. No British ship had Aegis. Polmar, the military analyst, says a U.S. carrier force would have destroyed the Argentine air force "in two days."

But there are missiles that could threaten a carrier—cruise missiles. They are flying torpedoes with large warheads, launched up to 350 miles from their targets and often moving at supersonic speed. Backfire bombers can carry them. About 30 Soviet surface ships can carry them. And so do 62 Soviet submarines, including the new Oscar class. Each Oscar has 24 cruise missiles. Two are at sea now, with another joining the fleet every two years.

. . . leads into a discussion of cruise missile threat.

"We do not have an adequate defense for cruise missiles," said Adm. Carroll of the Center for Defense Information. "It's been the bête noire of naval strategy for some time now. We've made progress. We've got Phalanx and such. But I'll guarantee you that if you take those carriers in range of Soviet land-based aircraft and cruise missiles, there will be enough cruise missiles coming through the defense to hit the ships. I don't know how many will get through, but say it's one out of five. And if one out of five hits our ships? It's all over."

Aegis is supposed to deal with cruise missiles, but its performance has not been flawless. Initially, it knocked down only four of 15 attacking missiles in tests. Later, that rose to 10 of 11, but doubts remain. Moreover, a missile doesn't have to sink a carrier to render it useless. Each carrier has four very weak points—its catapults. Without them, planes don't fly. The Navy thinks it is highly unlikely that any enemy will get so lucky as to put all four out of action at once. But then, naval history is replete with lucky moments.

Transition to submarine threat.

A carrier's greatest foe, however, is not in the air. It is the enemy it never sees. Gary Hart calls them the kings of the sea. And the Soviets have more of them than anyone. In March 1984, a Soviet nuclear-powered attack submarine rose up under *Kitty Hawk* in the Sea of Japan, bumping it and damaging both ships. It was an accident, not an attack. But the battle group had not detected the sub, even though at least five Small Boys were around *Kitty Hawk*.

Hair-raising incident.

Because it was peacetime, it was possible the escorts weren't "pinging" with sonar to find subs. The incident, however, illustrates how stealthy subs can be. They are a threat not only from their cruise missiles, but from their torpedoes. While the Navy believes its detection skills are good, they are not perfect. "We don't always know where they are," said Capt. Allen, "so we don't know whether we're being followed or not all the time."

Oddly, Allen has never been on a submarine at sea, despite being in the Navy for 27 years. Critics say that would be an excellent way for carrier captains to learn how their underwater adversaries work and think.

Summarizes the carrier's precarious nature; validity of critics' stance.

Given the air and sea threats to carriers, Lehman's "forward strategy" could end in the destruction of the heart of the Navy. It would be going right where the defenses are thickest. Stripped of even a few of its carriers, the Navy might then be unable to do its more important job, protecting the sea lanes. That, in turn, would jeopardize a war in central Europe.

"If we wail into battle against the Soviets depending on just 15 ships, we will, like the Spanish Armada, sail in expectation of a miracle," Hart writes in *America Can Win*. "Perhaps we will get one, although the precedent is not encouraging. Perhaps the opponent, despite numerous submarines and aircraft, will prove incompetent. But our survival, as a navy and a nation, would depend . . . on massive incompetence, not on our strength."

Even if the strategy worked and the carriers sank huge portions of the Soviet navy, the cornered Soviets might shift first to tactical and then strategic nuclear weapons to stave off surrender. In that case, the carriers' size wouldn't matter.

Wrap takes us back to where we came in: romance and adventure of carrier life.

Astern of *America*, they formed a necklace of lights in the night sky, 15 planes strung out in a row. They had lined up to take their turns coming home. It was 11:30 p.m.

On a catwalk hanging over the side of the flight deck, four landing-signals officers stood peering into the dark. LSOs can tell just by looking at wing lights, if a returning pilot is on the right glide path, dropping 100 feet for each quarter mile to the ship.

"You're high, high," an LSO said softly into his radio to the first inbound plane. It was too dark to see what kind it was.

No task in all of aviation is more difficult than landing on a carrier at night. While modern jets can all but fly themselves and the carrier has runway lights, pilots have none of the usual reference points, such as the lights of a city. The sky is black, the water is black. They cannot tell where one stops and the other starts. All they can see is a short line of light. They cannot even see the ship, let alone the deck. No matter what instruments can say and computers can do, that is frightening.

The first plane drew nearer. It crossed the stern. Sparks shot from the flight deck as the arresting hook hit first, searching for one of the four cables. It found one, yanking an A-7 to a halt in 350 feet, one-tenth of the distance a plane needs to land. The lights of the next plane grew larger.

"Foul deck! Foul deck!" said two LSOs.

Until the A-7 could be unhooked and moved aside, until the arresting cables were back in position, until deck crews had moved, the LSOs would keep telling the next pilot his runway was blocked. If necessary, they would wave him off. On this night, they would not have to; the crews were perfect.

Sparks flew, engines roared. In 16 minutes, all the planes were down. The ship grew quiet for the night, sailing on.

"Sometimes," said an LSO, "I can't believe what we do out here."

EDITORIAL OVERVIEW

This is a story written for people who *like* to read. It gives the lie to the theory that newspaper readers crave staccato bursts of information occupying their attention no longer than would a typical television ad.

Characteristic of a newspaper report, the article does not overtly reveal its author's assessment of the issues. Instead, it presents serious questions about carriers like *America* and offers answers from men who are committed to maintaining these ships. The only subjective impression we get is that Twomey had a great deal of fun working on this story.

As a result, he turns a potentially dry subject—the quarrel between military experts over a massively expensive warship that may be outmoded—into a fun read. He does so by using fictional techniques: characterization, dialog, anecdote, vivid description. He brings facts to life with metaphor, simile, repetition, and comparison, and he moves the facts along the way a fiction writer would move a narrative: scene by scene. Yet the story's architecture—lead, bridge, body, wrap-up—is typical of the classic feature article.

–30–

22

History Articles

History pieces are reports about the past. Like reports on contemporary issues, they challenge the writer to keep the copy interesting while reciting a collection of potentially dull facts. They tend to lack immediacy, unless tied to some current event such as a new historic preservation project or a centennial.

Still, readers love history. Such stories are especially popular in local and regional publications, where the audience feels some pride or interest in a region's past. People like to know what problems their forebears faced and how they tackled them.

For this reason, here—as in the report—it is often most effective to open a history story by focusing on someone who is or was involved in the action.

Once, for example, I was asked to write about a statewide historic preservation program. Acting on my first impulse, I wrote a cinematic lead that panned in on a particularly depressed small town and then focused on the physical restoration in progress. Boring! After some agony, I recalled an activist couple who had moved West from Maine. They had told me of their distress and horror at seeing their adopted town's elegant old high school demolished. By implication, they suggested the event launched their crusade to install a federally-funded redevelopment program. The story opened with those folks watching that old school tumble to the ground. And it worked.

If the story is set in the recent past, a nostalgic approach may succeed: "do you remember when . . . ." This usually hooks older readers and may interest younger ones who are curious about their elders' lives. But don't lay any money on nostalgia as a draw for youngsters.

Do set scenes that provide vivid description. Portray the story's actors as fully human, not as quaint caricatures or larger-than-life heroes.

Don't put thoughts in a historic figure's mind unless you have written proof that he or she was thinking those thoughts. One student wrote of an early explorer that he must have been exhilarated by a particular desert vista; actually, the 19th-century perspective on wilderness was entirely different from the electrified, air-conditioned, and romantic 20th-century viewpoint.

Similarly, avoid putting imagined quotes into a historic figure's mouth. It's fine to quote a diary, letter, or memoir that reports a person's specific remark, but never create your own dialogue for history pieces or any other kind of nonfiction.

Before you start to write, sketch a timeline so that you will have the chronology firmly in mind. Be sure the reader can follow the sequence of events as well as the larger logic of your story—don't jump from date to date without explicit, clear transitions. As you edit your final draft, check specifically for this concern. Readers can easily lose their way in a maze of unfamiliar dates and occurences.

Research for a history story depends as much or more on local sources as on the major resources we discussed in chapters 3 and 4. You will want to seek out two kinds of sources: *primary*, or reports directly from those who experienced or witnessed an event; and *secondary*, commentary by scholars and others not directly involved.

City libraries often have special collections for local history, and the personnel in charge of those sections can be very knowledgeable. Many university libraries also have fine local history collections. There you may find ample printed material on your subject. States, counties, and cities invariably host historical societies and archives, the mother lodes of letters, memoirs, diaries, maps, historic photographs, and printed sources—as well as experts who know the subject. State governmental archives are also invaluable; they are usually located in or near the capital city. Historical society museums often open their libraries to researchers working on a given project; their curators usually cooperate with journalists. Corporations that have been in business for many years may compile statistical and historical archives; among the most likely sources are banks and utilities.

Over the past decade, oral history has become a popular cause among academics. For this reason, university and college history departments often can direct you to elderly people who remember half a century of a region's history. Obviously, their first-hand accounts can give your story life. Some scholars collect taped interviews with old-timers, superb source material if you can gain access to it. The way to ingratiate yourself with these academics is to give them generous credit in your published piece.

THE FIRST 1040

by Nancy Shepherdson

American Heritage, March 1989

Lead is short and to the point. This story does not have a nut graf because the lead makes the story's subject very clear.

Near the top, Shepherdson focuses on the most amazing aspect of early-day income tax: people were happy to pay it. As she describes this strange attitude, she briefly explains why.

Note the easy-going, conversational tone. History pieces for popular magazines must not smack of stuffy library stacks. Despite the academic subject, this is still a *story.*

These quotes probably came from newspaper articles—secondary sources. Quotation is as vital to the history story as to any other kind of journalism.

On the evening of March 1, 1914, Americans all around the nation inaugurated what has become a spring ritual for millions of us. They raced to file the first Form 1040 at the last minute before the deadline, hurrying by motorcar or trolley or on foot.

In New York City stragglers braved a blizzard to reach the Customs House office of the Bureau of Internal Revenue, which, like district offices everywhere, stayed open until midnight. Their last-minute scurrying was front-page news in the *Times* the next day, and it saved them from being the first Americans to pay penalties for late filing. The weather, no matter how severe, was no excuse, as three men snowbound on a train from New York to Chicago found out. They arrived just after midnight and rushed to file. The tax collector, Samuel N. Fitch, was unyielding. "If they're late, they're late," he said, "and there is no use in coming in to-day."

Some citizens were reluctant to concede that the government had a right to share their income. A tax collector in Chicago was overheard saying into the telephone: "The penalty is up to $2,500 fine and maybe a year in prison. . . . Yes, a taxi would get you here the quickest." But amazingly from today's perspective, most Americans actually welcomed the tax.

The attitude made considerable sense. Nobody would owe any tax or even, usually, have to file a return if he or she earned less than three thousand dollars (four thousand if married) —and that was the equivalent of more than thirty-five thousand dollars (forty-seven thousand if married) today. In fact, the tax was deliberately designed to affect only the wealthiest one percent of the population, and revenues from it were intended to permit the reduction of crushing protective tariffs and excise taxes that disproportionately burdened the poor and the middle class by adding sharply to the prices of food, clothing, and other necessities.

One Missourian expressed joy in the tax in a note he attached to his return: "I have purposely left out some deductions I could claim, in order to have the privilege and the pleasure of paying at least a small income tax. . . . I had rather pay twice as much direct and certain tax to and for support of the Federal Government than to pay only half as much indirectly [in tariffs]." And the New York *Herald* observed the emergence of "the young man who overstates his income in order to be among those who are obliged to pay an income tax." The paper predicted that "many a $12 to $20 a week clerk will be waving an income tax receipt from the stool of his favorite quick lunch to show his value and standing in the commercial world."

The new Form 1040 required taxpayers to report income "of whatever kind," beginning, as we do now, with salaries, wages, and compensation for personal services. Most dividends were exempt, as long as the company issuing them had paid its corporate income tax. Gain on the sale of most types of property would receive no special treatment until 1921; capital losses were not recognized at all.

Only six categories of deductions were allowed: business expenses, interest on personal debt, other taxes paid, casualty losses not covered by insurance, bad debts, and depreciation of business property. Medical expenses and mortgage interest, considered "personal, living, or family expenses," were not deductible.

The new income tax's basic levy of 1 percent on incomes between three thousand and twenty thousand dollars was supplemented by a surtax of up to 6 percent on higher incomes. It was estimated that John D. Rockefeller would owe almost two million dollars in annual taxes, Andrew Carnegie almost six hundred thousand, and the extravagant Vanderbilts a mere one hundred thousand. The average worker—a man, woman, or child putting in perhaps twelve hours a day—earned eight hundred dollars per year, slightly more than one-quarter of the lowest taxable wage.

Proponents of the tax had long argued that it would offer the only fair way to shift the burden of taxation toward those with the greatest ability to pay. In an era when everyone knew, for instance, that William K. Vanderbilt had a garage on his Long Island estate with space for one hundred automobiles, the ostentatious wealthy were an irresistible target for reform-minded lawmakers—especially since many of the very rich actually benefited personally from the high tariffs protecting the industries they owned.

Attempts to tap Americans' earnings to support the government had begun back in the Massachusetts Bay Colony, which taxed tradesmen such as tailors, masons, and blacksmiths. The first income tax collected by the United States government was signed into law by Abraham Lincoln in 1862 to finance the Civil War. Most people with incomes of more than six hundred dollars willingly paid their share as long as the war lasted. The tax was repealed in 1872.

The short-lived Civil War tax gave rise to two institutions that are still very much with us. One was progressive rates, introduced not to make the burden equitable but simply to raise revenue. The other was the Internal Revenue Service, then known as the Bureau of Internal Revenue. Taxpayers were assessed by collectors through notices in newspapers and public places, which if not answered were followed up with personal visits. For a time the bureau tried paying commissions to its employees but it abandoned that idea when several agents, pocketing both tax payments and commissions, simply disappeared.

The Civil War tax forcefully demonstrated the revenue-raising power of an income tax, and the lesson was never forgotten. Between 1873 and 1879 fourteen income tax bills were introduced by congressmen from the South and Midwest, where income was lowest and the impact of tariffs greatest. A bill finally was passed in 1894 that would have put a flat 2 percent tax on incomes of more than four thousand dollars. It made Rep. David De Armond of Missouri nearly delirious: "The passage of the bill will make the dawn of

Factual description of the early tax. Probably gleaned from a secondary source. Wraps it up with surprising comment on the poverty of the average American in 1914.

Transition—contrasting conspicuous consumption with that $800 average annual wage—explains something about why many people welcomed the tax and moves the story into the history of how the tax came about.

Chronological reprise of early efforts to establish an income tax. This material probably summarizes one or more academic histories of taxation.

a brighter day, with more of sunshine, more of the songs of birds, more of that sweetest music, the laughter of children well fed, well clothed, well housed." Stockholders of several companies saw things differently and filed suits to challenge the tax's constitutionality. One of the cases, *Pollock v. Farmers' Loan and Trust Company,* ended in one of the most questionable Supreme Court decisions of all time.

The Court had to decide whether the tax was an indirect one, permitted by the Constitution, or a direct one, forbidden by Article I unless apportioned on the basis of population. The plaintiffs argued passionately that the Founding Fathers had considered any taxes on rents and personal property direct. The record of the Constitutional Convention gives no indication of this, but in May 1895 the Court declared the entire income tax legislation invalid, even though it had retroactively upheld the Civil War tax fifteen years before. Justice Stephen J. Field, who had voted with the majority in that case, was still sitting in 1895, but he had changed his mind. "The present assault upon capital is but the beginning," he wrote in his concurring opinion, and if it continues, "our political contests will become a war of the poor against the rich."

Justice Edward D. White's dissent seemed to support speculation that the Court was acting in self-interest: "If the permanency of its conclusions is to depend upon the personal opinions of those who from time to time may make up its membership, it will inevitably become a theater of political strife and its action will be without coherence or consistency."

Despite the ruling, the income tax idea would not die. Between 1895 and 1900 forty-two more income tax bills were introduced, exclusively by Democrats and Populists from the South and West. Even President Theodore Roosevelt came out for a tax during a 1906 speech. To the immense relief of fellow Republicans, he did not pursue the idea further.

One Democrat in the Tennessee legislature watched the development and demise of the 1894 tax especially closely. Cordell Hull, later Franklin Roosevelt's Secretary of State, represented a poor, rural district and was convinced that "wealth was shirking its share of the tax burdens." He was elected to Congress in 1906 and promoted the income tax idea almost to the point of obsession throughout the 60th Congress.

"I talked to some Congressmen so often they were no longer willing to listen," he later recalled. "House leaders . . . strongly favoring an income tax, would turn and walk in another direction when they saw me approaching." Unfortunately for Hull, the House was still dominated by Republican "stand-patters," who supported the tariff as a means of keeping wages (not to mention profits) high. He would not be deterred.

In 1909 Hull managed to get a bill considered as an amendment to the Republican-sponsored Payne Tariff Bill, but it was promptly defeated, and the tariff was approved and sent to the Senate, seemingly out of Hull's reach. Then, in a quirk of fate with lasting reverberations, Hull had the good fortune to share a sleeping car with Sen. Joseph W. Bailey of Texas, a strong advocate of the 1894 tax. By the time the train reached Tennessee, Hull had persuaded Bailey to sponsor an income tax amendment in the Senate.

Meanwhile a bipartisan alliance was emerging in the Senate among those who opposed increased tariffs and thus supported an income tax. To counter this movement, President Taft secretly worked out a compromise during golf games at Chevy Chase and clandestine evening carriage rides. If the Democrats and protax Republicans would drop the tax from the tariff bill, the administration and regular Republicans would back a resolution authorizing an income tax amendment to the Constitution—an amendment they doubted would ever be ratified.

The deal was struck. The Republicans got their tariff, but with prices soaring, the vast majority of Americans continued to blame the tariff for the high cost of living. The income tax amendment began to pass in state after state.

The deal backfires on tariff proponents. Suggests populist support for income tax.

On February 3, 1913, the Sixteenth Amendment was approved by Wyoming, the thirty-sixth state to do so and the last required. Only Connecticut, Florida, Rhode Island, and Utah had voted no. The amendment gave Congress the power to "lay and collect taxes on incomes, from whatever sources derived, without apportionment among the several States and without regard to any census or enumeration." A permanent income tax was now possible.

Congress went to work. Cordell Hull got the job of drafting a law and took on the task with relish, poring through a mountain of statistics on the economy and making a detailed study of income tax laws around the world. According to Hull's biographer, Harold B. Hinton, the congressman based the system on the government's need for revenue and the individual's ability to pay, with no thought of redistributing income. It soon became apparent, though, that the law's effect was to use the income of the rich to pay for services for the disadvantaged.

How Hull fashioned the 1914 income tax law despite opposition. This is given short shrift, but the story might have bogged down had Shepherdson dwelt on it in detail.

Debate on the House floor lasted just two days. More than a few representatives—particularly those who wanted to see the provision fail—suggested changes. Several proposals for higher rates, including one with a top level of 68 percent, were defeated. President Wilson urged that the exemption be fixed at three thousand dollars, to "burden as small a number of persons as possible with . . . what will at best be an unpopular law"; the House settled on a more generous four-thousand-dollar exemption because, according to one representative, that was the amount required to "maintain an American family according to the American standard and send the children through college."

The measure passed the House on May 8, 1913, substantially unchanged. In the Senate the debate lasted through a steamy summer. A demand for an increase in the surtax on very large incomes led to a compromise that set the maximum surtax at 6 percent on incomes of more than five hundred thousand dollars. An exemption of five hundred dollars for each child of a married couple was rejected; the final bill lowered the personal exemption to three thousand dollars for individuals and kept it at four thousand dollars for married taxpayers. Since then Congress has never stopped struggling with the problem of equalizing the tax burden on people in different family circumstances.

Lasting problems.

The Underwood-Simmons Tariff Act, with the income tax amendment attached, was approved by the Senate on September 9, 1913. It went to the President for his signature less than a month later and became law on October 3, effective retroactively to March 1, 1913.

What it was called, specifically; date the act became law.

By far the most controversial aspect of the final bill turned out to be "collection at the source," which had been tucked away in Hull's original proposal. Based on a system then in use in England, this required that any entity paying anyone three thousand dollars or more in income withhold 1 percent of it and pay it directly to the Treasury. Withholding on salaries has since become a routine part of our lives, but the original version meant, for

Some exotic aspects of the early law.

instance, that tenants would have to ensure the payment of taxes by their landlords. Corporations and banks were asked to collect taxes on interest earned, exempting only those who filed certificates declaring their income to be less than three thousand dollars a year. And the certificates weren't immediately available, even though withholding was supposed to begin November 1, 1913.

Collection at the source proved unworkable and was repealed in 1916; simple salary withholding was not introduced until 1943. The penalties for late filing in 1913 ranged from twenty dollars to one thousand dollars, depending on the amount owed. A fraudulent return could cost two thousand dollars or a year in prison or both.

People's reaction to the new law.

Humorous quote that could apply to today's income tax confusion.

Despite the simplicity of the form, it perplexed thousands. Very few regulations had been issued, and no tax rulings had yet been made. As *Leslie's Illustrated Weekly* predicted, the birth of Form 1040 had to mean "a rich harvest for lawyers." Sen. Elihu Root reportedly warned a friend who couldn't master the form: "I guess you will have to go to jail. If that is the result of not understanding the Income Tax law I shall meet you there. We will have a merry, merry time, for all of our friends will be there. It will be an intellectual center, for no one understands the Income Tax law except persons who have not sufficient intelligence to understand the questions that arise under it."

How-to articles appeared in all sorts of publications. "Don't get excited," counseled *The New York Times*. "Look Blank 1,040 squarely in the face." In 1915 the newspaper observed that many House members were going to the office of the sergeant at arms for help in completing their own returns. Ordinary taxpayers could get assistance too. Local district offices of the Bureau of Internal Revenue offered help both in person and by telephone.

The government's reaction.

Interesting item: where the "1040" designation came from.

The birth of a bureaucracy.

The bureau's Washington staff of 277 had only several weeks in late 1913 to create and distribute Form 1040, whose name simply indicated the next in an old series of bureau form numbers. The bureau had survived the repeal of the Civil War tax and all the years since but had been doing little more than enforcing the payment of excise taxes. With the passage of the new law, 477 new field agents were taken on, each at eight dollars per day, to examine returns.

Results of the first levy.

No money had to be sent in with any return that first year. Instead each taxpayer's computation of his liability was verified by the bureau's field agents, who then sent out bills. A *New York Times* editorial complained that this gave the taxpayer "the same option that the eel has about being skinned." Nonetheless, the process proceeded amazingly smoothly. By June 1, 1914, the tax bills were ready to be sent out, payable by the end of the month. When the receipts were tallied, more than twenty-eight million dollars had been collected. That was far less than the seventy million dollars Hull had predicted, but it was enough to prove to most members of Congress that a great resource had been discovered for raising revenue without grave consequences at the polls.

Political aftereffects; Supreme Court reverses itself.

Probably from Supreme Court records.

In fact the new tax created political capital for most of those involved. The average tariff rate had been lowered from a high of more than 40 percent to about 29 percent. There were, of course, court challenges. But in 1916 the Supreme Court, led by Justice White, the chief dissenter in the *Pollock* case, found the tax constitutional on all counts. Hull immediately declared, "We are now free to go ahead to revise the law to meet new needs." Later that year he proposed augmenting the tax to raise an additional seventy-five million dollars "without making it burdensome."

As everybody knows, taxes would never be that low—or that popular—again. The assassination of Archduke Franz Ferdinand in Sarajevo on June 28, 1914, changed everything. By 1919 the maximum tax rate had risen from 7 percent to 77 percent, and the Revenue Act of 1917 had lowered the minimum taxable income to one thousand dollars. As Hull had observed in a 1910 speech to the House, "We cannot expect always to be at peace. If this nation were tomorrow plunged into a war with a great commercial country . . . we would be helpless to prosecute [it] without taxing the wealth of the country in the form of incomes." It would take just one more great war, less than three decades later, to transform Hull's gentlemanly "class tax" into the mass tax we know today.

Allusive reference to what was to come.

Wrap reflects on the difference between the intention and the results.

EDITORIAL OVERVIEW

Nancy Shepherdson's writing shows she has a rare and wonderful gift: the ability to distill heavy source material into simple, clear language. She has undoubtedly used the *Congressional Record*, several stolid tomes on the history of taxation, records from the Supreme Court, memoirs, and perhaps some less-than-exciting biographies to produce this easy-to-read story. She also has read newspaper reports of the period.

By pulling quotes from primary and secondary sources, Shepherdson gives the copy something like immediacy: you feel what the events must have meant to those who lived through them. This characteristic is key to successful journalism, whether you are writing history pieces or current news reports. Focusing on people—humanizing the facts—will bring your story to life.

Although the story's structure is roughly chronological, the background material that begins in the tenth paragraph takes us back 52 years before the lead's time frame. In effect, the author begins *in medias res*—in the middle of things—by showing us how people responded to the first income tax levy and then filling in the background. This is a classic fictional technique.

–30–

23

Nonfiction Humor

Humorous stories are probably the only ones free-lancers should submit over the transom, without querying an editor. Two reasons for this:

1. There's no way an editor can tell from a three-paragraph query whether you can sustain your repartee through a whole feature; and

2. One man's joke is another man's affliction. What tickles one editor may simply bore another. Too, unless you are a professional humorist or you run across an intrinsically hilarious story, it's hard to be funny on assignment.

Some years ago, I proposed to the editor of a newspaper's Sunday magazine a take-off on a comedy of errors that befell a friend when she tried to set up a computer she had received through the mail. This particular editor and I saw the world from the same twisted perspective. Hashing over the woman's misadventures, we laughed till the tears ran down our faces. It was, we agreed as he handed over a contract, one of the most brilliant ideas we had ever concocted.

Six weeks later, it didn't seem the least bit funny. A couple of minor personal crises had temporarily darkened my mood, and I no longer saw much humor in the run-around my friend had gone through. Nor could I find anyone else with comparable experiences that might broaden the story. As the deadline grew nigh, I was in deep trouble.

Three days before the story was due, I met a computer buff who was a CompuServe addict. In desperation, I asked him to show me how the database worked, which he did. As he talked, it became apparent that he and other CompuServe fans viewed those electronic halls as actual, physical places: malls and libraries and meeting rooms. Ah, weirdness! By straining every synapse, I managed to crank out 1500 words describing this oddity of the technocratic psyche and pass it off as humor. Luckily, my editor was highly amused—but I'll never agree to be funny on contract again.

Writers use several devices in crafting humor. *Parody* makes fun of an individual or a circumstance by imitating certain features, usually weaknesses. The broad humor of *Mad* Magazine is largely parody. Much more sophisticated is "Dr. Science," the PBS minifeature by Duck's Breath Productions. With *irony* and *sarcasm*, the humorist says one thing but means another. Jessica Mitford used both to scathing effect in *The American Way of Death*. *Satire* is verbal caricature that deliberately distorts the image of a person, institution, or society. The classic satire most college students read, of course, is Jonathan Swift's *A Modest Proposal*; among the great modern satirists are James Thurber, Ken Kesey, and Woody Allen. *Punning* is play on words that knots together two disparate strings of thought: "Vaudeville speaks loudly and carries a big schtick."

All these techniques set logical contradictions on a collision course. They will work for nonfiction as long as you apply them with a light touch. The idea is to juxtapose details so that they underscore some implicit silliness or illogic.

If you can write humor, you will find a ready welcome in editorial offices across the land. One of journalism's most grievous deficits is widespread lack of wit—and that failing is keenly felt.

WHEN IS A RENAULT NOT A RENAULT?
WHEN IT'S A DACIA

by Alan Freeman

The Wall Street Journal, March 14, 1986

Last summer, Marke Bradnam's automobile began doing strange things. "I'd park the car, walk away and the windshield wipers would start going."

Not long after that, the 10-month-old car began falling apart. "The gearshift came off in my hand, and pieces of the shifting connector were on the road. I was doing about 30 miles per hour and shifting from third to fourth. I ended up in neutral."

Mr. Bradnam, a newspaper circulation-manager from Toronto, is one of about 2,000 Canadians who have bought Dacias since Romania began exporting the subcompact to Canada three years ago. He isn't alone in his

Lead focuses on a person involved in a pretty silly incident.

Bridge

complaints. Americans are supposed to get their first chance to buy the Dacia in the fall.

George Iny, a lawyer with the Automobile Protection Association, a Montreal-based consumer group, says the Dacia is "a little agricultural" in its handling, and he says it suffers from "unbelievably poor manufacturing and assembly quality." Sam Kassam, a garage owner who appears in court as an expert witness on behalf of angry car owners, is more blunt about the cars. "I personally despise them," he says. "I don't think they should be on the road."

A Renault Knockoff

Named for the Roman province that corresponds to modern-day Romania, the Dacia (which rhymes with gotcha) is built in Romania based on the design of the Renault 12, a model long since abandoned by the French auto maker.

It's also cheap. At $4,995 (Canadian) the car struck Mr. Bradnam as a bargain. The purchase, he says, "was part of a separation agreement that my wife and I have cars of equal value. It was the best deal, the cheapest on the market." The Bradnams sold their Toyota Camry and bought two Dacias.

Mr. Bradnam's problems began the day he picked up his new car. "I filled it with gas. By the time I got home, the whole back seat of the car and the floor were sopping wet with gas because there was a leak in the tank." In December, Canada's transport department ordered seven safety recalls involving the Dacia, including one for faulty fuel tanks.

But it was Mrs. Bradnam who initially had the most problems. In the first four months, the front headlights burned out, and she had to replace the battery, the starter, the windshield-wiper motor and the fan blower. Mr. Bradnam accompanied his wife to the dealer when the voltage regulator was changed for the third time.

Unstoppable

"While we were driving home, the passenger compartment filled up with blue smoke, the headlights went out, the windshield wipers stopped and the voltage regulation gauge died," says Mr. Bradnam. "We turned off the ignition, took out the key and the car kept running. Only after we shut off the headlight switch did the car finally stop."

The Dacia hasn't fared too well with the critics, either. When *Protect Yourself*, a Quebec consumer magazine, tested a Dacia supplied by the importer, it reported that the car "was extremely noisy, the luggage compartment light and AM radio didn't work; it leaked oil everywhere (I parked it), and to top it all off, it broke down at 1:00 a.m. on an expressway."

In a test conducted by *Road & Track* magazine, the Dacia finished last when rated against five other bargain imports sold in Canada, including the Lada from Russia and the Skoda from Czechoslovakia. The magazine called the Dacia the "crudest, slowest, noisiest sedan in the assembled company."

But the magazine did note that the Dacia had the most comfortable interior of all six cars—"at least at a standstill." And there was another asset. "Under its hood, Dacia still uses a large glass jar for its radiator overflow: in a pinch, it might be lifted and used for making borsch."

Ironic understatement . . .

. . . juxtaposed against seeming overstatement.

Ludicrously low price mentioned in this context makes the reader suspect one gets what one pays for.

Piles one fiasco atop another to great comic effect.

Ironic subhead. The term "unstoppable" often refers to football heroes and other aggressive winners.

More! This tale is unstoppable.

The worst of an obscure lot.

Nice sarcastic touch.

The first Romanian vehicles entered Canada in the late 1970s, when Pierre Villeneuve, a Montreal process-server, began importing the Aro, a four-wheel-drive utility vehicle. "The first batch wasn't too bad," recalls Mr. Villeneuve. "The second batch arrived in January. Of the 10 vehicles we took off the boat, eight had brakes that didn't work and three motors blew their pistons and head gaskets on the 12-mile drive to our plant."

Denis Duquet, the automotive columnist for the Montreal daily *La Presse*, calls the Aro "the worst car I've ever driven in my life. Driving it was like driving an old GMC truck with 200,000 miles on the odomoeter." And he will never forget the Aro's first-aid kit, which included splints and instruments for performing a tracheotomy.

By 1979, with 400 Aros sold, Mr. Villeneuve's fellow process servers were knocking on his door. His company, Aro Auto Canada Ltd., "was forced into bankruptcy," he says, by losses of about $500,000. Into the breach stepped Terra-Power Tractor Co., originally set up by the Romanian government to distribute Romanian tractors on the Canadian prairies. It established a division to handle cars and trucks.

At Terra-Power's warehouse near Montreal's airport, 15 employees, most of them Romanian nationals, install Canadian batteries, seat belts and headlights on newly arrived Dacias. On an office wall, three road maps with about 15 pins clustered in Quebec indicate the extent of Dacia's Canadian dealer network.

Flight from Bucharest

Victor Jigman, a 40-year-old Romanian on loan from Auto Dacia in Romania, oversees the operation. He says that Terra-Power began importing the Dacia because it felt there was room in Canada for a low-cost subcompact. "We figured it would be easy to sell 5,000 to 10,000 cars a year."

Sales haven't been quite that good, but Mr. Jigman denies that it is because the cars are unreliable. "It's true the Dacia is based on technology that's 10 to 15 years old, but it has been improved." Asked about complaints that parts are hard to find, he points to racks of mufflers, wheels, and other items with inscriptions in Romanian. "If a part is missing, in 48 hours it's on the first flight from Bucharest."

Mr. Jigman says he hasn't run into any special consumer problems. Dacia owners, however, complain that Terra-Power ignores their letters and calls. Philip Edmonston, the president of the Automobile Protection Association, says the Romanians have trouble dealing with a market-driven economy. "Over and over, we were told that North American owners don't really earn the right to drive cars because they aren't first-class mechanics."

At Auto Bumi, a Montreal Dacia dealer that claims to be Canada's largest, owner Michel Ionesco tells a visitor to his spartan showroom that the Dacia "is Renault 12, practically." But American Motors (Canada) Inc., Renault's Canadian affiliate, says it stopped selling the Renault 12 in 1979 and wants nothing to do with the Romanian facsimile. "We want to make it very clear that they aren't Renaults and have no connection with Renault whatsoever," says a spokesman.

Awe-inspiring deficiency.

An extreme simile added to the catalog of complaints.

Crazed incongruity.

Placing this remark after the litany of defects gives it an ironic twist.

This sequence makes Jigman seem oblivious or hopelessly naive.

Suspicions confirmed!

A remark so outrageous it's funny—especially coming after the catalog of faults.

"Satan, get thee from me!"

Three Vintages

Mr. Ionesco boasts that Dacia is "the cheapest front-wheel drive in Canada." It may also be the only car available simultaneously in new 1984, 1985 and 1986 models. A 1984 can be had for $3,995.

The low price for new Dacias may explain in part why Dacias are so hard to resell once used. Mr. and Mrs. Bradnam sold their Dacias at big losses. At a Montreal auto auction, a 1984 model recently went for $1,025.

Roland Ducharme, a Dacia owner from Granby, Quebec, has tried unsuccessfully to unload his car, which has been plagued with motor, heater, muffler, suspension and electrical problems, as well as leaks around the windshield. "I drove around with a For Sale sign for six months, and nobody showed any interest," he says. "Even the dealers don't want to buy it back."

A nod to the principle of journalistic objectivity: balances criticism with dealers' responses.

Not all Dacia owners are unhappy, however. When a consumer group in Sherbrooke, Quebec, publicized the complaints of a group of disgruntled owners recently, the local Dacia dealer responded with a petition signed by most of his customers, testifying that they were satisfied. One of them, Myles Doran, says he has had no problems since he bought the car in May. "It starts beautiful, even on the coldest nights."

Nor do the complaints worry Ole Spaten, the chairman of Auto Dacia of America, Inc., a Miami-based concern that, he says, recently signed an exclusive contract to import the whole line of Romanian vehicles into the U.S. "I don't fear the quality of the car," he says. "The reason it's doing so miserably in Canada is that [promoters] aren't aggressive enough and aren't professional enough."

But Mr. Spaten's plan to sign up 100 dealers by May and sell his first cars in September seems to be up in the air. Louis Morton, the president of North American Import-Export Co. of New Paltz, N.Y., says that he has his own agreement with Romania to get U.S. certification for the cars and he, too, plans to start importing them later this year.

Following yet another of the car's goofy characteristics, this ruefully funny crack makes a strong final quote.

Meanwhile, Mr. Ducharme holds on to his Dacia and keeps his fingers crossed, knowing that keys to Dacias are interchangeable. "We've always hoped it would be stolen," he says, "but thieves must know about it."

EDITORIAL OVERVIEW

This story may not be intrinsically funny, but Alan Freeman had the taste to recognize that cataloging the series of fiascoes associated with the Dacia would result in a hilarious article. At some point, bad luck when it is not tragic becomes laughable.

The order in which the facts are presented—the story's internal structure—builds the humor here. Setting off Dacia dealer Victor Jigman's defensive remarks against a long list of increasingly bizarre defects and complaints makes his comments sound unwittingly ironic, in a way that he could not have intended. Juxtaposing the Renault spokesman's disclaimer with dealer Michel Ionesco's proud claim that the Dacia imitates the Renault has a sarcastic effect. The marvelous wrap-up—Mr. Ducharme cannot even get a thief to steal the car—underscores the ludicrous series of events.

Manipulative? Yes, probably so. Is it unfair? That's hard to tell, from our vantage point. Criticism of the car comes from many different sources, including several consumer and automotive experts. Too, Freeman gives the Dacia dealers a chance to tell their side of the story, albeit after reporting that one was forced into bankruptcy. The Dacia and its misguided dealers most likely were fair game.

—30—

Appendix A
Basic Punctuation Rules

Here are the elementary rules of mechanics that editors suspect are no longer taught in high school or college. Learn them: to land a job in journalism, you'll need them. For more specific questions, refer to your publication's style sheet, to the *Associated Press Stylebook*, or to the University of Chicago *Manual of Style*.

COMMAS

1. *Use a comma to separate independent clauses that are joined by a coordinating conjunction* (but, and, or).

Pete shot the pictures, but he didn't write the story.

An independent clause is an utterance that has a subject and a verb; like a sentence, it could stand on its own. *Do not* join two independent clauses with a comma alone.

Wrong: Pete shot the pictures, he didn't write the story.

Join them with a comma and a conjunction, or with a semicolon.

Right: Pete shot the pictures, but he didn't write the story.
Pete shot the pictures; he didn't write the story.

2. *Use a comma to set off an adverbial clause that precedes a main clause.*

When Jennifer came down the stairs, she found Olive on the sofa with Popeye.

3. Use commas to set off items of a parenthetical nature (appositives) from the rest of a sentence.

Olive, Jennifer's cousin, was Popeye's wife.
Coreen drove in from Minot, North Dakota, last week.
We first saw him, I believe, on a Thursday.

4. Use commas to set off a nonrestrictive phrase or clause from the rest of a sentence. A "nonrestrictive" phrase is one that is not essential to the meaning of the sentence. A "restrictive" clause is essential to the meaning.

The ideals, which we love, are in danger. (Nonrestrictive)
The ideals which we love are in danger. (Restrictive)

Most authorities prefer the word "that," rather than "which," to introduce a restrictive clause:

The ideals that we love are in danger.

5. Direct quotation is usually set off from the rest of the sentence with a comma.

"Let's go to the hop," she said.
Rhonda said to Jill, "Let's go to the hop."
"Actually," Jill replied, "I'd rather visit the zoo."

But sometimes a quotation may be so closely linked to the sentence that no comma is needed:

He often greeted callers with a cheerful "What can I do for you today?"

Do not use a comma when the quoted statement ends with a question mark or exclamation point:

"Do you want it?" she asked.

No comma is used before an indirect quotation:

Jill said she'd rather visit the zoo.

Nor is a comma used before the title of a work in quotation marks:

Mark Twain wrote "Fenimore Cooper's Literary Offenses."

6. Use a comma to indicate direct address.

No, sir, I cannot tell a lie.
Tell me, Mary, did you see the murderer?

7. Use commas to separate a series of words, phrases, or short clauses:

Jeff bought pencils, erasers, a pen, some ink, and paper. [NOTE: The *Associated Press Stylebook* deletes the final comma in a series; sometimes, however, this usage can lead to ambiguity.]

Lenore went to Paris, took a good look at this year's styles, and decided to wear blue jeans.

I came, I saw, I conquered.

We'll win whether we play at home, whether we play on their court, or whether we have to use some other gym.

8. Use commas to set off items in a date.

On July 4, 1776, our forefathers . . .

9. Separate adjectives of equal weight with commas.

It was a long, slow haul.

But don't separate the adjectives if the one directly preceding the noun is part of a noun phrase—that is, if it seems to be an integral part of the noun.

She's an honest young woman.
The old oaken bucket

SEMICOLONS

1. Use a semicolon or a period to separate independent clauses.

John Glenn went to outer space; he also ran for Congress.
Johm Glenn went to outer space. He also ran for Congress.

2. Use a semicolon when an independent clause is introduced by however, therefore, yet, moreover, hence, thus, accordingly, or then.

He drove to Santa Fe; then he caught a plane for Denver.
I'd like to buy that expensive house; however, I also like to eat.

3. Use semicolons between phrases when one or more of the phrases includes a comma.

Denby summarizes the *A Fish Named Wanda*'s plot; gives an informed reaction; justifies his responses (both pro and con) with allusions to the movie and its actors; and puts the film in context, both as a comedy and as part of Charles Crichton's work.

4. Type semicolons outside quotation marks, unless the semicolon is part of the quoted material.

He was called "The Hulk"; however, he stood 5'2" in his stocking feet.

APOSTROPHES

1. Use an apostrophe to indicate letters omitted in a contraction.

isn't, wouldn't, haven't, ne'er-do-well
it's meaning *it is.*

2. Use an apostrophe to indicate possessives.

Tom's pen
The boy's home

3. When a plural possessive noun ends in s, add only an apostrophe:

The brothers' home

4. When a singular possessive noun ends in s, add 's.

The actress's costume
James's pizza

5. There is no apostrophe in any possessive pronoun.

its, his, hers, theirs, yours

6. Use an apostrophe to show the plural of a single letter but not for plurals of numerals.

Mind your p's and q's.
The 1980s

7. The apostrophe is commonly omitted in geographical names: Pikes Peak, Lees Ferry.

QUOTATION MARKS

1. Use double quotation marks (". . .") to enclose a direct quotation. Use single quotation marks ('. . .') to enclose a quotation within a direct quotation.

"I'm leaving," he said.
"It's true that we'll have to start over," he reflected, "but after all, 'what's past is prologue.' "

2. Use quotations with the titles of articles, chapters, short stories and poems, and unpublished works.

Read Poe's story, "The Pit and the Pendulum."
Her dissertation was titled "The Use of Pull-Toys by Mothers in Government Housing Projects."

Use italics for books, long poems, magazines, and newspapers. In typescript or longhand, underscore the passage to be italicized.

The Sun Also Rises
The Ancient Mariner
The New Yorker
The Los Angeles Times

3. Use quotation marks for the nickname of an individual, when the entire name is given.

Paul "Bear" Bryant

4. Use quotation marks to convey irony.

His "mansion" was a two-story condo.

5. Do not enclose slang or informal language in quotation marks; the effect is ironic and quickly stales.

6. The first word of a direct quotation begins with a capital letter.

He replied, "Leave it to me."

ITALICS

1. Indicate italic in typescript by underscoring.

2. Italicize titles of long literary works; see item 3 under "Quotation Marks."

3. Italicize foreign words and terms that have not come into common English use. Type familiar words in roman.

luminaria
papier-mâché

4. Use italic to distinguish a term under discussion.

For Oliver, the word *stop* had no meaning.

5. Avoid italicizing words for emphasis, unless you're trying to write like the Cosmo girl.

PARENTHESES

1. Avoid overuse. As a rule, if an aside is not worth placing in the narrative, it's not worth including at all.

2. Parenthetical material within a sentence does not begin with a capital letter or end with a period.

> She wrote to him (she was always writing letters) as soon as she arrived in Cairo.

3. Punctuation for the main sentence should remain outside the parentheses.

> He was on time (contrary to his habit), and we left.

4. If a separate sentence is set in parentheses, it takes a period before the closing parenthesis.

> (You would type it like this.)

HYPHENS

1. Use hyphens to combine words to make a single adjective preceding a noun.

> free-lance writer
> better-qualified applicant
> a red-orange sunset

2. Do not use a hyphen after words ending in **ly.**

> a freely given promise

3. The custom for hyphenating compound words changes rapidly. Use a recent-edition dictionary to confirm compound spellings.

4. Use hyphens in compound numbers from twenty-one to ninety-nine.

5. When typing copy for a typesetter, avoid breaking a word at the end of a line. Turn off the discretionary hyphen on your word processor.

DASHES

1. Use dashes to set off an abrupt change of thought.

> I buy all the scandal rags—I think they're a kick—and I read all the women's magazines.

2. *Use dashes to set off a parenthetic series within a phrase.*

He noticed his favorite dessert on the menu—soufflé Grand Marnier—and then ordered dinner with that in mind.

3. *Use a dash to indicate an author's name at the end of a quotation.*

"And when we think we lead, we are most led."—Byron

PERIODS AND ELLIPSIS POINTS

1. *Use a period at the end of a declarative or imperative sentence.*

2. *Use periods after initials and abbreviations.*

E. B. White
A.D., B.C.
A.M., P.M.
Calif.
Ph.D.

3. *Do not use periods after Post Office abbreviations for states.*

CA, NY, GA

4. *Some other abbreviations, such as* per cent *and* YMCA, *do not take periods. Use a dictionary to be sure.*

5. *Ellipsis points are used to show omitted material. Three points indicate that the material was part of the same sentence that appears; four points show that a sentence ended and a new one began in the omitted passage.*

The donkeys were all good . . . and willing to prove it. They had all been newly barbered, and. . . . were indescribably gorgeous.

Place four ellipsis points after a sentence whose final words have been omitted—i.e., three points and a period.

They say they do not have accidents on these French roads. . . .

6. *Do not use ellipsis points to indicate that the voice trails off, or for other imaginative effects.*

–30–

Appendix B
20 Rules for Good Writing

(Reprinted by permission of Writer's Digest School)

1. Prefer the plain word to the fancy.
2. Prefer the familiar word to the unfamiliar.
3. Prefer the Saxon word to the Romance.
4. Prefer nouns and verbs to adjectives and adverbs.
5. Prefer picture nouns and action verbs.
6. Never use a long word when a short one will do as well.
7. Master the simple declarative sentence.
8. Prefer the simple sentence to the complicated.
9. Vary your sentence length.
10. Put the words you want to emphasize at the beginning or end of your sentence.
11. Use the active voice.
12. Put statements in a positive form.
13. Use short paragraphs.
14. Cut needless words, sentences, and paragraphs.
15. Use plain, conversational language. Write like you talk. (Of course, you *don't* talk that way!—MVH)
16. Avoid imitation. Write in your natural style.
17. Write clearly.
18. Avoid gobbledygook and jargon.
19. Write to be understood, not to impress.
20. Revise and rewrite. Improvement is always possible.

Appendix C
List of Useful Editor's Marks

until ~~until~~ the end	delete
per cent	close up
percapita	insert space
ae	transpose
	begin new paragraph
. . . on the wavy grass. ¶ Adults who insist . . . or . . . on the wavy grass. Adults who insist . . .	no paragraph
⊏	move left
⊐	move right
⊐ title ⊏	center
⑧	spell it out
eighteen	use figures
New York	abbreviate
N.Y.	spell it out
STET	let it stand
word	another way of saying stet (dots beneath the letters to be retained)
∧	insert

⊙	insert period
⋀	insert comma
⋀	insert semicolon
⌄ ⌄	insert quotation marks
⊥/M	insert dash (one-em dash)
=	insert hyphen
⊥/N	insert one-en dash
a	make uppercase
X	make lowercase
A	typeset as small cap
<u>word</u>	italicize
<u>word</u>	boldface
Now is the time for all good	delete a block of copy
men and women and	
foxes and quick brown	
dogs to come to the aid of	
their countries.	

Appendix D
Glossary of Magazine and Newspaper Terms

a.a. "author's alteration": changes made at the writer's request.

Add in newspaper jargon, a page following the first page; numbered *add 1, add 2*, etc.

Advertorial advertising disguised as an article, plugging paid advertisers or businesses the publication hopes will buy ad space.

Artwork the design, typography, photography, and illustrations for a printed work, taken as a whole. Sometimes refers to photography or illustration.

Author's bio short biographical notice about the writer, usually printed on the article's first or last page.

Back matter columns and lightweight editorial placed at the end of the editorial well or near the back of a magazine.

Banner the title of a newspaper, as it appears on the front page.

Bleed a color illustration in which the color runs all the way to the edge of the page, or "bleeds" off the page.

Blow-in a card or other piece of advertising inserted loose between pages, rather than bound with the pages.

Bluelines printer's proofs. *To be in blueline:* to be at the stage just before the publication is printed, at which printer's proofs receive a final check. Corrections at this point are very costly.

Boards or flats cardboard forms with nonreproducing blue guidelines, used to lay out photo-ready copy for the printer.

Book jargon term for "magazine."

Box a block of copy enclosed by lines.

Brite a very short, usually upbeat filler.

Budget lines brief outline of a proposed story.

Bullet a graphic device used for emphasis: a raised dot.

Byline the writer's name, printed with the story.

Camera-ready copy typeset copy ready to paste on boards for printing; sometimes refers to the pasted-up boards.

Center spread the two pages in the center of the magazine; considered a prominent spot.

Column inch one inch of typeset print, one column wide.

Consumer magazine a publication, usually supported by advertising, that is sold to a general audience (as opposed to a trade or professional readership).

Content edit to read copy for logical sense, organization, style, completeness, and overall quality.

Controlled-circulation magazine a publication given free to a specific, limited audience.

Copy written material in manuscript or typeset form.

Copy editor an editor who reads manuscript copy for sense, grammatical and spelling correctness, appropriateness to the publication, etc., and marks the copy to fit the house style.

Copy reader strictly, a person who line edits manuscript copy. Sometimes this term is applied to proofreaders.

Cover lines mention of an article on the magazine's cover.

Credit acknowledgement of a photographer or artist, usually printed near a picture.

CRT or VDT cathode-ray tube or video display terminal; a word-processing terminal for staff members.

Cutline   caption.

Deadline   the last moment to complete a task. **Copy deadline**   the time articles are due to the editor.   **Printer's deadline**   the time all typeset, pasted-up copy and art are due to the printer.

Deck   subhead beneath the main head of a story.

Defamation   legal term meaning an untrue, malicious attack on an individual's character.

Demographics   the number and nature of a publication's readers, including such statistics as age range, average income, geographical distribution, and education.

Department   a column or regularly appearing feature, which appears in every issue of a magazine.

Dingbat   a graphic device used to mark the end of an article.

Double-truck spread   two facing pages containing a single photo or article.

Download   to copy into one computer data sent from another computer through a modem.

Dropped letter   a graphic device—a large letter at the beginning of a paragraph—which extends down two or more lines.

Dummy   a mock-up of an issue, roughing out the publication's design and contents.

Editorial   the written part of a newspaper or magazine that is not paid advertising. Sometimes used collectively to refer to editorial staff members.

Editorial well   a section in some magazines reserved for articles, with little or no advertising.

File copy   to hand in a story to an editor.

Filler   short, bright material used to fill space.

First rights   the right to be the first to publish a work.

Flush left   type that begins at the left margin

Flush right   type that lines up in with the right margin; sometimes refers to justified columns.

Four colors   full color; a printing process that combines four colors (red, yellow, blue, and black) to produce a wide variety of hues and shades.

Front matter columns and departments run near the front of a magazine; usually consisting of short features, letters, new-product roundups, and the like.

Froth see "puff."

Fulfillment maintenance of a publisher's mailing list.

Galleys proofs of typeset copy.

Graf paragraph.

Gutter the margins and crease where pages are bound together.

Head title of a story

House organ an in-house publication, or a controlled-circulation publication designed for a company's customers or employees.

Illustration a drawing, picture, or artwork other than a photograph.

Jump to continue a story to another page.

Jump head a shortened version of the head, marking a story's continuity on succeeding pages.

Jump the gutter to "bleed" a photograph or illustration across the bound center of a magazine; sometimes, to design a two-page spread so that the copy reads horizontally across both pages, rather than in conventional vertical columns.

Justified refers to typeset copy in which each line abuts the margin. Used alone, this term means the copy aligns straight against both left and right margins. However, either the left or the right margin may be justified, and the other left "ragged."

Keyline rule drawn around a photograph or illustration.

Kill fee amount paid to a free-lance writer when, through no fault of the writer, an assigned story cannot be used.

Layout the design of a page.

Lead a story's opening.

Leading the space between typeset lines.

Lede newspaperese for "lead."

Libel any statement not made in the public interest which exposes a person to public ridicule or injures his reputation in any way.

Line edit to read and correct copy, line by line, checking for spelling, punctuation, and grammatical accuracy.

Logo   the title of a magazine, as it appears on the cover.

Masthead   a notice in a magazine or newspaper listing the staff members and usually giving the address of the editorial offices. Newspaper mastheads do not name all the editors.

Modem   a device allowing two or more computers to communicate over telephone lines.

One-time rights   the right to publish a work once, but not necessarily to be the first to publish it.

Pasteup   the careful placement of copy, photographs, and illustration on boards, according to a preconceived design.

Payment on acceptance   an arrangement whereby writers or artists are paid when an editor receives and accepts their work.

Payment on publication   an arrangement whereby writers or artists are not paid for their work until it appears in print.

Photo-ready copy   same as "camera-ready copy."

Press release   a self-interested announcement sent to the media in an attempt to obtain free editorial coverage.

Proofreader   a person who carefully reads typeset galleys for mechanical accuracy.

Puff or puffery   breathless prose hyping a product, event, company, or individual; unduly cheerful writing; a naive approach to a subject. Sometimes called *froth*.

Pull quote or teaser   line or quote selected from a story, set in large bold-face type and used as a design element to pique reader interest.

q.a.   "query the author"—ask the author to clarify a point in a manuscript.

Query or query letter   an article proposal presented as a business letter.

Quotes   quotations; quotation marks.

Ragged right   typeset copy with an unjustified right margin.

Raised or standing letter   a graphic device: a large letter at the beginning of a paragraph that protrudes above the line.

Reprint rights   the right to reproduce a work after it has been printed somewhere else.

Roman type   the most commonly used type, as opposed to *italic* or boldface.

Rule a line (layout artist's term).

Running foot or Running head a notation appearing at the bottom or top of each page and identifying the publication, its date, and the page number.

SASE (pronounced "say-zee") self-addressed, stamped envelope.

Second rights the right to be the second publisher of a work.

Separation a process whereby the colors in a photograph or illustration are broken out into several hues, preparatory to printing.

Serial rights the right to reproduce a work in a regularly appearing publication, such as a magazine or newspaper.

Sidebar a short article related to a longer one.

Slug a one- or two-word working title for an article.

Slush pile a stack of unsolicited articles awaiting an editor's attention.

Spread two facing pages, over which a single article or department may be laid out.

Subhead subtitle.

Syndication rights right to reproduce a work in several different publications at once.

Take page.

Trade or business magazine a magazine whose audience consists of members of a given trade or profession.

Upload to send data from one computer to another through a modem or over a network.

Work for hire an agreement whereby a free-lance writer signs over all rights to a work, becoming in effect a temporary employee of the company that hires him or her—without benefits and at the higher self-employed tax rate.

Wrap a satisfying ending for a story.

—30—

Appendix E
The Society of Professional
Journalists Code of Ethics

The Society of Professional Journalists, Sigma Delta Chi believes the duty of journalists is to serve the truth.

We believe the agencies of mass communications are carriers of public discussion and information, acting on their Constitutional mandate and freedom to learn and report the facts.

We believe in public enlightenment as the forerunner of justice and in our Constitutional role to seek the truth and report the facts.

We believe those responsibilities carry obligations that require journalists to perform with intelligence, objectivity, accuracy and fairness.

RESPONSIBILITY

The public's right to know of events of importance and interest is the overriding mission of the mass media. The purpose of distributing news and enlightened opinion is to serve the general welfare. Journalists who use their professional status as representatives of the public for selfish or other unworthy motives violate a high trust.

FREEDOM OF THE PRESS

Freedom of the press is to be guarded as an inalienable right of people in a free society. It carries with it the freedom and the responsibility to discuss, question and challenge actions and utterances of our government and of our public and private institutions. Journalists uphold the right to speak unpopular opinions and the privilege to agree with the majority.

ETHICS

Journalists must be free of obligation to any interst other than the public's right to know the truth.

1. Gifts, favors, free travel, special treatment or privileges can compromise the integrity of journalists and their employers. Nothing of value should be accepted.
2. Secondary employment, political involvement, holding public office and service in community organizations should be avoided if it compromises the integrity of journalists and their employers. Journalists and their employers should conduct their personal lives in a manner that protects them from conflict of interest, real or apparent. Their responsibilities to the public are paramount. This is the nature of their profession.
3. So-called news communications from private sources should not be published or broadcast without substantiation of their claims to news value.
4. Journalists will seek news that serves the public interst, despite the obstacles. They will make constant efforts to ensure that the public's business is conducted in public and that public records are open to public inspection.
5. Journalists acknowledge the newsman's ethic of protecting confidential sources of information.
6. Plagiarism is dishonest and unacceptable.

ACCURACY AND OBJECTIVITY

Good faith with the public is the foundation of all worthy journalism.

1. Truth is our ultimate goal.
2. Objectivity in reporting the news is another goal that serves as the mark of an experienced professional. It is a standard of performance toward which we strive. We honor those who achieve it.
3. There is no excuse of inaccuracies or lack of thoroughness.
4. Newspaper headlines should be fully warranted by the contents of the articles they accompany. Photographs and telecasts should give an accurate picture of an event and not highlight a minor incident out of context.

5. Sound practice makes clear distinction between news reports and expressions of opinion. News reports should be free of opinion or bias and represent all sides of an issue.
6. Partisanship in editorial comment that knowingly departs from the truth violates the spirit of American journalism.
7. Journalists recognize their responsibility for offering informed analysis, comment and editorial opinion on public events and issues. They accept the obligation to present such material by individuals whose competence, experience and judgment qualify them for it.
8. Special articles or presentations devoted to advocacy or the writer's own conclusions and interpretations should be labeled as such.

FAIR PLAY

Journalists at all times will show respect for the dignity, privacy, rights and well-being of people encountered in the course of gathering and presenting the news.

1. The news media should not communicate unofficial charges affecting reputation or moral character without giving the accused a chance to reply.

2. The news media must guard against invading a person's right to privacy.

3. The media should not pander to morbid curiosity about details of vice and crime.

4. It is the duty of news media to make prompt and complete correction of their errors.

5. Journalists should be accountable to the public for their reports and the public should be encouraged to voice its grievances against the media. Open dialogue with our readers, viewers and listeners should be fostered.

PLEDGE

Journalists should actively censure and try to prevent violations of these standards, and they should encourage their observance by all newspeople. Adherence to this code of ethics is intended to preserve the bond of mutual trust and respect between American journalists and the American people.

Appendix F
American Society of Journalists and Authors Code of Ethics and Fair Practices

PREAMBLE

Over the years, an unwritten code governing editor-writer relationships has arisen. The American Society of Journalists and Authors (ASJA) has compiled the major principles and practices of that code that are generally recognized as fair and equitable.

The ASJA has also established a Committee on Editor-Writer Relationships to investigate and mediate disagreements brought before it, either by members or by editors. In its activity, this committee shall rely on the following guidelines.

1. TRUTHFULNESS, ACCURACY, EDITING

The writer shall at all times perform professionally and to the best of his or her ability, assuming primary responsibility for truth and accuracy. No writer shall deliberately write into an article a dishonest, distorted, or inaccurate statement.

Editors may correct or delete copy for purposes of style, grammar, conciseness, or arrangement, but may not change the intent or sense without the writer's permission.

2. SOURCES

A writer shall be prepared to support all statements made in his or her manuscripts, if requested. It is understood, however, that the publisher shall respect any and all promises of confidentiality made by the writer in obtaining information.

3. IDEAS

An idea shall be defined not as a subject alone, but as a subject combined with an approach. A writer shall be considered to have a proprietary right to an idea suggested to an editor and to have priority in the development of it.

4. ACCEPTANCE OF AN ASSIGNMENT

A request from an editor that the writer proceed with an idea, however worded and whether oral or written, shall be considered an assignment. (The word "assignment" here is understood to mean a definite order for an article.) It shall be the obligation of the writer to proceed as rapidly as possible toward the completion of an assignment, to meet a deadline mutually agreed upon, and not to agree to unreasonable deadlines.

5. CONFLICT OF INTEREST

The writer shall reveal to the editor, before acceptance of an assignment, any actual or potential conflict of interest, including, but not limited to, any financial interest in any product, firm, or commercial venture relating to the subject of the article.

6. REPORT ON ASSIGNMENT

If in the course of research or during the writing of the article, the writer concludes that the assignment will not result in a satisfactory article, he or she shall be obliged to so inform the editor.

7. WITHDRAWAL

Should a disagreement arise between the editor and writer as to the merit or handling of an assignment, the editor may remove the writer on payment of mutually satisfactory compensation for the effort already expended, or the writer may withdraw without compensation and, if the idea for the assignment originated with the writer, may take the idea elsewhere without penalty.

8. AGREEMENTS

The practice of written confirmation of all agreements between editors and writers is strongly recommended, and such confirmation may originate with the editor, the writer, or an agent. Such a memorandum of confirmation should list all aspects of the assignment including subject, approach, length, special instructions, payments, deadline, and guarantee (if any). Failing prompt contradictory response to such a memorandum, both parties are entitled to assume that the terms set forth therein are binding.

9. REWRITING

No writer's work shall be rewritten without his or her advance consent. If an editor requests a writer to rewrite a manuscript, the writer shall be obliged to do so, but shall alternatively be entitled to withdraw the manuscript and offer it elsewhere.

10. BYLINES

Lacking any stipulation to the contrary, a byline is the author's unquestioned right. All advertisements of the article should also carry the author's names. If the author's byline is omitted from a published article, no matter what the cause or reason, the publisher shall be liable to compensate the author financially for the omission.

11. UPDATING

If delay in publication necessitates extensive updating of an article, such updating shall be done by the author, to whom additional compensation shall be paid.

12. REVERSION OF RIGHTS

A writer is not paid by money alone. Part of the writer's compensation is the intangible value of timely publication. Consequently, if after six months the publisher has not scheduled an article for publication, or within twelve months has not published an article, the manuscript and all rights therein should revert to the author without penalty or cost to the author.

13. PAYMENT FOR ASSIGNMENTS

An assignment presumes an obligation upon the publisher to pay for the writer's work upon satisfactory completion of the assignment, according to the agreed terms. Should a manuscript that has been accepted, orally or in writing, by a publisher or any representative or employee of the publisher, later be deemed unacceptable, the publisher shall nevertheless be obliged to pay the writer in full according to the agreed terms.

If an editor withdraws or terminates an assignment, due to no fault of the writer, after work has begun but prior to completion of the manuscript, the writer is entitled to compensation for work already put in; such compensation shall be negotiated between editor and author and shall be commensurate with the amount of work already completed. If a completed assignment is not acceptable, due to no fault of the writer, the writer is nevertheless entitled to payment; such payment, in common practice, has varied from half the agreed-upon price to the full amount of that price.

14. TIME OF PAYMENTS

The writer is entitled to payment for an accepted article within ten days of delivery. No article payment should ever be subject to publication.

15. EXPENSES

Unless otherwise stipulated by the editor at the time of an assignment, a writer shall assume that normal, out-of-pocket expenses will be reimbursed by the publisher. Any extraordinary expenses anticipated by the writer shall be discussed with the editor prior to incurring them.

16. INSURANCE

A magazine that gives a writer an assignment involving any extraordinary hazard shall insure the writer against death or disability during the course of travel or the hazard, or, failing that, shall honor the cost of such temporary insurance as an expense account item.

17. LOSS OF PERSONAL BELONGINGS

If, as a result of circumstances or events directly connected with a perilous assignment and due to no fault of the writer, a writer suffers loss of personal belongings or professional equipment, or incurs bodily injury, the publisher shall compensate the writer in full.

18. COPYRIGHT, ADDITIONAL RIGHTS

It shall be understood, unless otherwise stipulated in writing, that sale of an article manuscript entitles the purchaser to first North

American publication rights only, and that all other rights are retained by the author. Under no circumstances shall an independent writer be required to sign a so-called "all rights transferred" or "work made for hire" agreement as a conditon of assignment, of payment, or of publication.

19. REPRINTS

All revenues from reprints shall revert to the author exclusively, and it is incumbent upon a publication to refer all requests for reprint to the author. The author has a right to charge for such reprints, and must request that the original publication be credited.

20. AGENTS

According to the Society of Authors' Representatives, the accepted fee for an agent's services has long been 10 percent of the writer's receipts, except for foreign rights representation. An agent may not represent editors or publishers. In the absence of any agreement to the contrary, a writer shall not be obliged to pay an agent a fee on work negotiated, accomplished and paid for without the assistance of the agent.

21. TV AND RADIO PROMOTION

The writer is entitled to be paid for personal participation on TV or radio programs promoting periodicals in which the writer's work appears.

22. INDEMNITY

No writer should be obliged to indemnify any magazine or book publisher against any claim, actions, or proceedings arising from an article or book.

23. PROOFS

The editor shall submit edited proofs of the author's work to the author for approval, sufficiently in advance of publication, so that any errors may be brought to the editor's attention. If for any reason a publication is unable to so deliver or transmit proofs to the author, the author is entitled to review the proofs in the publication's office.

Index

Davidson, Sara, 9

Deadlines, working against, 147; importance of, 148, 152

Dedera, Don, 157

Dénouement, example of, 201

Description (literary technique), in lead, 81-82, 93; examples of, 189-90, 192, 195, 200, 213-14, 222, 223, 224, 225, 226, 231, 233; importance to history articles, 243

Destination stories, 212

Details, importance of, 51-52; use of, 214, 216, 218, 231, 247

Development of article, 84-86

Dialog Information Services, 45

Dictionary of American Biography, 38

Dictionary of National Biography, 38

Didion, Joan, 9

Direct address, punctuation of, 258

Directory of American Scholars, 38

Ditzen, Walt, 111

"Doctor Science," 251

Dow Jones News-Retrieval, 45

Duck's Breath Productions, 251

Dun and Bradstreet Million-Dollar Directory, 32, 39

Dun and Bradstreet Reference Book of Corporate Managements, 39

Ecodefense: A Field Guide to Monkeywrenching, by Dave Foreman and Bill Haywood, 46

Economy, editing for, 112-13, 226

Editing, content (substantive), 109-10; checklist, 114

Editing, line, 114-16; checklist, 116

Editor and Publisher, 106

Editor and Publisher International Yearbook, 17, 21

Editorial, contrasted with feature article, 7

Editor (magazine), and writers, 143, 151-52; typical responsibilities, 144-45, 148; qualities of, 150-51; payment of free-lance writers, 154; problems between writer and, 153-54

Editor's marks (list), Appendix C

Education Index, 36

Elements of Style, The, by William Strunk and E. B. White, 41, 126

Ellipsis points, use of, 263

Employment, ethical concerns, 133

Encyclopaedia Britannica, 39

Encyclopedia Americana, 39

Encyclopedia of Associations, 43

Enterprise story, 186

Esquire, 9

Essay and General Literature Index, 36

Essay, contrasted with feature article, 7

Ethics, importance of, xviii; 132-41; defined, 132; see also employment, taste, travel

Euphemism, 103

European Travel and Life, 212

Expenses (for writers), 152

Experts, locating, 41-43

Exposition (literary technique), 233-34, 238

Fact-checking, importance of, 114

Fact-finding, 32-35

Facts on File, 40

Fair comment, 141

Family Circle, 19

Family Circus, 111, 112

"Fam trips" (familiarization trips), see travel, free

Feature article, described, 3, 6-8; for newspapers, xviii, 185-86; growth of, in newspapers, 4-5; difference between, in magazines and newspapers, 4, 185-87; for magazines, 4, 186-87; structure of, 75-86; progress from assignment to publication, 146-50; types of, 185-87; length of, 241

Fee, see Editor; Payment

Feminism, effect on journalism, 5

Fenn, Donna, 82

Fictional techniques, in nonfiction: see literary devices; literary technique

Fiction, elements of, 88-90

Field and Stream, 27

50 Plus, 34

Filler, contrasted with feature article, 7, 187

First rights, 169

Focus, 19, 235

"Fog Index," 117

"Footed bowl," 76

Foreign serial rights, 169

Foreign words and terms, italicizing, 261

Foreshadowing (literary device), 95; examples of, 199, 215

Formulas, for readability, 117-18

Forthcoming Books in Print, 37

Freeman, Alan, "When Is a Renault Not a Renault? When It's a Dacia," The Wall Street Journal, March 14, 1986 (example of humorous article), 251-54

Friendly Exchange, 27, 148

F & S Index International, 39

F & S Index of Corporations and Industries, 39

Kramer, Mark, 9
Krazy Kat, 37

Lanzmann, Claude, 55
Latinate words, 100
Lead, of article, 75; differences in magazines and newspapers, 78; types of, 78-83; length of, 81; examples of, 191, 199, 204, 209, 213-14, 221-22, 230, 244, 251; focusing on a person, 242
Levels of the Game, by John McPhee, 77-78
Libel, defined, 139-41; defenses against, 140
Library of Congress—National Union Catalog, 37
Library, uses of, 43
Liebling, A. J., 9
Lipman, Joanne, 190
Literary agents, 163-64
Literary devices, *see* allusion; anecdote; cataloguing; foreshadowing; iconography; irony; metaphor; parody; pathetic fallacy; punning; repetition; sarcasm; satire; simile
Literary technique, in nonfiction, xviii, 8-9, 13, 14, 88-96; *see also* characterization; conflict; description; exposition; imagery; narrative; plot; point of view; prosody; quotation; setting; suspense; theme; voice (narrative)
Los Angeles Times, The, index, 36; story from, 191-96

Macintosh (computers), 179
Mad Magazine, 251
Magazine Index, 34, 36; on-line, 45
Magazine industry, guides to, 17
Magazines, evolution of, 5; masthead, 15-16; departments, 15-16; significance of appearance, 16; computerization of, 144; editorial staff of, 144-46;
Malott, Adele, 148
Manning, Reg, 111
Manuscript preparation, 119-30; hard copy for magazines, 120-21; hard copy for newspapers, 121; mailing, 130
Manuscripts, locating, 44
Manuscript style, 116
Market, importance of, xviii
Marketing (for free-lance writers), 160
Masthead, of magazine, 15; of newspaper, 15-16
Mauldin, Bill, 37, 111
McCall's, 82, 204
McDonald's Corporation, 32

McNichol, Kristy, 189
McPhee, John, 9, 77, 91
Meade, Marion, 117
Mearn's quail, 26
"Menorah," 77
Meredith Publishing Services, contract of, 173-75
Metaphor, 106; 196; examples of, 192, 194, 230
Michaud, Stephen G., 81, 84, 86
Microsoft Word, 180
Miller, Arthur, 52
Mitchell, Joseph, 9
Mitford, Jessica, 251
Modem, 177
Modern Maturity, 32, 34
Modest Proposal, A, by Jonathan Swift, 251
Money, article from, 204-11
Monthly Catalog of U.S. Government Publications, 43
Moon, William Least Heat, 9
Morris, William and Mary, 102
Mother Jones, 9
Ms., 34
"Mush-words," 102-3
Music Index, 36

Nancy, 111, 112
Narrative, in lead, 80-81; examples of, 199, 222
National Council on Aging, 32
National Cyclopedia of American Biography, 39
National Faculty Directory, 38
National Geographic, 81-82
National Geographic Traveler, 212
National Magazine Award, 204
National Trade and Professional Associations of the United States, 43
National Union Catalog of Manusript Collections, 44
National Wildlife, 27
National Writers Union, 164
Nation's Business, 34
New Choices, 34
New Journalism, 8-9
News feature, 186
Newspapers, writing for, 17, 20-21; editorial staff of, 144; computerization of, 144
News report, contrasted with feature article, 6-7
New York, 9; article from, 221-26
New Yorker, The, 52, 92, 117
New York Times Biographical Service, 38
New York Times Obituary Index, 38

Public relations, free-lance, ethical concerns, 134; jobs, 165
Public relations officers and agents, 41-42, 49-50
Publisher's Weekly, 38, 83
Pulitzer Prize, 196, 230
Pull quotes (teasers, pullouts), 121
Punctuation, importance of, 106-7; editing for, 114-15
Punning (literary device), 251; use of, 218

Query letter, defined, 21; importance of, 21-22; form of, 22; contents of, 22; tone of, 22-23; mailing, 26
Quotation marks, use of, 260-61
Quotation ("quotes"), linking out of context, 72; purposes, 93-94; when and how to use, 94-95; attributions of, 94-95; lifting, 135-36; dialect suggested in, 191; examples of, 191, 205, 230, 231, 234, 235, 238, 244, 246; punctuation of, 258, 259, 260 262

Rand-McNally *Road Atlas to the United States, Canada, and Mexico,* 41
"Readability Formula," 117
Reader, importance of, 11; to understand, 14; as reflected in editorial, 14-15; as reflected in advertising, 15; of newspapers, 15
Reader's Digest, 80; article cited, 95-96; story from, 199-201
Reader's Guide to Periodical Literature, 36
Record-keeping, 160
Redbook 202
Redundancy, 104
Reference works, 34; indexes to periodicals, 35-37; bibliographies, 37; card catalogues, 37; indexes to book reviews, 37; biographical indexes, 38-39; business, 39; miscellaneous, 39; recommended for writers, 39-41
Regional stories, 212
Reiss, Marguerite, 95-96; "Nightmare Hunt," *Reader's Digest,* November 1985 (example of personal experience story), 199-201
Rejection of assigned article, 155
Repetition (literary device), 230-31
Report, 186, 174-76, 228-41; described, 228; importance of research, 228-29; techniques to enliven, 229; market, 229; types, 229-30; example of, 230-41
Research Centers Directory, 44

Research, importance of, xviii, 30-31, 51, 72-73, 221, 228-29, 232, 236; steps to, 30; organization of, 64-74; Main Street Historical Preservation Program as example of, 65; computerized, 177-78; for history articles, 243; examples of use, 244-45, 246; turning research into a story, 249; *see also* databases; experts; fact-finding; interviewing; manuscripts; notes; public records; reference works; sources; subject headings
Research paper, contrasted with feature article, 6
Restrictive phrase, 115-16, 258
Review, contrasted with feature article, 7
Revision, techniques of, 109-18; importance of, 109; goal of, 109
Rhetorical question, as lead, 80
Rhodes, Richard, 9
Richmond Times-Dispatch, 137
Rights: North American, 169; Foreign Serial, 169
Robb, Charles S., Governor of Virginia, 137
Robbins, Michael W., "Dream Weekends," *New York,* April 28, 1986 (example of roundup article), 221-26
Rodale's Synonym Finder, 40
Roget's Thesaurus, 40
Ross, Lillian, 9
Rumors, reporting of, 137
Running heads, typing, 120, 121

Sacramento Bee, 138
Sanders, Colonel Harland, 32
Sarcasm (literary device), 251
Satire (literary device), 251
Savvy, 79, 204
Scanlon, John, 190
Scene-setting, in lead, 81; examples of, 193, 194
Schwadel, Francine, 78, 83, 85-86
Science, 34
Scott, Jerry, 111
Seasonal story, 186
Second person, in lead, 82
Self-publishing, 164-65
Semicolon, use of, 259
Sentence fragments, 100
Serial comma, 258-59
Serial rights, 169
Service information, examples of, 223, 226
Service piece (roundup), 186, 220-27; advantages, for beginners, 220-21;

Transitional statement, *see* capsule statement

Travel and Leisure, 212

Travel article, 187, 212-19; importance of description, 212; types of, 212; ethical concerns, 213

Travel, free, 133, 213

Travel-Holiday, 212

"Truth," as journalistic goal, 136

Turley, Keith, 189-90

Twain, Mark, 103

Twomey, Steve, "How Super Are Our Supercarriers?" *The Philadelphia Inquirer*, October 5, 1986 (example of report), 230-41

Updike, John, 91, 117

USA Today, 98

Vanity presses, 164-65

Vanos, Nick, 138

Vanos, Peter, 138

Verbs, use of, 99-100; verbs of being vs. verbs of action, 99; agreement, 115; examples, 199, 231

Video releases, canned, 134-35

Village Voice, The, 9

Voice, narrative (literary device), 216, 219

Wall Street Journal, The, index, 36; analysis of articles in, 78 ff., 82, 190, 254-55; reading levels of, 98; article from, 251-54

Washington Information Directory, 43

Washington Post, The, 137; index, 36

Webster's Biographical Dictionary, 40

Webster's Instant Word Guide, 40

Webster's New Biographical Dictionary, 39

Webster's New Unabridged Dictionary, 40

Western Horseman, 11

Western Outdoors, 27

West, Richard, 9

"Which" or "that," use of, 258

Who's Who (British), 38

Who's Who in American Law, 38

Who's Who (Marquis), 38

Who's Who of American Women, 38

Williams, J.R., 111

Williams, Maureen Smith, 204

Wolfe, Tom, 9, 51

Women in Communications, Inc., 164

Word choice, importance of, 103

WordPerfect, 180

Word processing programs, characteristics desirable for writers, 180-81

Word processors, ease of learning, 178

WordStar, 180

Work for hire, 139, 170

Work habits (for writers), 160-61

World Almanac and Book of Facts, 40, 41

Wrapup, 75; described, 86; examples of, 195-6, 201, 209, 218, 240-41, 249, 254

Writer-editor relations, 138; 143-55; importance of communication, 147-48

Writer's groups, 164

Writer's guidelines, 17, 126

Writer's Market, 17, 41

Writers, quality of, xvii; characteristics of, xviii; free-lance, as sources of story ideas, 12; 20; jobs for, 21, 165; empathy a skill of, 28; and potential conflicts of interest, 133-34; average free-lance income, 157

Writing, free-lance (as business), 157-66; disadvantages, 157-58, 159; advantages, 157; need for professionalism, 158, 161-62

XyWrite, 180

Zinsser, William, xvii